The United States: MAKING A NEW NATION

Reading Support and Intervention

www.harcourtschool.com

Printed in the United States of America

ISBN-13: 978-0-15-349431-4
ISBN-10: 0-15-349431-X

3 4 5 6 7 8 9 10 054 15 14 13 12 11 10 09 08 07

Contents

Unit 4

Introduction

Today's students are growing up in the Information Age. Our concept of literacy is expanding and changing. In our technological society, students need to understand and evaluate information in many forms—websites, e-mail, Internet advertisements, trade books, newspapers, and magazines—in addition to their textbooks.

WHY is it important to offer reading support to students in the context of social studies instruction? To succeed in social studies, students must be able to read and make meaning from expository text. The structure of social studies text is very different from the more familiar structure of stories and fiction selections. The organizational pattern of social studies text is likely to be different from texts in other content areas.

Students come to us with varying levels of English proficiency and literacy, as well as a variety of backgrounds and experiences. As we assess and plan for the individual needs of our students in grades 3–6, we identify students who are struggling to comprehend grade-level expository texts. This puts them at a disadvantage. In order for students to learn about the world, past and present, they must be able to connect ideas within a text and also to connect prior knowledge to ideas in a text.

Research shows that we can help students better understand and remember what they read by

- using **direct vocabulary instruction** to teach words that are important to concepts in their reading.
- providing **systematic fluency practice,** through rereadings and feedback, to help students improve their fluency.
- teaching students how and when to **use comprehension strategies** to understand expository text.

HOW can we effectively offer reading support to students in the context of social studies instruction? Teachers need an organized, systematic way to help struggling students access on-grade level texts and materials. *Reading Support and Intervention* gives social studies teachers a practical guide for helping these students. Materials include

- A guide that supplements the *Harcourt Social Studies Teacher Edition* with clear and specific suggestions for supporting struggling readers throughout each lesson.
- Student pages that provide vocabulary and concept words, as well as fluency practice, for each lesson. Graphic organizers are also provided to help students focus on important concepts and monitor their comprehension.
- Procedure Cards for teaching vocabulary, fluency, previewing, and comprehension of expository text.
- Student Cards to guide students in using helpful strategies as they read their social studies text in cooperative learning groups.
- Word Cards that represent the vocabulary words taught in the *Harcourt Social Studies Student Edition,* along with their glossary definitions.

Using *Reading Support and Intervention*

Each lesson in *Reading Support and Intervention* corresponds to lessons in the *Harcourt Social Studies Teacher Edition.* The instructional model presented in this book is best suited for small groups of students who need direct and explicit reading instruction at different times during the social studies lesson. The information presented below will show how to use *Reading Support and Intervention* in conjunction with *Harcourt Social Studies* lessons.

BEFORE . . . starting a new lesson in *Harcourt Social Studies*

Teach Vocabulary Strategies

- *Reading Support and Intervention* lesson
- Procedure Card 1
- *Reading Support and Intervention* student vocabulary/fluency page
- Word Cards

Help Build Fluency

- *Reading Support and Intervention* lesson
- Procedure Card 2
- *Reading Support and Intervention* student vocabulary/fluency page

DURING . . . the lesson in *Harcourt Social Studies*

Support Text Comprehension

- *Reading Support and Intervention* Preview the Lesson
- Procedure Card 3
- *Reading Support and Intervention* Build Comprehension of Expository Text
- *Reading Support and Intervention* student comprehension page
- Procedure Card 4
- Student Cards 1–3

AFTER . . . the lesson in *Harcourt Social Studies*

Facilitate Responses to Expository Text

- *Reading Support and Intervention* student comprehension page
- *Reading Support and Intervention* Summarize/Review and Respond
- Leveled Readers
- Procedure Card 5
- Student Cards 1–3

Teaching Vocabulary

WHAT does research tell us about the importance of direct vocabulary instruction? As students read expository texts, they are sure to encounter words whose meanings they do not know. Such words may represent key social studies concepts that students are unfamiliar with. Students will not be able to comprehend the text without knowing what the words mean.

Research has shown that the direct teaching of specific words before reading will result in improved reading comprehension. The vocabulary words identified in each *Harcourt Social Studies* lesson are included on the student vocabulary/fluency pages in *Reading Support and Intervention.* Students practice reading aloud vocabulary words along with additional concept words that should be helpful to struggling readers. The program introduces Additional Words that appear in the lesson and that are important to understanding key concepts. Some of these words may be unfamiliar to students who are reading below grade level. Others may be words introduced in earlier lessons in *Harcourt Social Studies* that are also important in the upcoming lesson. Reviewing the meanings of the words and reading them in text-related sentences will help students read the lesson and understand it better.

Word Cards are provided in *Reading Support and Intervention* to aid in direct vocabulary instruction.

Teaching Fluency

WHY do we need to teach fluency in the context of social studies instruction? Fluency is the ability to read a text quickly and with accuracy. Fluent readers recognize words in print and group the words into chunks, such as phrases and clauses. As a result, these students can focus their attention on making connections between concepts and on understanding what they read. By helping less-fluent readers improve their fluency, we help them become better social studies learners.

HOW can we teach fluency? Research tells us that repeated oral readings of a text, with the teacher providing guidance or feedback, helps students improve their fluency and their comprehension. *Reading Support and Intervention* provides sentences with Vocabulary and Additional Words in context, as well as suggestions for fluency practice. The teacher models fluent reading and guides students in oral rereadings.

Previewing the Lesson

HOW can previewing the lesson help struggling readers better understand the text? Research tells us that good readers intuitively set a purpose for reading. Previewing a lesson helps students become familiar with the text so that they can set a purpose for reading it. After previewing, they read to learn about the topics they have previewed, to find out specific information about those topics, and to answer specific questions.

We also know that students learn by connecting new information to information they already know. Previewing activates students' prior knowledge about concepts they will encounter in the lesson. The preview helps them understand the chronology of historic events and helps them see how these events are related to other events that preceded and followed them.

Building Comprehension of Expository Text

WHAT strategies can students use to increase their understanding of expository text? Research has identified specific strategies that students can use to improve their reading comprehension. Strategies emphasized in *Reading Support and Intervention* include

- monitoring comprehension.
- using graphic organizers.
- answering questions.

HOW can we help students monitor their comprehension? Students who monitor their understanding as they read are better able to master social studies content. In order to monitor their comprehension, students must learn to think metacognitively. That is, they must learn to think about their thinking. As they read, good readers assess whether or not they understand the content. They choose and use appropriate strategies, such as rereading portions of the text, adjusting their reading rate according to the difficulty of the material, restating passages in their own words, and pausing occasionally to summarize what they have just read.

The Preview the Lesson and the Build Comprehension of Expository Text sections in *Reading Support and Intervention* provide opportunities for you to teach strategies for monitoring comprehension. As you guide students through the lesson and observe where they have problems, you can suggest appropriate strategies to help resolve the difficulty. Explain how the strategy can help them and when to apply it.

Students can also use the KWL, SQ3R or QAR strategy to help them monitor their comprehension as they read. Student Cards are available that provide guidance in using these strategies.

Summarizing the Lesson

WHY is using graphic organizers an important strategy for social studies? Graphic organizers include webs, charts, graphs, and diagrams. The purpose of a graphic organizer is to show how concepts are related. Graphic organizers such as time lines and flowcharts show how events are related chronologically. Other types of graphic organizers show cause-and-effect relationships, comparisons and contrasts between concepts, or how details relate to a main idea.

Completing the *Reading Support and Intervention* graphic organizer for each lesson helps students focus on important concepts in the lesson. Filling in the organizer as they read also helps them monitor their comprehension of the material. The completed organizer gives them a tool that they can use to recall relationships in the text and to summarize what they read.

WHAT does research tell us about the value of answering questions? Having students answer questions about their reading is a traditional strategy that teachers have used to guide and assess learning. Recent research confirms the value of this strategy. Answering questions improves students' comprehension of social studies concepts by

- giving them a purpose for reading the text.
- focusing their attention on the content.
- encouraging them to monitor their comprehension and think metacognitively.
- helping them review what they have learned and relate it to other knowledge.

Support metacognitive thinking and strategy use by asking students to explain how they figured out correct answers or how they can find answers that they do not know.

HOW can Leveled Readers help struggling readers? The Leveled Readers were specifically produced to match the content of *Harcourt Social Studies*. The readers are categorized into three reading levels: Basic, Proficient, and Advanced. These readers can help build fluency when used for small-group reading, shared reading, echo reading, choral reading, or reading at home.

LESSON 1

States and Regions

Vocabulary Strategies

Preteach Additional Vocabulary After teaching the Vocabulary words on Student Edition page 14, explain to students that there are several other important words they will see in this lesson. Use Procedure Card 1, along with the suggestions below, to introduce the words.

northernmost	Have students identify the word *north* and suffixes *-ern* and *-most.* Ask students to locate Alaska on the map on page 15 and explain why it is the northernmost state.
similar	Remind students that similar things are alike in some way. *Similar* and *different* are antonyms, or opposites.
culture	Tell students that a culture is a way of life that a group of people share.
area	Explain that the amount of land that makes up a place is called its area. On the map on page 15, have students compare states of noticeably different sizes, such as Texas and Louisiana, and tell which has the greater area.
ranks	Have students use the following context to determine the meaning of *ranks:* "In land area, Canada is the largest country in North America. The United States ranks second."

WORD CARDS To help teach the lesson vocabulary, use the Word Cards on pages 233–234.

Build Fluency

Use page 4 and the steps on Procedure Card 2 to reinforce vocabulary and build fluency. Read each vocabulary word aloud and have students repeat it. Then have students work in pairs to reread the words. Follow a similar procedure with the phrases and sentences. Continue to help students build fluency by having them reread "You Are There" in the Student Edition.

Text Comprehension

Before Reading

Preview the Lesson Guide students in previewing the lesson using Procedure Card 3. Point out the following features of the lesson on Student Edition pages 14–19.

- **Pages 14–15** Read the lesson title and the "What to Know" question, and have students predict topics they will learn about in this lesson. Preview the photographs of the Derby Line library on page 14. Have students locate their state on the map on page 15 and use the key to locate and identify its capital.
- **Pages 16–17** Have students examine the map of the regions of the United States and read the labels. Students should locate their own state and identify the region in which it is located.

- **Pages 18–19** Preview the photographs showing scenes in Canada and Mexico. Have students examine the graph on page 19 and answer the caption questions. Point out that Canada, which is largest in land area, has the smallest population. Then preview the Review questions.

During Reading

Build Comprehension of Expository Text Present the graphic organizer on page 5. Have students preview the organizer by filling in the lesson title and comparing the two main heads in the organizer with the matching subheads in the Student Edition pages 14–19. Tell students that the section subheads provide additional help with identifying important information. Use Procedure Card 4, the Reading Check questions in *Harcourt Social Studies*, and the directed reading suggestions below.

- **Page 14** After students have read "You Are There," have them locate the border of Vermont and Canada on the map on page 15. Explain that the country of Canada is divided into provinces, as the United States is divided into states.
- **Pages 15–17** Have students read "A Nation of 50 States." Then guide them in filling in the information in the first box of the organizer. Point out the connection to the box with the subhead "Regions of the United States." Tell students that they will find the names of the regions and how states in each region are similar under the section subhead "Regions of the United States" in the text. Then they can write the information in the organizer.
- **Pages 18–19** After students have read "A Country in North America," point out the subheads in the two boxes that match the section subheads in the text. Students can locate and write information about history that Canada shares with the United States and about history that Mexico shares with the United States.

After Reading

Summarize Have students use their completed graphic organizers to summarize the lesson. Then have them compare their summaries to the lesson summary on page 19.

Review and Respond Work through the Review questions with students. Use Transparency 1 (Compare and Contrast) to discuss comparisons and contrasts in the lesson.

Draw a Map Suggest that students look at a map of North America to help them draw their own maps. Remind them to give the map a title, to label each country on the map, and to include a compass rose to make clear the relative locations of the countries.

Leveled Readers Use the Leveled Readers and Procedure Card 5 to build fluency and comprehension.

Name ______________________________ Date ____________

DIRECTIONS **Read aloud the words in Part A. Practice reading aloud the phrases and the sentences in Part B.**

Part A

Vocabulary Words	Additional Words
contiguous	northernmost
region	similar
relative location	culture
continent	area
population	ranks

Part B

1. Forty-eight states / of the United States / are contiguous, / but Alaska and Hawaii / are separated from the other states.

2. Alaska, / our northernmost state, / shares a border / with the country of Canada.

3. The five regions of the United States / are based on their relative location.

4. The states in each region / often have similar kinds of land, / and the people who live there / often earn their living in similar ways.

5. The states in each region / may also share / a history and culture.

6. The United States / is in the continent of North America.

7. Of the countries in North America, / the United States / ranks second / in land area.

8. In population, / the United States / is the largest country / in North America.

YOU ARE THERE **Turn to Student Edition page 14. Practice reading aloud "You Are There" three times. Try to improve your reading each time. Record your best time on the line below.**

Number of words 83 My Best Time ________ Words per Minute ________

Name ______________________ Date ______________

Lesson Title ______________________

A Nation of 50 States

Number of contiguous states ____________

States that are separated

____________ and ____________

Regions of the United States

Names of regions

How states in a region are similar

Canada

A Country in North America

Mexico

Canada, Our Northern Neighbor

Shared history with United States

Mexico, Our Southern Neighbor

Shared history with United States

LESSON 2 The Land

Vocabulary Strategies

Preteach Additional Vocabulary After teaching the Vocabulary words on Student Edition page 22, explain to students that there are several other important words they will see in this lesson. Use Procedure Card 1, along with the suggestions below, to introduce the words.

geographer	Point out the root *geo,* meaning "Earth." Discuss the relationship between the words *geography* and *geographer.*
extends	Have students substitute synonyms *stretches* and *reaches* for *extends* in this sentence: "From Florida, the Coastal Plain extends west into Texas and the country of Mexico."
valley	Ask a volunteer to draw a sketch of two mountains and point out the valley between them.
glacier	Tell students that a glacier is a huge mass of ice that very slowly moves across the land.
interior	Point out that the first two letters of this word spell *in,* which can help students remember that *interior* means the inside of a house or the inner part of a body of land, away from the coast.

WORD CARDS To help teach the lesson vocabulary, use the Word Cards on pages 233–234.

Build Fluency

Use page 8 and the steps on Procedure Card 2 to reinforce vocabulary and build fluency. Read each vocabulary word aloud and have students repeat it. Then have students work in pairs to reread the words. Follow a similar procedure with the phrases and sentences. Continue to help students build fluency by having them reread "You Are There" in the Student Edition.

Text Comprehension

BEFORE READING

Preview the Lesson Guide students in previewing the lesson using Procedure Card 3. Point out the following features of the lesson on Student Edition pages 22–29.

- **Pages 22–23** Read the lesson title and discuss the "What to Know" question. Preview the photograph of New York Harbor in the 1890s and the portrait of Robert Louis Stevenson.
- **Pages 24–25** Have students examine the landforms map on page 24 and answer the map skill question. Preview the photograph on page 25, and then have students locate the Appalachian Mountains, the Coastal Plain, and the Interior Plains on the map on page 24.
- **Pages 26–27** Preview the photograph of the Rocky Mountains. Have students read and discuss the Fast Fact.

- **Pages 28–29** Preview the photographs. Have students locate the Central Valley in California on the map on page 24 and identify landforms on the Pacific Coast. Preview the Review questions on page 29.

During Reading

Build Comprehension of Expository Text Present the graphic organizer on page 9. Have students preview the organizer by filling in the lesson title and comparing the six main heads in the organizer with the matching subheads in the Student Edition pages 22–29. Tell students that the section subheads provide additional help with identifying important information. Use Procedure Card 4, the Reading Check questions in *Harcourt Social Studies*, and the directed reading suggestions below.

- **Page 22** After students have read "You Are There," ask them to show on the map on page 24 the direction in which the great great-grandparents would have traveled across the United States starting from New York City.
- **Page 23** Have students read "Landform Regions." Then guide them in filling in the information in the first box in the organizer. Point out the subhead "A Long Journey" that matches the section subhead in the text.
- **Pages 24–25** After students have read "The Coastal Plain," have them record information in the box with that head in the organizer. Point out the arrow that shows which landform region comes next. Have students read "The Appalachians" and fill in that box. Tell them to use the subhead "A Long Range" to locate information in the text.
- **Pages 26–27** Have students read "The Interior Plains," and write information in that box of the organizer, following the arrow from the previous box. Follow a similar procedure to have them read and write information about "The Rocky Mountains and Beyond."
- **Pages 28–29** After students have read "More Mountains and Valleys," they can complete the last box in the organizer. You may also want to have them list on the reverse side of their organizer sheets the valleys mentioned in this section of the lesson and then write a summary statement about what Stevenson learned on his journey across the United States.

After Reading

Summarize Have students use their completed graphic organizers to summarize the lesson. Then have them compare their summaries to the lesson summary on page 29.

Review and Respond If students need additional help with comparing and contrasting, use Focus Skill Transparency 1.

Make Flash Cards Suggest that students go back through the lesson and jot down the names and descriptions of the landform regions. Then they can use these notes to help them make their flash cards. You may want to have students work in pairs to make the flash cards and then use the cards to quiz each other.

Leveled Readers Use the Leveled Readers and Procedure Card 5 to build fluency and comprehension.

Name ______________________________ Date ______________

DIRECTIONS **Read aloud the words in Part A. Practice reading aloud the phrases and the sentences in Part B.**

Part A

Vocabulary Words		Additional Words	
landform	climate	geographer	glacier
environment	erosion	extends	interior
mountain range	prairie	valley	

Part B

1. To better study the land, / geographers/ often divide it / into landform regions.
2. In the late 1800s, / Robert Louis Stevenson / took a trip / across the United States / that would teach him / about the nation's landforms / and climate.
3. From Florida, / the Coastal Plain / extends west into Texas / and the country of Mexico.
4. The region of valleys and hills / on the eastern side of the Appalachian Mountains / is called the Piedmont.
5. The Appalachians / are a mountain range / running from southern Canada / to central Alabama.
6. Their peaks / were worn down / by glaciers / and by erosion / caused by rain and wind.
7. The eastern part of the Interior Plains / is sometimes called / a tall-grass prairie.
8. When Stevenson's train / stopped in the middle of Nebraska, / he saw that the environment / was yet again different.

YOU ARE THERE **Turn to Student Edition page 22. Practice reading aloud "You Are There" three times. Try to improve your reading each time. Record your best time on the line below.**

Number of words 84 My Best Time ________ Words per Minute ________

Name ______________________ Date ____________

Lesson Title ______________________

Landform Regions

Why each is unique ______________________

____

A Long Journey Across ______________________

The Coastal Plain

Description ______________________

Gets __________ farther __________

The Appalachians

Eastern side ______________________

Description ______________________

A Long Range Where ______________________

____

Description ______________________

____

The Interior Plains

Eastern part ______________________

Description ______________________

The Great Plains Description

____

The Rocky Mountains and Beyond

Part of United States ______________________

Description ______________________

The Intermountain Region

Part of this land ______________________

More Mountains and Valleys

Mountain Ranges to the West

____

____

The Journey Ends

Where ______________________

LESSON 3 Bodies of Water

Vocabulary Strategies

Preteach Additional Vocabulary After teaching the Vocabulary words on Student Edition page 30, explain to students that there are several other important words they will see in this lesson. Use Procedure Card 1, along with the suggestions below, to introduce the words.

shape	Point out that *shape* is a noun in phrases such as "the shape of the United States" but is also used as a verb, as in this sentence: "Hundred of bays and sounds also shape the coastline."
offshore	Have students identify the two shorter words that make up this compound word. Explain that an offshore island is located close to the mainland.
source	Tell students that the source of something is where it begins. Have students locate Lake Itasca, the source of the Mississippi River, on the map on page 32.
empty	Discuss the difference between saying that someone empties a bucket of water and saying that a river empties into a larger body of water. The river, unlike the bucket, is still full of water.
continental	Have students identify the word *continent* and suffix *-al,* meaning "about" or "related to." Have them locate the Continental Divide on the map on page 32.

WORD CARDS To help teach the lesson vocabulary, use the Word Cards on pages 233–236.

Build Fluency

Use page 12 and the steps on Procedure Card 2 to reinforce vocabulary and build fluency. Read each vocabulary word aloud and have students repeat it. Then have students work in pairs to reread the words. Follow a similar procedure with the phrases and sentences. Continue to help students build fluency by having them reread "You Are There" in the Student Edition.

Text Comprehension

Before Reading

Preview the Lesson Guide students in previewing the lesson using Procedure Card 3. Point out the following features of the lesson on Student Edition pages 30–35.

- **Pages 30–31** Read the lesson title and the "What to Know" question. Encourage students to name familiar bodies of water in the United States. Preview the photograph of Lake Michigan, and have students read the Fast Fact.
- **Pages 32–33** Have students examine the map on page 32 and answer the map skill question. Ask students to point out bodies of water found in or near their own state. Then have students read Children in History on page 33 and discuss the Make It Relevant question. Tell students that Mark Twain wrote *The Adventures of Tom Sawyer.*

- **Pages 34–35** Preview the photograph of the Continental Divide and the Review questions on page 34, and the biography of Marjory Stoneman Douglas on page 35.

During Reading

Build Comprehension of Expository Text Present the graphic organizer on page 13. Have students preview the organizer by filling in the lesson title and comparing the four main heads in the organizer with the matching subheads in the Student Edition pages 30–34. Tell students that the section subheads provide additional help with identifying important information. Use Procedure Card 4, the Reading Check questions in *Harcourt Social Studies,* and the directed reading suggestions below.

- **Page 30** After students have read "You Are There," point out that the photograph on pages 30–31 shows sailboats on Lake Michigan and also the tall buildings of the city of Chicago.
- **Page 31** Have students read "Inlets and Lakes." Then guide them in filling in the information in the two boxes with the subheads "Gulfs and Inlets" and "Our Largest Lakes" that match the section subheads in the text.
- **Page 32** After students have read "Rivers," point out the box with the subhead "River Systems." Students can write information about the largest river system in the United States in this box.
- **Pages 33–34** Have students read "Rivers in the East" and write information in the box with the subhead "Rivers and Population" that matches the section subhead in the text. Follow a similar procedure to have students read "Rivers in the West" and complete the organizer.

After Reading

Summarize Have students use their completed graphic organizers to summarize the lesson. Then have them compare their summaries to the lesson summary on page 34.

Review and Respond If students need additional help with comparing and contrasting, use Focus Skill Transparency 1.

Draw a Poster Provide or point out to students an appropriate map to help them locate the river nearest to your city or town. If students require more information about the river, landforms, nearby cities, or tributaries, suggest or provide helpful sources of information, such as encyclopedias, atlases, or websites.

Leveled Readers Use the Leveled Readers and Procedure Card 5 to build fluency and comprehension.

Name ______________________________ Date ____________

DIRECTIONS **Read aloud the words in Part A. Practice reading aloud the phrases and the sentences in Part B.**

Part A

Vocabulary Words		Additional Words	
inlet	river system	shape	empty
gulf	drainage basin	offshore	continental
sound	fall line	source	
tributary			

Part B

1. Hundreds of inlets / along the Atlantic and Pacific coasts / help define the shape / of the United States.
2. The largest gulf bordering the United States / is the Gulf of Mexico.
3. Hundreds of bays and sounds, / which are long inlets / that separate offshore islands / from the mainland, / also shape the coastline.
4. Every river / begins at a source / and ends at a mouth, / where it empties / into a larger body of water.
5. The Mississippi River and its tributaries / create the largest river system / in the United States.
6. The drainage basin / of the Mississippi River system / includes most of the land / between the Rocky and Appalachian Mountains.
7. Many cities / have been built / where rivers flow into oceans, / but other cities / lie inland / along the Fall Line.
8. Rivers that begin east of the Continental Divide / eventually reach the Atlantic Ocean.

YOU ARE THERE **Turn to Student Edition page 30. Practice reading aloud "You Are There" three times. Try to improve your reading each time. Record your best time on the line below.**

Number of words 63 My Best Time ________ Words per Minute ________

Name ______________________________ Date ______________

Lesson Title ______________________________

Inlets and Lakes

Gulfs and Inlets

Large gulfs ______________________________

____

Largest bays and sounds provide

____

Our Largest Lakes

Known as ______________________________

How many ______________________________

Waterway links ______________________________

____

Rivers

River Systems

Largest in the United States

____

Rivers in the East

Rivers and Population

Where many cities have been built

____

Where other cities lie ______________________________

____

How people now use fast-moving water ______________________________

Rivers in the West

Rivers and the Continental Divide

Where rivers that begin east of the Continental Divide eventually reach

____

Where most rivers that begin west of the Continental Divide empty

____

Lesson 4 Climate and Vegetation

Vocabulary Strategies

Preteach Additional Vocabulary After teaching the Vocabulary words on Student Edition page 36, explain to students that there are several other important words they will see in this lesson. Use Procedure Card 1, along with the suggestions below, to introduce the words.

orbit	Students may know that the orbit of a planet or an object such as a space station is the path it follows around a larger body in space. Explain that we also use *orbit* as a verb. For example, we say, "Earth orbits the sun."
tilted	Have students use an object such as a book to show the difference between something that is level and something that is tilted.
axis	Use a globe of Earth or the diagram on page 37 to point out the imaginary line that is called Earth's axis. Point out also that Earth is tilted on its axis.
distinct	Discuss the meaning of *distinct* in this sentence: "Some places have four distinct seasons."
precipitation	Tell students that precipitation is moisture that falls to the ground. Precipitation may be in the form of rain, snow, or hail.

WORD CARDS To help teach the lesson vocabulary, use the Word Cards on pages 235–236.

Build Fluency

Use page 16 and the steps on Procedure Card 2 to reinforce vocabulary and build fluency. Read each vocabulary word aloud and have students repeat it. Then have students work in pairs to reread the words. Follow a similar procedure with the phrases and sentences. Continue to help students build fluency by having them reread "You Are There" in the Student Edition.

Text Comprehension

Before Reading

Preview the Lesson Guide students in previewing the lesson using Procedure Card 3. Point out the following features of the lesson on Student Edition pages 36–39.

- **Pages 36–37** Read the lesson title and have students recall the meaning of *climate*. Then discuss the "What to Know" question. Preview the photograph of the Rocky Mountains, and ask students to name some other outdoor activities people might do in the mountains. Have students examine the diagram of the four seasons and discuss the question in the caption.
- **Pages 38–39** Have students look at the map of climate regions on page 38 and use the key to find out what climate region they live in. Preview the photograph of desert plants and the Review questions on page 39.

During Reading

Build Comprehension of Expository Text Present the graphic organizer on page 17. Have students preview the organizer by filling in the lesson title and comparing the two main heads in the organizer with the matching subheads in the Student Edition pages 36–39. Tell students that the section subheads provide additional help with identifying important information. Use Procedure Card 4, the Reading Check questions in *Harcourt Social Studies,* and the directed reading suggestions below.

- **Page 36** After students have read "You Are There," discuss what the paragraph shows about the climate of the Rocky Mountains.
- **Page 37** Before students read "Climate," point out that the organizer has a separate box for each section subhead. Have students use the organizer to set a purpose for reading this section of the lesson. As they read or after reading, students can list in the first box of the organizer three factors affecting climate and then, in the second box, write an effect for each cause.
- **Pages 38–39** Follow a similar procedure to the one used in the previous section. Point out that the information students will write in the first box is found under the main head "Vegetation" in the text, while the information for the second box will be under the section subhead "Vegetation Regions."

After Reading

Summarize Have students use their completed graphic organizers to summarize the lesson. Then have them compare their summaries to the lesson summary on page 39.

Review and Respond If students need additional help with comparing and contrasting, use Focus Skill Transparency 1.

Write a Poem Review briefly what students know about writing a poem. Be sure they understand the importance of imagery and rhythmical language and the fact that poems do not have to rhyme. Suggest that students begin by brainstorming words and phrases about the climate and vegetation of your region that they can use in their poems.

Leveled Readers Use the Leveled Readers and Procedure Card 5 to build fluency and comprehension.

Name ______________________________ Date ______________

DIRECTIONS **Read aloud the words in Part A. Practice reading aloud the phrases and the sentences in Part B.**

Part A

Vocabulary Words	Additional Words
elevation	orbit
natural vegetation	tilted
arid	axis
tundra	distinct
	precipitation

Part B

1. Factors affecting the climate of a place / include its distance from the equator / and from large bodies of water, / and its elevation.
2. Earth's orbit around the sun / causes changes in seasons / —summer, / autumn, / winter, / and spring.
3. Because Earth is tilted on its axis / as it orbits the sun, / places get different amounts of sunlight and heat / at different times of the year.
4. Some places / have four distinct seasons.
5. The natural vegetation / that grows in a place / varies / depending on the soil.
6. The vegetation / also varies / because of temperature / and precipitation.
7. Only plants that can grow in an arid climate / can grow in deserts.
8. Most of the United States / can be divided / into four main vegetation regions, / which are forest, / grassland, / desert, / and tundra.

YOU ARE THERE **Turn to Student Edition page 36. Practice reading aloud "You Are There" three times. Try to improve your reading each time. Record your best time on the line below.**

Number of words 63 My Best Time ________ Words per Minute ________

Name ______________________ Date ______________

Lesson Title: ______________________

Climate

Factors Affecting Climate

1. ______________________

2. ______________________

3. ______________________

Earth and the Sun

CAUSE →	EFFECT
Earth's orbit around the sun	______________________
Earth is tilted on its axis	______________________

Vegetation

Why natural vegetation varies

1. ______________________

2. ______________________

3. ______________________

Vegetation Regions

	Region	Type of Vegetation
1.	____________	____________
2.	____________	____________
3.	____________	____________
4.	____________	____________

LESSON 5 People and the Environment

Vocabulary Strategies

Preteach Additional Vocabulary After teaching the Vocabulary words on Student Edition page 40, explain to students that there are several other important words they will see in this lesson. Use Procedure Card 1, along with the suggestions below, to introduce the words.

route	Tell students that a route is the path or way that people use to travel from one place to another.
alters	Have students substitute the synonym *changes* for *alters* in this sentence: "A human feature is something created by people, such as a building or a road, that alters the land."
ore	Point out that this word, the name for a mineral from which we get a substance such as iron or other metal, is a homonym of *or* and *oar*.
century	Tell students that *century* is from the Latin root *centum*, meaning "hundred." Other words from this root include *cent*, *centimeter*, and *per cent*.
negative	Explain that the root of this word is the Latin *negare*, "to say no." An antonym of *negative* is *positive*.

WORD CARDS To help teach the lesson vocabulary, use the Word Cards on pages 235–238.

Build Fluency

Use page 20 and the steps on Procedure Card 2 to reinforce vocabulary and build fluency. Read each vocabulary word aloud and have students repeat it. Then have students work in pairs to reread the words. Follow a similar procedure with the phrases and sentences. Continue to help students build fluency by having them reread "You Are There" in the Student Edition.

Text Comprehension

BEFORE READING

Preview the Lesson Guide students in previewing the lesson using Procedure Card 3. Point out the following features of the lesson on Student Edition pages 40–45.

- **Pages 40–41** Read the lesson title and the "What to Know" question. Ask students to predict some of the ways that people change the environment. Preview the photographs, and have students read the Fast Fact. Discuss changes that people have made to the environment shown in the photographs.
- **Pages 42–43** Preview the photographs on page 42. Have students identify the oil rig in the smaller photograph and the crop being harvested in the larger one. Then have students examine the map on page 43 and use the map key to answer the map skill question about natural resources where you live.
- **Pages 44–45** Have students examine and discuss the illustration of the Hoover Dam and how it operates. Then preview the Review questions.

During Reading

Build Comprehension of Expository Text Present the graphic organizer on page 21. Have students preview the organizer by filling in the lesson title and comparing the three main heads in the organizer with the matching subheads in the Student Edition pages 40–45. Tell students that the section subheads provide additional help with identifying important information. Use Procedure Card 4, the Reading Check questions in *Harcourt Social Studies*, and the directed reading suggestions below.

- **Page 40** After students have read "You Are There," point out the connection with the photographs on pages 40–41 and the Fast Fact about the John A. Roebling bridge.
- **Page 41** Have students read "Patterns of Land Use." Then guide them in writing information in the first box of the organizer. Point out the subhead that matches the section subhead in the text.
- **Pages 42–43** After students have read "Using the Land," call attention to the two boxes below this head in the organizer with subheads that match the section subheads. Students can list in the first box three ways that people use the land. In the second box, they should list two kinds of natural resources and a word that describes the second type of resource.
- **Pages 44–45** Have students read "Changing the Environment" and complete the three boxes with subheads that match the section subheads.

After Reading

Summarize Have students use their completed graphic organizers to summarize the lesson. Then have them compare their summaries to the lesson summary on page 45.

Review and Respond If students need additional help with comparing and contrasting, use Focus Skill Transparency 1.

Write a Paragraph Discuss the topic of conserving natural resources and specific things that students can do to help in this effort. You may want to jot down ideas on the board or on chart paper. Tell students to choose one idea to write about. Remind them to begin the paragraph with a topic sentence and then to write two or more additional sentences to give supporting details.

Leveled Readers Use the Leveled Readers and Procedure Card 5 to build fluency and comprehension.

Name ________________________________ Date ______________

DIRECTIONS **Read aloud the words in Part A. Practice reading aloud the phrases and the sentences in Part B.**

Part A

Vocabulary Words		Additional Words
natural resource	modify	route
renewable resource	land use	alters
nonrenewable resource	efficiency	ore
	irrigation	century
		negative

Part B

1. Settlers / set up communities / where there was farmland, / fresh water, / and transportation routes, / such as rivers.
2. Landforms and climate / can influence land use.
3. A human feature / is something created by people, / such as a building or a road, / that alters the land.
4. Some natural resources / are renewable resources / that can be made again / by people or nature.
5. During the last century, / people began to realize / that the supply of nonrenewable resources, / such as ores,/ is limited.
6. Americans use tools / to modify the land / and to gather and use natural resources.
7. Irrigation / can sometimes have negative effects, / such as causing pollution / in waterways.
8. Today, / engineers have learned much / about energy efficiency.

YOU ARE THERE **Turn to Student Edition page 40. Practice reading aloud "You Are There" three times. Try to improve your reading each time. Record your best time on the line below.**

Number of words 76 My Best Time _______ Words per Minute _______

Name ______________________ Date ______________

Lesson Title: ______________________

Patterns of Land Use

Factors Encouraging Settlement

What can affect where people settle ______________________

Where people avoided settling ______________________

How patterns have changed ______________________

____

Using the Land

How People Use the Land

1. ______________________
2. ______________________
3. ______________________

Natural Resources

1. ______________________
2. ______________________

Supply is ______________________.

Changing the Environment

Using Water Changes to the environment ______________________

____

____

Using the Land How people modify the environment ______________________

____

____

Balancing the Changes

How ______________________

LESSON 1 Early People

Vocabulary Strategies

Preteach Additional Vocabulary After teaching the Vocabulary words on Student Edition page 52, explain to students that there are several other important words they will see in this lesson. Use Procedure Card 1, along with the suggestions below, to introduce the words.

origin	Tell students that a synonym for *origin* is *beginning*.
descendant	Explain that *descendant* (one who comes later in a family line) is the antonym of *ancestor* (one who came earlier in a family line.)
government	Discuss what students know about government and what governments do.
mound	Ask a volunteer to draw a picture of a mound, a rounded hill of earth.
burial	Tell students that this word is formed from *bury* by changing *y* to *i* and adding the suffix *-al*. Burial is the act of burying a person who has died.

WORD CARDS To help teach the lesson vocabulary, use the Word Cards on pages 239–240.

Build Fluency

Use page 24 and the steps on Procedure Card 2 to reinforce vocabulary and build fluency. Read each vocabulary word aloud and have students repeat it. Then have students work in pairs to reread the words. Follow a similar procedure with the phrases and sentences. Continue to help students build fluency by having them reread "You Are There" in the Student Edition.

Text Comprehension

BEFORE READING

Preview the Lesson Guide students in previewing the lesson using Procedure Card 3. Point out the following features of the lesson on Student Edition pages 52–59.

- **Pages 52–53** Discuss the "What to Know" question. Preview the time line and the illustration. Discuss students' ideas about who these people are and what they are doing. Preview the map of land routes and have students answer the map skill question.
- **Pages 54–55** Preview the illustration on page 54 and have students read and discuss the meaning of the story "How the Robin Got His Red Breast." Call attention to the illustration of a woolly mammoth on page 55, and ask students to describe what is happening in the picture.
- **Pages 56–57** Preview the map of early civilizations, and have students answer the map skill question. On page 57, preview the photograph of Mayan ruins. Have students point out the location of the Mayan civilization on the map on page 56.

- **Pages 58–59** Have students examine the painting of Cahokia. Discuss the caption and how people today may have ideas about what Cahokia looked like. Have students locate Cahokia on the map on page 56. Preview the illustration on page 59, and have students locate Mesa Verde on the map. Then preview the Review questions.

During Reading

Build Comprehension of Expository Text Present the graphic organizer on page 25. Have students preview the organizer by filling in the lesson title and comparing the five main heads in the organizer with the matching subheads in the Student Edition pages 52–59. Tell students that the section subheads provide additional help with identifying important information. Use Procedure Card 4, the Reading Check questions in *Harcourt Social Studies,* and the directed reading suggestions below.

- **Page 52** After students have read "You Are There," discuss the two different ways it describes that early people obtained food—hunting animals and gathering wild plants.
- **Pages 53–54** Have students read "The Land Bridge Story." Then guide them in summarizing the theory and writing the summary in the first box of the graphic organizer. Next have them read "Other Theories" and write in that box of the organizer why some scientists have other theories and what many Native Americans believe.
- **Page 55** Have students look at the organizer to set a purpose for reading "Early Ways of Life." As they read or after reading, students can fill in the information about how and why early ways of life changed.
- **Pages 56–57** After students have read "The Olmec and the Maya," point out that the subheads in the two smaller boxes in the organizer match the section subheads in the text. Tell students to use the subheads to find and list information about Olmec achievements and Mayan culture.
- **Pages 58–59** As students read "Other Civilizations," or after reading, they can complete the organizer by filling in information about two other civilizations. Tell students that the section subheads can help them identify these civilizations.

After Reading

Summarize Have students use their completed graphic organizers to summarize the lesson. Then have them compare their summaries to the lesson summary on page 59.

Review and Respond If students need additional help with comparing and contrasting, use Focus Skill Transparency 1.

Write a Paragraph Suggest that students take notes as they reread passages that tell about theories of how people arrived in the Americas. Remind students to begin the paragraph with a topic sentence and to tell information in their own words.

Leveled Readers Use the Leveled Readers and Procedure Card 5 to build fluency and comprehension.

Name ______________________________ Date ______________

DIRECTIONS **Read aloud the words in Part A. Practice reading aloud the phrases and the sentences in Part B.**

Part A

Vocabulary Words		Additional Words
ancestor	civilization	origin
theory	tradition	descendant
migration	class	government
artifact		mound
		burial

Part B

1. Scientists / have several theories / to explain how the ancestors / of present-day Native Americans / arrived in North America.
2. Many scientists believe / that a migration / took place / across a land bridge / from Asia / to North America.
3. Native American origin stories / have come from descendants / of early people / in the Americas.
4. Artifacts / can tell scientists / a great deal / about life long ago.
5. The Mayan civilization / was influenced / by Olmec traditions.
6. The Maya / were divided into social classes / and had no central government.
7. The earliest civilization of Mound Builders, / the Adena, / built large earth mounds / that they used for burials.

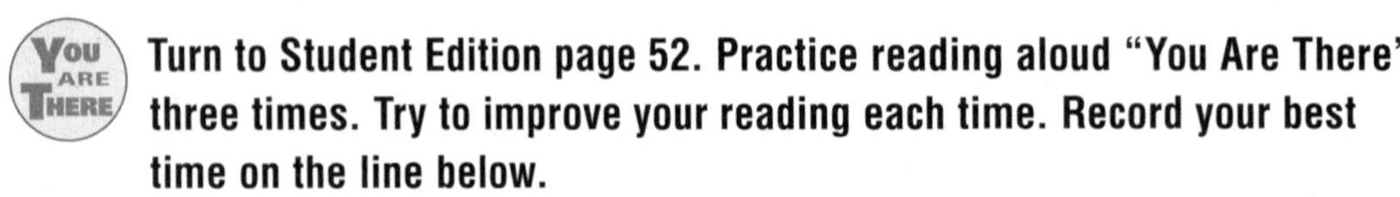

Turn to Student Edition page 52. Practice reading aloud "You Are There" three times. Try to improve your reading each time. Record your best time on the line below.

Number of words __85__ My Best Time ______ Words per Minute ______

Name ______________________ Date ____________

Lesson Title: ______________________

The Land Bridge Story

Theory

Other Theories

Why

What many Native Americans believe

Early Ways of Life

How ways of life changed

Why ways of life changed

The Olmec and the Maya

The Olmec Civilization Achievements

The Mayan Civilization Culture

Other Civilizations

Who

What they built

Who

What their houses were like

LESSON 2 The Eastern Woodlands

Vocabulary Strategies

Preteach Additional Vocabulary After teaching the Vocabulary words on Student Edition page 62, explain to students that there are several other important words they will see in this lesson. Use Procedure Card 1, along with the suggestions below, to introduce the words.

shelter	Give examples of shelters, such as a tent and an apartment building. Have students give other examples.
moccasin	Tell students that this name for a type of leather shoe made by Native Americans comes from an Algonquian language.
goods	Point out that this word looks and sounds like the familiar adjective *good* with *s* added. Explain that *goods* is a noun often used to means items that are bought and sold.
dispute	Tell students that a synonym for *dispute* is *disagreement*. Ask students to suggest other synonyms.
dome	Display a picture of the United States Capitol in Washington, D.C. or another building with a dome. Have students draw and label dome shapes.

WORD CARDS To help teach the lesson vocabulary, use the Word Cards on pages 239–242.

Build Fluency

Use page 28 and the steps on Procedure Card 2 to reinforce vocabulary and build fluency. Read each vocabulary word aloud and have students repeat it. Then have students work in pairs to reread the words. Follow a similar procedure with the phrases and sentences. Continue to help students build fluency by having them reread "You Are There" in the Student Edition.

Text Comprehension

BEFORE READING

Preview the Lesson Guide students in previewing the lesson using Procedure Card 3. Point out the following features of the lesson on Student Edition pages 62–67.

- **Pages 62–63** Read the "What to Know" question and discuss students' ideas about how the geography and climate of the Eastern Woodlands might have affected the Native Americans there. Preview the illustration of Iroquois youngsters playing lacrosse, and have students read the Fast Fact. Preview the photograph of the Eastern Woodlands and ask what resource it shows.
- **Pages 64–65** Have students examine the illustration of an Iroquois village and read the labels. Then have them answer the question in the caption.
- **Pages 66–67** Preview the engraving and discuss how it helps us learn about the Algonquian people. On page 67, preview the picture of an Algonquian bowl and then the Review questions.

During Reading

Build Comprehension of Expository Text Present the graphic organizer on page 29. Have students preview the organizer by filling in the lesson title and comparing the three main heads in the organizer with the matching subheads in the Student Edition pages 62–67. Tell students that the section subheads provide additional help with identifying important information. Use Procedure Card 4, the Reading Check questions in *Harcourt Social Studies,* and the directed reading suggestions below.

- **Page 62** After students have read "You Are There," ask whether they think they would enjoy playing this Iroquois game and why or why not.
- **Page 63** Have students read "Life in the Eastern Woodlands." Tell them to write in each box in the organizer a way that the people of the Eastern Woodlands used trees as a natural resource.
- **Pages 64–65** After students have read about the Iroquois, have them write information for each category below the heading "The Iroquois" in the graphic organizer. Point out that the section subheads in the text can help students locate information.
- **Pages 66–67** After students have read about the Algonquians, have them write information for each category below the heading "The Algonquians" in the organizer. Discuss similarities and differences that the organizer shows between the Iroquois and the Algonquians.

After Reading

Summarize Have students use their completed graphic organizers to summarize the lesson. Then have them compare their summaries to the lesson summary on page 67.

Review and Respond If students need additional help with comparing and contrasting, use Focus Skill Transparency 1.

Give a Speech Have students recall what the Iroquois League was and why it was formed, rereading passages in the lesson as necessary. Remind students that speakers will need to state their opinions clearly and give strong reasons to support those opinions.

Leveled Readers Use the Leveled Readers and Procedure Card 5 to build fluency and comprehension.

Name ______________________________ Date ______________

DIRECTIONS **Read aloud the words in Part A. Practice reading aloud the phrases and the sentences in Part B.**

Part A

Vocabulary Words		Additional Words
division of labor	wampum	shelter
confederation	palisade	moccasin
longhouse	wigwam	goods
		dispute
		dome

Part B

1. Native Americans of the Eastern Woodlands / used trees / to make canoes / and shelters.
2. The women / used animal skins / to make clothing / and moccasins.
3. Division of labor / made it possible / for people to produce more goods.
4. To protect against enemies, / many Iroquois / built palisades around their villages, / where they lived in shelters / called longhouses.
5. Like many other Native Americans, / the Iroquois / traded wampum for goods.
6. The Five Nations / formed a confederation / called the Iroquois League.
7. The league / set up a Grand Council / to settle disputes among the people.
8. Some Algonquians / built wigwams / by bending and tying trunks of small trees / into dome shapes.

YOU ARE THERE **Turn to Student Edition page 62. Practice reading aloud "You Are There" three times. Try to improve your reading each time. Record your best time on the line below.**

Number of words 71 My Best Time ________ Words per Minute ________

Name ______________________________ Date ______________

Lesson Title: ______________________________

Life in the Eastern Woodlands

A Common Resource

The Iroquois
Where ______________________
Language ______________________
Villages ______________________
Shelters ______________________
Food ______________________
Government ______________________
____
____

The Algonquians
Where ______________________
Language ______________________
Villages ______________________
Shelters ______________________
Food ______________________
Government ______________________
____
____

LESSON 3 The Plains

Vocabulary Strategies

Preteach Additional Vocabulary After teaching the Vocabulary words on Student Edition page 70, explain to students that there are several other important words they will see in this lesson. Use Procedure Card 1, along with the suggestions below, to introduce the words.

prairie	Ask students to draw sketches of flat or rolling land with grass and wildflowers. Have them label the pictures with the word *prairie*.
fertile	Explain that fertile land is land where crops grow well. Discuss why fertile land is important for farming.
independent	Tell students that a synonym for *independent* is *free*.
decision	Point out the similarity in spelling between this word and *decide*. When we decide something, we make a decision.
unity	Tell students that this word is from the Latin root *unus*, which means "one." The word *unity* means joining together as one. Discuss related words such as *united* in United States.

WORD CARDS To help teach the lesson vocabulary, use the Word Cards on pages 241–242.

Build Fluency

Use page 32 and the steps on Procedure Card 2 to reinforce vocabulary and build fluency. Read each vocabulary word aloud and have students repeat it. Then have students work in pairs to reread the words. Follow a similar procedure with the phrases and sentences. Continue to help students build fluency by having them reread "You Are There" in the Student Edition.

Text Comprehension

BEFORE READING

Preview the Lesson Guide students in previewing the lesson using Procedure Card 3. Point out the following features of the lesson on Student Edition pages 70–75.

- **Pages 70–71** Read the "What to Know" question. Discuss what students know about the geography and climate of the Plains. Preview the illustration and have students read the Fast Fact. Have them examine the diagram of a buffalo, read the labels, and answer the question in the caption.
- **Pages 72–73** Have students examine the illustration of Great Plains Life, read the captions, and identify activities they see in the illustration.
- **Pages 74–75** Have students read the Primary Sources feature and discuss the document-based question. Preview the illustration of a tribal leader and the Review questions.

During Reading

Build Comprehension of Expository Text Present the graphic organizer on page 33. Have students preview the organizer by filling in the lesson title and comparing the four main heads in the organizer with the matching subheads in the Student Edition pages 70–75. Tell students that the section subheads provide additional help with identifying important information. Use Procedure Card 4, the Reading Check questions in *Harcourt Social Studies,* and the directed reading suggestions below.

- **Page 70** After students have read "You Are There," discuss the reasons that the buffalo hunt was so important to these people.
- **Page 71** Have students read "Life on the Plains." Then have them list in the first diagram in the organizer ways that the Plains Indians used the different parts of the buffalo. Tell students to use information from the text and from the diagram in this section of the lesson.
- **Page 72** After students have read "Farmers and Hunters," have them list in the Farming box the important crops grown by Plains groups. In the Hunting box, students should list the names of animals that Plains groups hunted.
- **Page 73** Have students read "A Nomadic Society." Then tell them to write labels below the two pictures in the organizer that show important items made by people of the Great Plains.
- **Pages 74–75** After students have read "Plains Cultures," have them write in the organizer important details from this section of the lesson. Point out that the subheads "Government" and "Traditions and Religious Beliefs" match the section subheads in the text.

After Reading

Summarize Have students use their completed graphic organizers to summarize the lesson. Then have them compare their summaries to the lesson summary on page 75.

Review and Respond If students need additional help with comparing and contrasting, use Focus Skill Transparency 1.

Draw a Building Plan Suggest that students look back at information in the lesson and the illustration on pages 72–73 to help them write accurate instructions. You might provide one or more samples of directions with lists of materials and numbered steps for students to use as models for formats and style. Remind them to write the instructions in their own words.

Leveled Readers Use the Leveled Readers and Procedure Card 5 to build fluency and comprehension.

Name ______________________________ Date ______________

DIRECTIONS **Read aloud the words in Part A. Practice reading aloud the phrases and the sentences in Part B.**

Part A

Vocabulary Words		Additional Words
lodge	travois	prairie
sod	council	fertile
scarce	ceremony	independent
tepee		decision
		unity

Part B

1. Millions of buffalo / once roamed / the dry prairie land / of the Plains region.
2. Native American groups of the Central Plains / farmed / in the fertile valleys of the Missouri River / and the Platte River.
3. They built / large round earthen lodges, / sometimes covered by sod.
4. Wood was scarce / in the western part / of the Interior Plains.
5. The Great Plains Indians / built shelters called tepees.
6. They carried goods / on a travois / pulled by a dog.
7. The ten groups of Cheyenne / were independent of each other / in many ways, / but each group / sent its leaders / to meet in a council of chiefs.
8. All the Cheyenne groups / had to follow / the council's decisions.
9. Ceremonies / such as the sun dance / showed the people's respect for nature / and helped build a sense of unity.

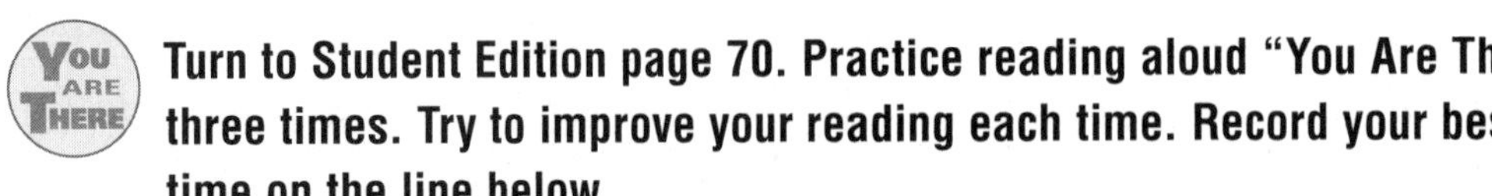

Turn to Student Edition page 70. Practice reading aloud "You Are There" three times. Try to improve your reading each time. Record your best time on the line below.

Number of words ___87___ My Best Time ________ Words per Minute ________

Name ______________________ Date ______________

Lesson Title ______________________________

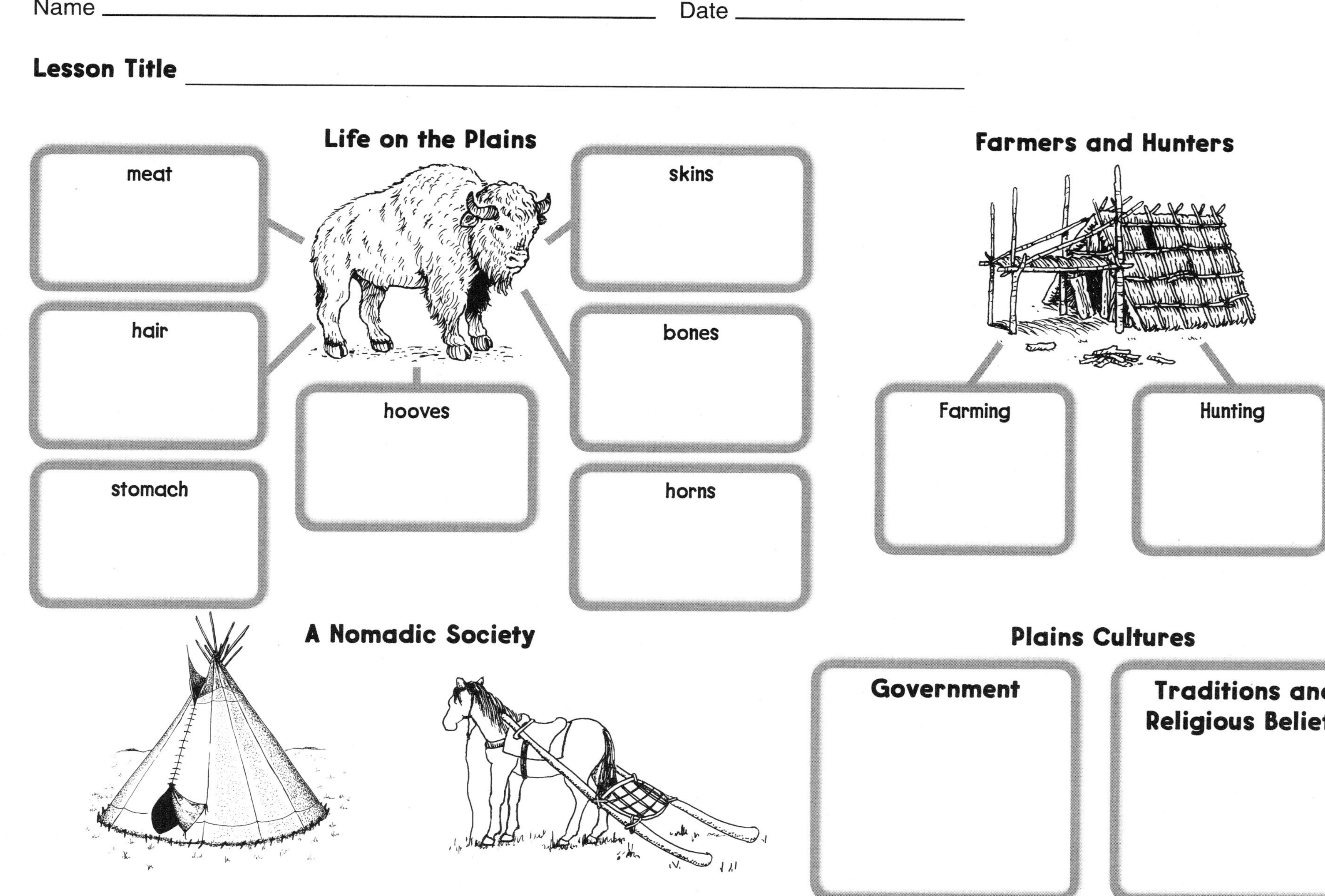

LESSON 4 The Southwest and the West

Vocabulary Strategies

Preteach Additional Vocabulary After teaching the Vocabulary words on Student Edition page 76, explain to students that there are several other important words they will see in this lesson. Use Procedure Card 1, along with the suggestions below, to introduce the words.

mesa	Tell students that *mesa* means "table" in Spanish, or ask a Spanish-speaking student to give the meaning. Discuss why this name is used for a raised landform with a flat top.
canyon	Explain that this word came into English from the Spanish word *cañón*. Discuss the similarities and differences between a canyon and a valley.
pottery	Point out the shorter word *pot* in this word. Tell students that pottery includes pots and other objects, such as vases and plates, that are shaped from clay and then heated.
brush	Tell students that this word has multiple meanings. Twigs and branches are sometimes called brush.
salmon	Pronounce the word for students, pointing out the silent *l*. Have students draw the outline of a fish and write *salmon* in the outline to remind them that a salmon is a kind of fish.

WORD CARDS To help teach the lesson vocabulary, use the Word Cards on pages 241–244.

Build Fluency

Use page 36 and the steps on Procedure Card 2 to reinforce vocabulary and build fluency. Read each vocabulary word aloud and have students repeat it. Then have students work in pairs to reread the words. Follow a similar procedure with the phrases and sentences. Continue to help students build fluency by having them reread "You Are There" in the Student Edition.

Text Comprehension

BEFORE READING

Preview the Lesson Guide students in previewing the lesson using Procedure Card 3. Point out the following features of the lesson on Student Edition pages 76–81.

- **Pages 76–77** Read the "What to Know" question and review briefly what students have learned about effects of geography and climate in the Eastern Woodlands and the Plains. Preview the diagram of a pueblo. Have students read the Fast Fact and the labels and answer the question in the caption.
- **Pages 78–79** Have students read Children in History and discuss the Make It Relevant question. Preview the illustrations and captions.
- **Pages 80–81** Preview the illustration of a Chumash couple and the Review questions on page 80. Then preview the biography of Navajo poet Luci Tapahonso on page 81.

During Reading

Build Comprehension of Expository Text Present the graphic organizer on page 37. Have students preview the organizer by filling in the lesson title and comparing the three main heads in the organizer with the matching subheads in the Student Edition pages 76–80. Tell students that the section subheads provide additional help with identifying important information. Use Procedure Card 4, the Reading Check questions in *Harcourt Social Studies,* and the directed reading suggestions below.

- **Page 76** After students have read "You Are There," remind them that they learned about the Ancient Puebloans in Lesson 1.
- **Page 77** Have students read "The Southwest" and fill in important details in the first box of the organizer. Point out that the subhead "Adapting to the Southwest" matches the section subhead and can help students locate information.
- **Page 78** After students have read "Pueblo Culture," have them fill in the next box in the organizer. Point out the subhead "Religion and Government" and the arrows between this box and the one above. Explain that the two-headed arrows show a direct connection between the information in these two sections of the lesson.
- **Pages 79–80** Have students read "Groups to the West." Tell them to summarize the ways of life of the three groups under the section subhead "Ways of Life" in the organizer and then to fill in the information under the subhead "Trading for Needed Goods."

After Reading

Summarize Have students use their completed graphic organizers to summarize the lesson. Then have them compare their summaries to the lesson summary on page 80.

Review and Respond If students need additional help with comparing and contrasting, use Focus Skill Transparency 1.

Draw a Map Suggest that students reread parts of the lesson to find clues about the areas where the people of the Southwest and West lived. Then students can use that information to shade in those areas on their maps.

Leveled Readers Use the Leveled Readers and Procedure Card 5 to build fluency and comprehension.

Name ______________________ Date ____________

DIRECTIONS **Read aloud the words in Part A. Practice reading aloud the phrases and the sentences in Part B.**

Part A

Vocabulary Words		Additional Words	
adapt	adobe	mesa	brush
staple	hogan	canyon	salmon
surplus	trade network	pottery	

Part B

1. The Pueblo peoples / of the desert Southwest / were able to adapt their ways of life / to a land of mesas, / canyons, / cliffs, / and mountains.
2. Even in the dry environment, / the Pueblo people / were able to grow their staple foods / of corn, / beans, / and squash.
3. They found ways / to collect water / and to store / a surplus of food.
4. The Navajo / built hogans / by covering wooden frames / with mud or adobe.
5. The Pueblo and the Navajo / sometimes traveled far / to trade their pottery and baskets / with other tribes.
6. The Shoshone / lived part of the year / in the Great Basin / and built shelters with dry brush.
7. The Nez Perce, / who lived to the northwest, / made long spears and nets / to catch salmon.
8. Native Americans / in the Plateau, / Great Basin, / and California cultural regions / formed large trade networks / to get goods / from faraway places.

YOU ARE THERE **Turn to Student Edition page 76. Practice reading aloud "You Are There" three times. Try to improve your reading each time. Record your best time on the line below.**

Number of words 98 My Best Time ________ Words per Minute ________

Name ______________________ Date ____________

Lesson Title: ______________________

The Southwest

Land ______________________

Adapting to the Southwest

Staple foods ______________________

Also grew ____________ used to weave ______________________

Pueblo Culture

What shaped their lives ______________________

What they depended on for resources not found nearby ______________________

Religion and Government

Who led Navajo ceremonies ______________________

What had a strong role in the government of the Pueblo ______________________

Groups to the West

Ways of Life

People ____________ Way of Life ______________________

People ____________ Way of Life ______________________

People ____________ Way of Life ______________________

Trading for Needed Goods

What people formed ____________ Why ______________________

LESSON 5 The Northwest and the Arctic

Vocabulary Strategies

Preteach Additional Vocabulary After teaching the Vocabulary words on Student Edition page 82, explain to students that there are several other important words they will see in this lesson. Use Procedure Card 1, along with the suggestions below, to introduce the words.

stranded	Point out the *-ed* ending. Explain that a strand is a strip of land along the edge of a body of water. The word *stranded* can mean "washed up on shore."
rank	Tell students that synonyms include *position* and *level*. Give examples, such as higher and lower ranks in the armed forces.
totem pole	Point out the totem poles in the illustration on page 85, and discuss their significance.
unique	Tell students that this word, like *unity* and *unite*, is from the Latin root *unus*, meaning "one." *Unique* describes something that is the only one of its kind.
caribou	Ask if students know what a reindeer is. Explain that *caribou* is another name for *reindeer*, large deer that live in northern regions.

WORD CARDS To help teach the lesson vocabulary, use the Word Cards on pages 243–244.

Build Fluency

Use page 40 and the steps on Procedure Card 2 to reinforce vocabulary and build fluency. Read each vocabulary word aloud and have students repeat it. Then have students work in pairs to reread the words. Follow a similar procedure with the phrases and sentences. Continue to help students build fluency by having them reread "You Are There" in the Student Edition.

Text Comprehension

BEFORE READING

Preview the Lesson Guide students in previewing the lesson using Procedure Card 3. Point out the following features of the lesson on Student Edition pages 82–87.

- **Pages 82–83** Read the "What to Know" question and ask how students think these regions may differ from those they have learned about previously. Discuss how the artifacts and the scene shown in the illustration differ from those of other regions.
- **Pages 84–85** Have students examine the illustration of a Northwest Coast village, read the labels, and answer the question in the caption.
- **Pages 86–87** Preview the illustrations of Inuit life. Discuss how these scenes of the Arctic are like and unlike those of the Pacific Northwest on the preceding pages. Then preview the Review questions.

During Reading

Build Comprehension of Expository Text Present the graphic organizer on page 41. Have students preview the organizer by filling in the lesson title and comparing the three main heads in the organizer with the matching subheads in the Student Edition pages 82–87. Tell students that the section subheads provide additional help with identifying important information. Use Procedure Card 4, the Reading Check questions in *Harcourt Social Studies*, and the directed reading suggestions below.

- **Page 82** After students have read "You Are There," talk about why whales may have been an important resource for peoples of the Northwest and the Arctic.
- **Page 83** Have students read "A Region of Plenty" and fill in information about the land of the Northwest Coast. Tell students they can locate information about groups and their food sources under the section subhead "People of the Northwest Coast." Guide students in recording that information in the organizer.
- **Pages 84–85** After students have read "Resources and Trade," explain that the two-headed arrows between the first two boxes in the organizer show that both sections of the lesson are about the same region. Point out that the organizer box is structured the same way as the section in the text. Students should write in the organizer information from the introductory paragraph and from each of the three subsections.
- **Pages 86–87** Have students read "Lands of the North" and complete the organizer, using the subheads to help them locate information.

After Reading

Summarize Have students use their completed graphic organizers to summarize the lesson. Then have them compare their summaries to the lesson summary on page 87.

Review and Respond If students need additional help with comparing and contrasting, use Focus Skill Transparency 1.

Write a Poem Discuss how poetry uses colorful language to express ideas in an interesting way. You may want to read several short poems as examples. Suggest that students begin by listing ideas, words, and phrases to include in their poems. Remind them that poems do not have to rhyme.

Leveled Readers Use the Leveled Readers and Procedure Card 5 to build fluency and comprehension.

Name ______________________ Date ______________

DIRECTIONS **Read aloud the words in Part A. Practice reading aloud the phrases and the sentences in Part B.**

Part A

Vocabulary Words		Additional Words	
harpoon	potlatch	stranded	unique
clan	kayak	rank	caribou
economy	igloo	totem pole	
barter			

Part B

1. Most Pacific Northwest groups / captured only whales / that had become stranded / on the shore.
2. Makah clans, / in which each person / held a specific rank, / made important decisions / about village life.
3. The people of the Northwest Coast / made almost everything from wood, / including totem poles.
4. Trading / was a large part / of the region's economy.
5. The Chinook / developed a unique language / that allowed them to barter goods / on behalf of two groups / who spoke very different languages.
6. Northwest Coast groups / expressed their good fortune / through a potlatch.
7. The Inuit and the Aleut / in the Arctic region / hunted foxes, / caribou, / and polar bears.
8. They also used / harpoons and kayaks /to hunt seals, / walruses, / and whales.
9. During the winter, / some Inuit / lived in igloos.

YOU ARE THERE **Turn to Student Edition page 82. Practice reading aloud "You Are There" three times. Try to improve your reading each time. Record your best time on the line below.**

Number of words 76 My Best Time ______ Words per Minute ______

Name ______________________ Date ____________

Lesson Title: ______________________

A Region of Plenty

Resources and Trade

Land ____________

People of the Northwest Coast

Groups ____________

____

Important resources ____________

____

Important resource

____

Family Shelters

Type ____________

Who lived there ____________

The Dalles

What it was ____________

Best-known traders ____________

A Potlatch

What it was ____________

Lands of the North

Arctic Groups

____________ and ____________

Life in the Arctic

Resources ____________

____

Houses ____________

____

Life in the Sub-Arctic

Where ____________

People ____________

Resources ____________

CAUSE	→	EFFECT
		farming not possible

LESSON 1

Exploration and Technology

Vocabulary Strategies

Preteach Additional Vocabulary After teaching the Vocabulary words on Student Edition page 110, explain to students that there are several other important words they will see in this lesson. Use Procedure Card 1, along with the suggestions below, to introduce the words.

compass	Explain that a compass is a tool used for finding direction. If possible, display a compass and demonstrate its use.
astrolabe	Read this context clue: "They used the astrolabe to figure out the positions of the sun, moon, and stars." Discuss how knowing the positions of objects in the sky can help sailors figure out where they are on the sea.
longitude	Have students identify lines of longitude on a map or globe.
latitude	Have students identify lines of latitude on a map or globe.
risky	Point out the root word *risk* with the suffix *-y* added to form an adjective. Give synonyms, such as *dangerous* and *uncertain*.

WORD CARDS To help teach the lesson vocabulary, use the Word Cards on pages 245–246.

Build Fluency

Use page 44 and the steps on Procedure Card 2 to reinforce vocabulary and build fluency. Read each vocabulary word aloud and have students repeat it. Then have students work in pairs to reread the words. Follow a similar procedure with the phrases and sentences. Continue to help students build fluency by having them reread "You Are There" in the Student Edition.

Text Comprehension

BEFORE READING

Preview the Lesson Guide students in previewing the lesson using Procedure Card 3. Point out the following features of the lesson on Student Edition pages 110–117.

- **Pages 110–111** Read the "What to Know" question. Discuss the difficulties of traveling long distances by land hundreds of years ago. Preview the time line and the illustrations of the explorer Marco Polo and the first printing press.
- **Pages 112–113** Preview the illustration of a caravel on pages 112–113. Discuss why people may have wanted faster ships.
- **Pages 114–115** Preview the map on page 114 and the painting on page 115. Ask students to explain what each of these illustrations shows.
- **Pages 116–117** Preview the illustration, and have students read Children in History. Discuss the Make It Relevant question. Then preview the Review questions on page 117.

During Reading

Build Comprehension of Expository Text Present the graphic organizer on page 45. Have students preview the organizer by filling in the lesson title and comparing the four main heads in the organizer with the matching subheads in the Student Edition pages 110–117. Tell students that the section subheads provide additional help with identifying important information. Use Procedure Card 4, the Reading Check questions in *Harcourt Social Studies*, and the directed reading suggestions below.

- **Page 110** After students have read "You Are There," discuss how the invention of the printing press made a difference in people's lives.
- **Page 111** Have students read "A Rush of New Ideas." Then guide them in locating and filling in the information in the web at the top left of the graphic organizer.
- **Pages 112–113** As students read "The World Awaits," have them fill in the information in the next part of the organizer. Then discuss briefly other important concepts, making sure students understand that Europeans at that time did not know that North America or South America even existed.
- **Pages 114–117** Have students read "The Business of Exploring" and fill in brief details about Christopher Columbus. Before students read the final section, ask what they think the subhead "Two Worlds Meet" means, and what the two worlds were. After reading, students should complete the organizer.

After Reading

Summarize Have students use their completed graphic organizers to summarize the lesson. Then have them compare their summaries to the lesson summary on page 117.

Review and Respond Work through the Review questions with students. Use Transparency 2 (Main Idea and Details) to discuss main ideas and details mentioned in the lesson.

Write a Conversation Discuss with students how the cultures of a Spanish sailor and a Taino leader in 1492 may have differed. You may want to have students work with partners to write and then act out their conversations.

Leveled Readers Use the Leveled Readers and Procedure Card 5 to build fluency and comprehension.

Name ______________________ Date ______________

DIRECTIONS **Read aloud the words in Part A. Practice reading aloud the phrases and the sentences in Part B.**

Part A

Vocabulary Words		Additional Words	
technology	entrepreneur	compass	latitude
navigation	cost	astrolabe	risky
expedition	benefit	longitude	
empire	Reconquista		

Part B

1. In the 1400s, / Europeans / wanted to buy and then resell / Asian goods, / but they lacked the technology / to travel to Asia / by sea.
2. Prince Henry of Portugal / started a school / with the aim of making better ships, / maps, / and tools for navigation.
3. Prince Henry / hired scientists / to improve two navigational tools / —the compass and the astrolabe.
4. Sailors used the compass / to help them find their longitude, / and the astrolabe / to help them find their latitude.
5. Europeans / made expeditions to Asia / and also traded with rich empires / in North Africa.
6. Explorers / had to be entrepreneurs / and persuade others that the cost / was worth the risk / of an expedition.
7. The benefit / was the chance / of finding riches / worth many times the cost.
8. Christopher Columbus's idea / of sailing west to reach Asia / was risky, / but after the Reconquista, / Spain's king and queen / agreed to help him.

YOU ARE THERE **Turn to Student Edition page 110. Practice reading aloud "You Are There" three times. Try to improve your reading each time. Record your best time on the line below.**

Number of words 86 My Best Time ______ Words per Minute ______

Name ______________________ Date ____________

Lesson Title: ______________________

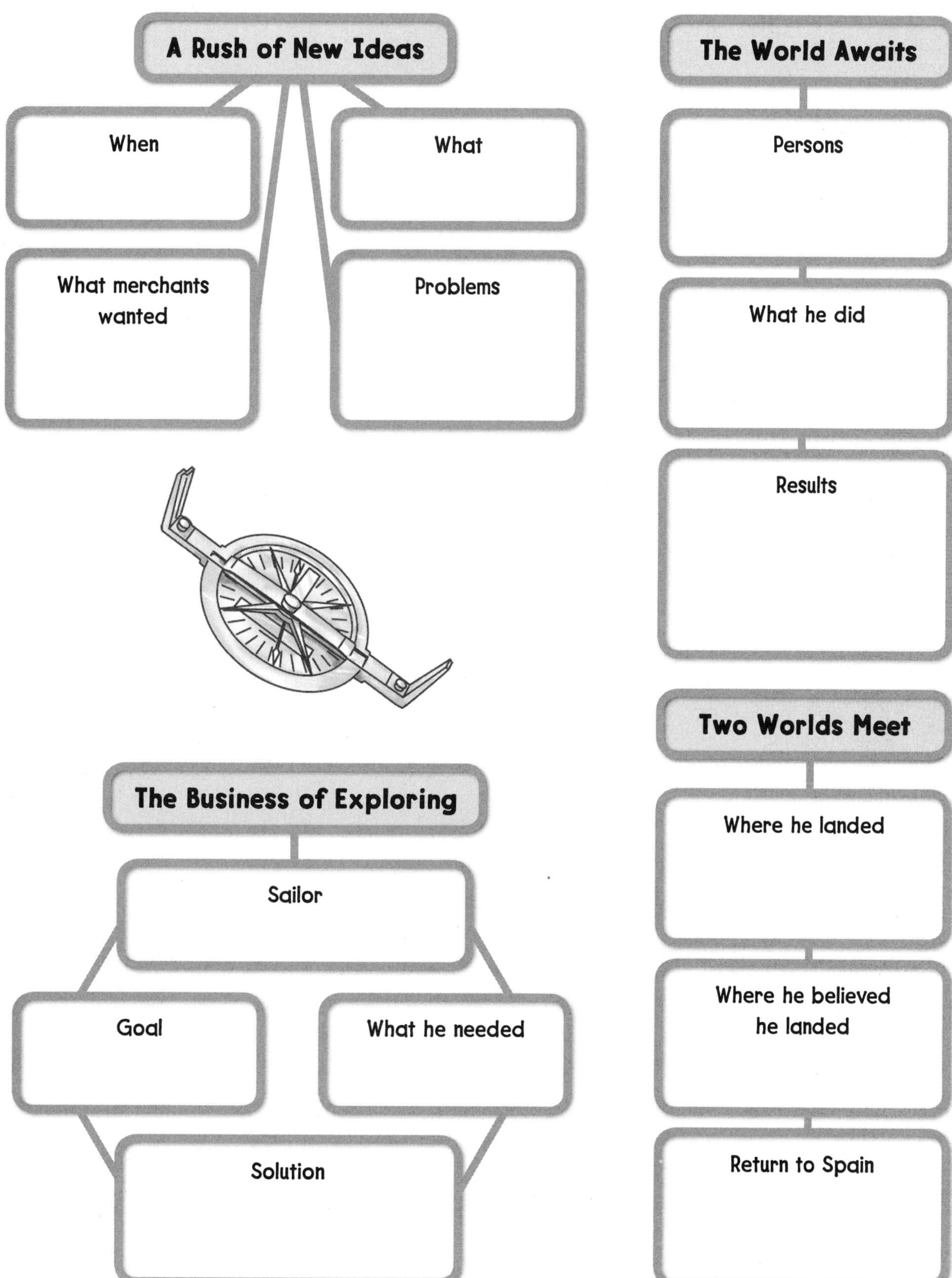

LESSON 2 A Changing World

Vocabulary Strategies

Preteach Additional Vocabulary After teaching the Vocabulary words on Student Edition page 120, explain to students that there are several other important words they will see in this lesson. Use Procedure Card 1, along with the suggestions below, to introduce the words.

inspired	Have students give examples of people or events that have inspired them to try something new or to attempt to do something difficult.
claim	Explain that when an explorer claimed land for a country, it meant that the country now owned that land.
course	Have students use the context of this sentence from the lesson: "In May 1497, Cabot and a crew of 18 sailed west on a course far north of Columbus's first route."
sign	Discuss familiar types of signs, such as street signs and stop signs. Ask what kind of signs someone might look for in a wilderness area or on a sea voyage.
settle	Tell students that this word has multiple meanings. Read and discuss these context sentences: "Balboa was one of the first Europeans to settle in the Americas." "The Catholic rulers of Spain and Portugal asked Catholic Church leaders to settle such a case."

WORD CARDS To help teach the lesson vocabulary, use the Word Cards on pages 245–246.

Build Fluency

Use page 48 and the steps on Procedure Card 2 to reinforce vocabulary and build fluency. Read each vocabulary word aloud and have students repeat it. Then have students work in pairs to reread the words. Follow a similar procedure with the phrases and sentences. Continue to help students build fluency by having them reread "You Are There" in the Student Edition.

Text Comprehension

BEFORE READING

Preview the Lesson Guide students in previewing the lesson using Procedure Card 3. Point out the following features of the lesson on Student Edition pages 120–125.

- **Pages 120–121** Read the "What to Know" question. Have students recall what they have learned about Columbus's voyage in 1492. Preview the time line, pointing out the names of explorers Cabot, Balboa, and Magellan. Then preview the illustrations. Have students locate the year on the time line when Cabot reached Newfoundland and Labrador in present-day Canada.
- **Pages 122–123** Preview the illustration of mapmakers on page 122 and of the explorer Balboa on page 123. Have students locate on the time line on page 120 the event shown in the illustration on page 123.

- **Pages 124–125** Have students examine the map showing voyages of exploration. Have them answer the map skill question. Then preview the illustration of Spanish coins and the Review questions on page 125.

During Reading

Build Comprehension of Expository Text Present the graphic organizer on page 49. Have students preview the organizer by filling in the lesson title and comparing the four main heads in the organizer with the matching subheads in the Student Edition pages 120–125. Tell students that the section subheads provide additional help with identifying important information. Use Procedure Card 4, the Reading Check questions in *Harcourt Social Studies,* and the directed reading suggestions below.

- **Page 120** After students have read "You Are There," ask how they think the mystery may be solved.
- **Page 121** Have students read "England Explores." Then guide them in writing in the organizer important information about John Cabot's expedition.
- **Page 122** After students have read "A New Map of the World," discuss what Vespucci realized and why it was important. Then have students complete the next box in the organizer.
- **Page 123** Before students read "Reaching the Pacific," set a purpose for reading—to find out who reached the Pacific and how. Have students fill in the organizer as they read or after reading.
- **Pages 124–125** Either as they read or after reading "A New View of the World," students can fill in the information to complete the organizer.

After Reading

Summarize Have students use their completed graphic organizers to summarize the lesson. Then have them compare their summaries to the lesson summary on page 125.

Review and Respond If students need additional help identifying main ideas and details, use Focus Skill Transparency 2.

Make a Table of Explorers Tell students to look back over the lesson and write down names of explorers and the areas they explored. Discuss how to make a chart with headings such as "Explorer" and "Area Explored." Have students display their charts, trace the routes on the map, and describe the distances to classmates.

Leveled Readers Use the Leveled Readers and Procedure Card 5 to build fluency and comprehension.

Name ______________________________ Date ______________

DIRECTIONS **Read aloud the words in Part A. Practice reading aloud the phrases and the sentences in Part B.**

Part A

Vocabulary Words	Additional Words	
isthmus	inspired	sign
treaty	claim	settle
	course	

Part B

1. Columbus's trips to the Indies / inspired several European rulers / to send ships west.
2. The rulers / were eager to claim lands / and riches / of their own.
3. In May, 1497, / John Cabot and a crew of 18 / sailed west / on a course / far north of Columbus's first route.
4. Amerigo Vespucci / sailed down the coast / of South America, / looking for signs / that he had reached Asia.
5. The Spanish explorer Balboa / was one the first Europeans / to settle in the Americas.
6. He and other explorers / crossed the Isthmus of Panama / and reached / the Pacific Ocean.
7. Spain and Portugal / both claimed the same land, / so they asked Catholic Church leaders / to settle the case.
8. Later, / Spain and Portugal / signed a treaty / to move the dividing line / that the leaders / had drawn.

You ARE THERE **Turn to Student Edition page 120. Practice reading aloud "You Are There" three times. Try to improve your reading each time. Record your best time on the line below.**

Number of words 83 My Best Time ________ Words per Minute ________

Name ______________________________ Date ______________

Lesson Title: ______________________________

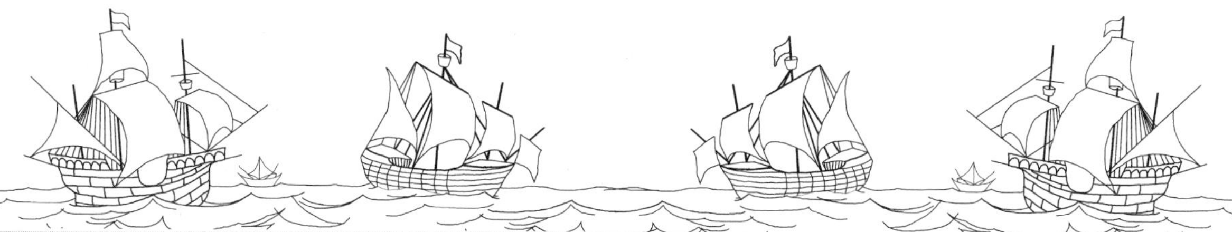

England Explores

Explorer ______________________________ Year ______________

What he thought he had found ______________________________

What he actually may have found ______________________________

A New Map of the World

Explorer ______________ Where he sailed ______________________

What he realized ______________________________

What was named for him ______________________________

Reaching the Pacific

Explorer ______________________________ Year ______________

What he did ______________________________

____

A New View of the World

Explorer ______________ What he named ______________________

Sailors on one of his ships were ______________________________.

New lands were divided between ______________________________.

LESSON 3

Spanish Explorations

Vocabulary Strategies

Preteach Additional Vocabulary After teaching the Vocabulary words on Student Edition page 128, explain to students that there are several other important words they will see in this lesson. Use Procedure Card 1, along with the suggestions below, to introduce the words.

convert	Explain that to convert people is to cause them to change their religion.
encouraged	Point out the root word *courage* and prefix *en-*, meaning "put into." To encourage someone is to put courage into them. The *-ed* ending shows that the action took place in the past.
fountain	Students may have seen fountains in parks or other public places. Explain that a fountain may also be a natural source of water flowing from the earth.
Protestant	Point out the word *protest* and suffix *-ant*. Tell students that a Protestant was someone who protested against leaders of the Catholic Church. Help students pronounce *Protestant* correctly.
banned	Point out that this past-tense verb is a homophone of *band*. Tell students that to ban something is to forbid it.

WORD CARDS To help teach the lesson vocabulary, use the Word Cards on pages 245–248.

Build Fluency

Use page 52 and the steps on Procedure Card 2 to reinforce vocabulary and build fluency. Read each vocabulary word aloud and have students repeat it. Then have students work in pairs to reread the words. Follow a similar procedure with the phrases and sentences. Continue to help students build fluency by having them reread "You Are There" in the Student Edition.

Text Comprehension

BEFORE READING

Preview the Lesson Guide students in previewing the lesson using Procedure Card 3. Point out the following features of the lesson on Student Edition pages 128–135.

- **Pages 128–129** Read the "What to Know" question, making sure that students understand the word *conquer*. Have students recall why earlier European explorers came to the Americas. Preview the time line and the painting on page 128. Have students locate on the time line the event mentioned in the caption for the illustration on page 129.
- **Pages 130–131** Have students examine the illustrations of the Spanish conquistador and Aztec warrior, read the labels, and discuss the question in the caption. Then preview the map showing the movement of conquistadors in North America, and have students answer the map skill question.

- **Pages 132–135** Preview the illustration of de Soto's expedition. On page 134, preview the illustration of Saint Ignatius and the Review questions. Then preview the biography of the explorer Estevanico on page 135.

During Reading

Build Comprehension of Expository Text Present the graphic organizer on page 53. Have students preview the organizer by filling in the lesson title and comparing the four main heads in the organizer with the matching subheads in the Student Edition pages 128–134. Tell students that the section subheads provide additional help with identifying important information. Use Procedure Card 4, the Reading Check questions in *Harcourt Social Studies*, and the directed reading suggestions below.

- **Page 128** After students have read "You Are There," ask whether they think the soldiers will find a Fountain of Youth, and why or why not.
- **Page 129** Have students read "The Spanish Explore Florida." Then guide them in summarizing and writing information in the organizer. Point out that the section subhead in the text can help them find this information.
- **Pages 130–131** After students have read "Early Conquistadors," have them summarize in the organizer what Cortés wanted and what he did, and then what Coronado wanted and what he did.
- **Page 132** Have students read "Expeditions Continue" and add information about Pizarro and de Soto to the organizer, using the section subheads in the text to help them locate information about each of these conquistadors.
- **Pages 133–134** Before students read "Missionaries to America," point out that the previous sections of this lesson have all been about conquistadors. Now students will read about a different group who came to America. After reading, have students complete the final box in the organizer.

After Reading

Summarize Have students use their completed graphic organizers to summarize the lesson. Then have them compare their summaries to the lesson summary on page 134.

Review and Respond If students need additional help identifying main ideas and details, use Focus Skill Transparency 2.

Write a Journal Tell students to choose one of the explorers from this lesson and reread passages that tell about the places that person explored. Then students can write journal entries written from the point of view of someone traveling with the explorer.

Leveled Readers Use the Leveled Readers and Procedure Card 5 to build fluency and comprehension.

Name ______________________ Date ______________

DIRECTIONS **Read aloud the words in Part A. Practice reading aloud the phrases and the sentences in Part B.**

Part A

Vocabulary Words		Additional Words
grant	conquistador	convert
reform	missionary	encouraged
Reformation		fountain
Counter-Reformation		Protestant
		banned

Part B

1. Some Spanish explorers / came to the Americas / to find adventure and riches, / while others / wanted to convert Native Americans / to Christianity.
2. The King of Spain / encouraged the explorers / and offered grants / to those who led expeditions.
3. Juan Ponce de León / set out to find / a so-called Fountain of Youth, / but instead / he landed in what is now / the state of Florida.
4. The conquistador Cortés / conquered the Aztecs / in what is now / Mexico.
5. During the Reformation, / Martin Luther and other Protestants / called for reforms / in the Catholic Church.
6. The Catholic Church / tried to keep its power / through the Counter-Reformation, / and banned books / that went against its teachings.
7. The Church / sent missionaries / to convert Native Americans / to the Catholic religion.

YOU ARE THERE **Turn to Student Edition page 128. Practice reading aloud "You Are There" three times. Try to improve your reading each time. Record your best time on the line below.**

Number of words 89 My Best Time ______ Words per Minute ______

Name ______________________________ Date ______________

Lesson Title: ______________________________

The Spanish Explore Florida

Explorer ______________ Set out to find ______________

What he did ______________________________

____

Early Conquistadors

What Cortés wanted ______________________________

What Cortés did ______________________________

What Coronado wanted ______________________________

What Coronado did ______________________________

____

Expeditions Continue

What Pizarro did ______________________________

What de Soto did ______________________________

____

Missionaries to America

What happened in Europe ______________________________

Why the Church sent missionaries ______________________________

____

LESSON 4 Other Nations Explore

Vocabulary Strategies

Preteach Additional Vocabulary After teaching the Vocabulary words on Student Edition page 138, explain to students that there are several other important words they will see in this lesson. Use Procedure Card 1, along with the suggestions below, to introduce the words.

waterway	Have students identify the two shorter words that make up this compound word. Tell students that a river is one kind of waterway.
navigator	Write *navigate, navigation,* and *navigator,* and have students compare them. Explain that the suffix *-or* often shows that a person performs an action, as in a sailor who sails, or an actor who acts.
inland	On a map, have students point out inland areas, or areas away from coasts.
rapids	Cover final *s* and ask what the adjective *rapid* means. (fast, quick) Explain that adding *s* creates a noun that means a stretch of fast-moving water in a river or stream.
adrift	Tell students that something set adrift moves or drifts along wherever the wind or water takes it. A synonym for *adrift* is *afloat.*

WORD CARDS To help teach the lesson vocabulary, use the Word Cards on pages 247–248.

Build Fluency

Use page 56 and the steps on Procedure Card 2 to reinforce vocabulary and build fluency. Read each vocabulary word aloud and have students repeat it. Then have students work in pairs to reread the words. Follow a similar procedure with the phrases and sentences. Continue to help students build fluency by having them reread "You Are There" in the Student Edition.

Text Comprehension

BEFORE READING

Preview the Lesson Guide students in previewing the lesson using Procedure Card 3. Point out the following features of the lesson on Student Edition pages 138–143.

- **Pages 138–139** Read the "What to Know" question and preview the time line. Discuss what the time line shows about what explorers found. Preview the illustrations of Henry Hudson and of a ship searching for the Northwest Passage.
- **Pages 140–141** Preview the illustration of the St. Lawrence River. Have students read and discuss the Fast Fact.
- **Pages 142–143** Have students examine the time line on page 142 and answer the question in the caption. Have students compare this time line with the time line on page 138. Then preview the illustration and the Review questions on page 143.

During Reading

Build Comprehension of Expository Text Present the graphic organizer on page 57. Have students preview the organizer by filling in the lesson title and comparing the three main heads in the organizer with the matching subheads in the Student Edition pages 138–143. Tell students that the section subheads provide additional help with identifying important information. Use Procedure Card 4, the Reading Check questions in *Harcourt Social Studies,* and the directed reading suggestions below.

- **Page 138** After students have read "You Are There," call attention to the illustration on this page and discuss its connection with the information in the paragraph.
- **Page 139** Have students read "The Northwest Passage." Then guide them in filling in the information about the Northwest Passage in the organizer.
- **Pages 140–141** After students have read "Verrazano and Cartier," have them write information about each of these explorers in the organizer. Point out that there is not enough space to write every detail, so students will need to summarize.
- **Pages 142–143** Have students read "Hudson's Voyages" and complete the organizer. Point out that the three explorers made many voyages and searched for the Northwest Passage over a wide area, but none of them was able to find it.

After Reading

Summarize Have students use their completed graphic organizers to summarize the lesson. Then have them compare their summaries to the lesson summary on page 143.

Review and Respond If students need additional help identifying main ideas and details, use Focus Skill Transparency 2.

Write a Scene Tell students to choose one of the explorers and to use information from the lesson to help them write their scenes. Point out that students may find information in "You Are There," in captions for illustrations, and from the Fast Fact on page 141, as well as from passages in the text.

Leveled Readers Use the Leveled Readers and Procedure Card 5 to build fluency and comprehension.

Name ______________________________ Date ______________

DIRECTIONS **Read aloud the words in Part A. Practice reading aloud the phrases and the sentences in Part B.**

Part A

Vocabulary Words	Additional Words	
Northwest Passage	waterway	rapids
mutiny	navigator	adrift
	inland	

Part B

1. Explorers in the 1500s / began searching / for a route they called / the Northwest Passage.
2. The first country to find this waterway / would control an important new trade route / between Europe and Asia / and gain great riches.
3. Giovanni da Verrazano / searched the coastlines / of North America and South America / but did not find / the Northwest Passage.
4. Jacques Cartier, / a French navigator, / traveled up the St. Lawrence River / and went inland / as far as what is now Montreal.
5. Instead of reaching the Pacific, / Cartier reached river rapids / that his boat could not pass.
6. An English explorer / named Henry Hudson / made four voyages / in search of the Northwest Passage.
7. After a cold winter / and much suffering, / Hudson's crew / mutinied.
8. They set Hudson / and eight others / adrift / in a small boat.

YOU ARE THERE **Turn to Student Edition page 138. Practice reading aloud "You Are There" three times. Try to improve your reading each time. Record your best time on the line below.**

Number of words 70 My Best Time ________ Words per Minute ________

Name ______________________ Date ____________

Lesson Title: ______________________

The Northwest Passage

What European rulers wanted to find

____

____

Why ______________________

____

Verrazano and Cartier

Giovanni da Verrazano	Jacques Cartier
What he did ______________________	What he did ______________________
______________________	______________________
______________________	______________________
What he did not find ______________________	What he did not find ______________________

Hudson's Voyages

Explorer ______________________ How many voyages ______________________

What he did ______________________

____

What he did not find ______________________

LESSON 1 The Spanish Colonies

Vocabulary Strategies

Preteach Additional Vocabulary After teaching the Vocabulary words on Student Edition page 148, explain to students that there are several other important words they will see in this lesson. Use Procedure Card 1, along with the suggestions below, to introduce the words.

overpower	Tell students that synonyms for *overpower* include *conquer* and *defeat.*
colonist	Have students compare *colony* and *colonist.* Point out the suffix *-ist,* which often shows that the noun names a person, as in *artist* and *guitarist.* A colonist is a person who lives in a colony.
landowner	Help students break the compound word into the smaller words *land* and *owner* and use the meanings of the smaller words to figure out the meaning of the compound word.
permanent	Tell students that synonyms for *permanent* are *lasting* or *long-lasting.* An antonym is *temporary.*
settlement	Discuss what it means to settle in a new place and how the words *settle, settler,* and *settlement* are related.

WORD CARDS To help teach the lesson vocabulary, use the Word Cards on pages 249–250.

Build Fluency

Use page 60 and the steps on Procedure Card 2 to reinforce vocabulary and build fluency. Read each vocabulary word aloud and have students repeat it. Then have students work in pairs to reread the words. Follow a similar procedure with the phrases and sentences. Continue to help students build fluency by having them reread "You Are There" in the Student Edition.

Text Comprehension

BEFORE READING

Preview the Lesson Guide students in previewing the lesson using Procedure Card 3. Point out the following features of the lesson on Student Edition pages 148–153.

- **Pages 148–149** Read the "What to Know" question and have students recall how Spain claimed land in the Americas. Preview the time line and the illustration of a Spanish fort.
- **Pages 150–151** Preview the illustration of a sugar mill in Brazil. Have students examine the map of New Spain and answer the map skill question.
- **Pages 152–153** Have students study the graph. Explain that it shows how the number of Europeans in the Western Hemisphere changed over time. Have students answer the question in the caption. Then preview the Review questions on page 152 and the biography of Bartolomé de Las Casas on page 153.

During Reading

Build Comprehension of Expository Text Present the graphic organizer on page 61. Have students preview the organizer by filling in the lesson title and comparing the three main heads in the organizer with the matching subheads in the Student Edition pages 148–152. Tell students that the section subheads provide additional help with identifying important information. Use Procedure Card 4, the Reading Check questions in *Harcourt Social Studies*, and the directed reading suggestions below.

- **Page 148** After students have read "You Are There," ask who they think the newcomers are and what animals they ride. Invite students to predict what will happen.
- **Page 149** Have students read "New Spain." Then guide them in writing a sentence in the "Effect" box in the organizer to tell what happened as a result of Spain's wish to protect the lands it had claimed in the Americas.
- **Page 150** After students have read "Slavery in the Americas," have them write sentences in the boxes to tell what happened because Spain and Portugal needed workers in their colonies, and then what happened that caused colonists to capture Africans to be enslaved workers.
- **Pages 151–152** Have students read "Settling the Borderlands" and then write sentences about three kinds of places that were built in the Americas as a result of Spain's wish to protect its empire by settling the borderlands.

After Reading

Summarize Have students use their completed graphic organizers to summarize the lesson. Then have them compare their summaries to the lesson summary on page 152.

Review and Respond If students need additional help identifying main ideas and details, use Focus Skill Transparency 2.

Write a Report Tell students that their textbook is one resource they can use for information on the topic of why Spain set up missions. You may also wish to suggest or provide additional research materials for students to use. Remind students to take notes as they read and to write the information in their reports in their own words.

Leveled Readers Use the Leveled Readers and Procedure Card 5 to build fluency and comprehension.

Name ______________________ Date ____________

DIRECTIONS **Read aloud the words in Part A. Practice reading aloud the phrases and the sentences in Part B.**

Part A

Vocabulary Words		Additional Words
colony	presidio	overpower
plantation	mission	colonist
slavery	hacienda	landowner
borderlands		permanent
		settlement

Part B

1. Spain, / which claimed / large parts of the Americas, / also tried to overpower Native American tribes / and take their lands.
2. Spain / formed the colony of New Spain / in 1535 / to protect its lands / and to govern the people there.
3. Many colonists / came to New Spain / to start plantations.
4. Both Spain and Portugal / forced Native Americans into slavery / to grow crops / and to mine gold and silver.
5. Bartolomé de Las Casas / was a landowner / who spoke out in favor of better treatment / of the Native Americans.
6. Spanish soldiers / built presidios / to protect the borderlands.
7. In 1565, / Spanish settlers / built the first permanent European settlement / in what is now / the United States.
8. Spanish missionaries / built missions / in the borderlands, / and some settlers / built haciendas.

YOU ARE THERE **Turn to Student Edition page 148. Practice reading aloud "You Are There" three times. Try to improve your reading each time. Record your best time on the line below.**

Number of words 75 My Best Time ________ Words per Minute ________

Name ____________________ Date ____________

Lesson Title: ____________________

New Spain

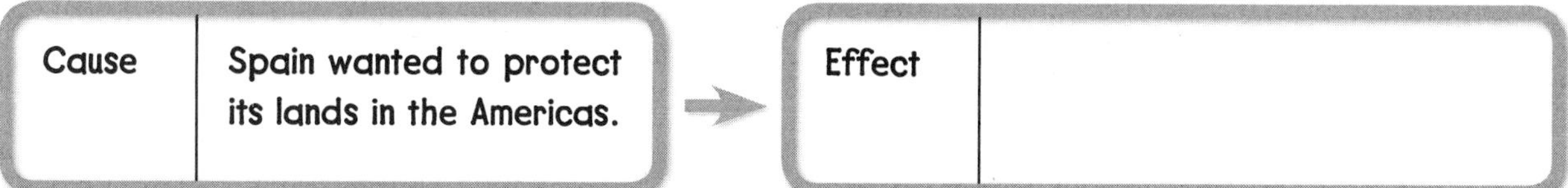

Slavery in the Americas

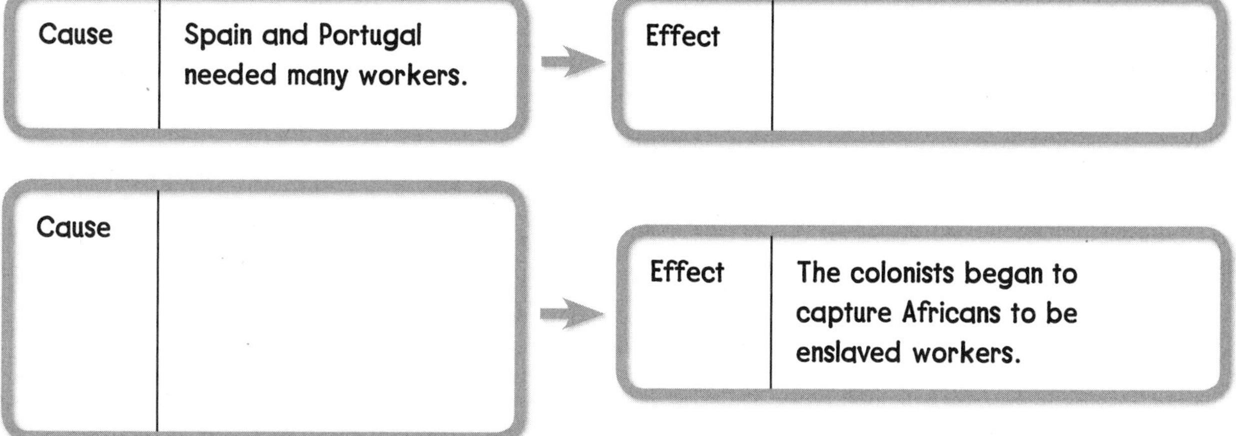

Settling the Borderlands

Cause	Spain wanted to protect its empire by settling the borderlands.

Effect	

Effect	

Effect	

Lesson 2 The Virginia Colony

Vocabulary Strategies

Preteach Additional Vocabulary After teaching the Vocabulary words on Student Edition page 154, explain to students that there are several other important words they will see in this lesson. Use Procedure Card 1, along with the suggestions below, to introduce the words.

lumber	Ask whether students have ever been to a lumberyard, where wood is sold in the form of boards used to build things. Explain that after trees have been cut down and sawed into pieces, the wood is called lumber.
merchant	Tell students that someone who buys and sells goods is called a merchant. This word is from the Latin root *mercari,* meaning "trade." Other words with this root include *market* and *merchandise.*
company	Discuss known meanings. Be sure students understand that a business can also be called a company. Give examples of well-known businesses that have the word *company* in their names.
governor	Ask students to name the governor of their state. Explain that a governor is the leader of a government. Point out the similarity between the words *governor* and *government.*

WORD CARDS To help teach the lesson vocabulary, use the Word Cards on pages 249–252.

Build Fluency

Use page 64 and the steps on Procedure Card 2 to reinforce vocabulary and build fluency. Read each vocabulary word aloud and have students repeat it. Then have students work in pairs to reread the words. Follow a similar procedure with the phrases and sentences. Continue to help students build fluency by having them reread "You Are There" in the Student Edition.

Text Comprehension

Before Reading

Preview the Lesson Guide students in previewing the lesson using Procedure Card 3. Point out the following features of the lesson on Student Edition pages 154–159.

- **Pages 154–155** Read the "What to Know" question. Discuss whether English settlers may have had the same reasons for coming to the Americas as Spanish settlers in New Spain. Preview the time line and the illustrations of Queen Elizabeth I and of the Lost Colony.
- **Pages 156–157** Preview the portrait of John Smith and the photograph of the reconstruction of Jamestown. On page 157, preview the illustration of Africans arriving in Jamestown.

- **Pages 158–159** Preview the illustration of the Powhatan defending their land and the Review questions on page 158. Have students look at the biography of Pocahontas on page 159. Explain that students may have heard from other sources, some of them partly fiction, about this Native American young woman.

During Reading

Build Comprehension of Expository Text Present the graphic organizer on page 65. Have students preview the organizer by filling in the lesson title and comparing the three main heads in the organizer with the matching subheads in the Student Edition pages 154–158. Tell students that the section subheads provide additional help with identifying important information. Use Procedure Card 4, the Reading Check questions in *Harcourt Social Studies*, and the directed reading suggestions below.

- **Page 154** After students have read "You Are There," invite them to tell what they think may happen to this group of settlers.
- **Page 155** Have students read "England Attempts a Colony." Call attention to the structure of the organizer, which is a sequence chart with events in time order. Guide students in recording and summarizing in the organizer information about the first English colony, the next colony, and then about the Virginia Company. Point out that the subheads in the boxes match the section subheads in the text, which will help students locate information.
- **Page 156** After students have read "Jamestown," have them complete the next section in the organizer. Point out the two subheads that match the section subheads in the text.
- **Pages 157–158** After reading "Growth and Government," students can complete the graphic organizer, using the three section subheads to locate information.

After Reading

Summarize Have students use their completed graphic organizers to summarize the lesson. Then have them compare their summaries to the lesson summary on page 158.

Review and Respond If students need additional help identifying main ideas and details, use Focus Skill Transparency 2.

Construct a Time Line Suggest that students review the lesson and jot down events and dates to include on their time line. Then they can plan and construct a time line that is neat and easy to read.

Leveled Readers Use the Leveled Readers and Procedure Card 5 to build fluency and comprehension.

Name ______________________ Date ____________

DIRECTIONS **Read aloud the words in Part A. Practice reading aloud the phrases and the sentences in Part B.**

Part A

Vocabulary Words		Additional Words
raw material	stock	lumber
represent	legislature	merchant
royal colony	cash crop	company
indentured servant	profit	governor

Part B

1. England's rulers / knew they would benefit / from the lumber / and other raw materials / that colonies in America / would provide.
2. In the early 1600s, / a group of English merchants / set up the Virginia Company / to start a new colony / in Virginia.
3. In return for money / to set up the company, / owners received stock.
4. Colonists in Jamestown / began growing tobacco / as a cash crop.
5. The Virginia Company / sold tobacco / all over Europe / and made huge profits.
6. Growing tobacco / required many workers, / so the Virginia Company / brought indentured servants / to Virginia.
7. Colonists / set up a legislature, / called the House of Burgesses, / and elected members / to represent them.
8. In 1624, / King James I / made Virginia a royal colony / and picked a governor, / who shared power / with the House of Burgesses.

YOU ARE THERE **Turn to Student Edition page 154. Practice reading aloud "You Are There" three times. Try to improve your reading each time. Record your best time on the line below.**

Number of words 76 My Best Time ________ Words per Minute ________

Name ______________________ Date ______________

Lesson Title: ______________________

England Attempts a Colony

The Lost Colony

First colony When ______________

Where ______________

What happened ______________

____

Next Colony When ______________

What happened ______________

____

The Virginia Company

When ______________

Who ______________

What they wanted ______________

____

____

Jamestown

England's First Permanent Colony

Leader ______________

What happened ______________

The Powhatan Confederacy

What happened ______________

Growth and Government

Leader ______________ Cash crop ______________

Newcomers Arrive Who ______________ ______________

The House of Burgesses When ______________

What it was ______________

The Powhatan Wars What happened ______________

____

LESSON 3 The Plymouth Colony

Vocabulary Strategies

Preteach Additional Vocabulary After teaching the Vocabulary words on Student Edition page 162, explain to students that there are several other important words they will see in this lesson. Use Procedure Card 1, along with the suggestions below, to introduce the words.

passage	Tell students that this word has multiple meanings. Discuss meanings that students know, and explain that *passage* can also mean "journey," especially a journey by sea or by air.
site	Give *place* and *location* as synonyms for *site.* Point out that *site* is a homophone of the familiar word *sight.*
benefited	Identify the base word *benefit* from the Latin *bene* + *facere,* meaning "to do good." Other words from the root *bene* include *beneficial, benefactor, beneficiary,* and *benevolent.*
cooperation	Explain that cooperation means working together. Discuss recent examples of cooperation in your classroom.
prosper	Tell students that to prosper is to succeed or to do well. This word is from the Latin *prosperus,* which means "favorable."

WORD CARDS To help teach the lesson vocabulary, use the Word Cards on pages 251–252.

Build Fluency

Use page 68 and the steps on Procedure Card 2 to reinforce vocabulary and build fluency. Read each vocabulary word aloud and have students repeat it. Then have students work in pairs to reread the words. Follow a similar procedure with the phrases and sentences. Continue to help students build fluency by having them reread "You Are There" in the Student Edition.

Text Comprehension

BEFORE READING

Preview the Lesson Guide students in previewing the lesson using Procedure Card 3. Point out the following features of the lesson on Student Edition pages 162–167.

- **Pages 162–163** Read the "What to Know" question. Ask students why they think an area of North America came to be called New England. Preview the time line and the painting of Pilgrims boarding the *Mayflower* to sail from England to America.
- **Pages 164–165** Preview the illustration on page 164, discussing briefly how women's rights have changed since the time of the Plymouth colony. Then preview the illustration on page 165, and have students read the Fast Fact.

- **Pages 166–167** Have students look at the painting on page 166. Discuss the caption question about how the artist viewed the first Thanksgiving. Preview the photograph of the Plymouth Plantation Historical Site and the Review questions on page 167.

During Reading

Build Comprehension of Expository Text Present the graphic organizer on page 69. Have students preview the organizer by filling in the lesson title and comparing the four main heads in the organizer with the matching subheads in the Student Edition pages 162–167. Tell students that the section subheads provide additional help with identifying important information. Use Procedure Card 4, the Reading Check questions in *Harcourt Social Studies*, and the directed reading suggestions below.

- **Page 162** After students have read "You Are There," ask how they would feel about taking such a voyage. What might make it worthwhile for them?
- **Page 163** Have students read "The Pilgrims' Journey." Point out that the section subhead "Seeking Religious Freedom" explains why these people made their journey. Guide students in filling in the information under this same subhead in the organizer
- **Pages 164–165** After students have read "The Mayflower Compact," have them complete the next section in the organizer. Point out the subhead that matches the section subhead in the text. Follow the same procedure for "Building a Colony." Tell students to list under "How" several ways that the colonists were helped.
- **Pages 166–167** Tell students to read "Plymouth Grows" and then to complete the graphic organizer, using the section subheads to locate information.

After Reading

Summarize Have students use their completed graphic organizers to summarize the lesson. Then have them compare their summaries to the lesson summary on page 167.

Review and Respond If students need additional help identifying main ideas and details, use Focus Skill Transparency 2.

Write a Speech Discuss with students why the Mayflower Compact was written and what it said. Encourage them to look back at the text to recall details. Tell students to choose a position, either in favor of signing the Mayflower Compact or against it. Remind them to make clear statements of their opinions and supporting reasons in their speeches.

Leveled Readers Use the Leveled Readers and Procedure Card 5 to build fluency and comprehension.

Name ________________________________ Date ______________

DIRECTIONS **Read aloud the words in Part A. Practice reading aloud the phrases and the sentences in Part B.**

Part A

Vocabulary Words	Additional Words
pilgrim	passage
compact	site
self-government	benefited
majority rule	cooperation
	prosper

Part B

1. A group of English people / who had moved to the Netherlands / to follow their religious beliefs / came to be known as Pilgrims.
2. The Virginia Company / agreed to pay / the Pilgrims' passage to North America / on a ship called the *Mayflower.*
3. Because they arrived / in a place with no government, / the men aboard the *Mayflower* / signed a compact.
4. The Mayflower Compact / included a very new idea, / self-government, / and also / the idea of majority rule.
5. The settlers / chose a site / on a harbor, / with fresh water / and good land for growing crops / nearby.
6. The colonists / lived in peace with the Wampanoag, / and both groups / benefited from their cooperation.
7. After the colony's leaders / decided to divide the land / among the colonists, / the colonists / began to prosper from their farming.

YOU ARE THERE **Turn to Student Edition page 162. Practice reading aloud "You Are There" three times. Try to improve your reading each time. Record your best time on the line below.**

Number of words 84 My Best Time ________ Words per Minute ________

Name ______________________________ Date ______________

Lesson Title: ______________________________

The Pilgrims' Journey

Seeking Religious Freedom

Who ______________ Going where ______________

When ______________ Ship ______________

The Mayflower Compact

Self-Government

What the signers agreed ______________________________

Two important ideas ______________________________

Building a Colony

Help from Native Americans

Who helped the colonists ______________________________

How ______________________________

____

____

Plymouth Grows

Growing Prosperity

How colonists prospered ______________________________

Trouble Starts

When ______________ Why ______________________________

____

LESSON 4 The French and the Dutch

Vocabulary Strategies

Preteach Additional Vocabulary After teaching the Vocabulary words on Student Edition page 170, explain to students that there are several other important words they will see in this lesson. Use Procedure Card 1, along with the suggestions below, to introduce the words.

partnership	Point out the root word *partner* and suffix *-ship*, meaning "state or condition." Other words with this suffix include *friendship* and *leadership*.
warehouse	Have students identify the elements of this compound word. (*ware* + *house*) Explain that *ware* means goods or articles for sale, and that a warehouse is a building used to store these goods.
mouth	Tell students that this word has multiple meanings. Draw a river growing wider and emptying into the sea. Label the mouth of the river.
hardship	Have students identify the root word *hard* and suffix *-ship,* and recall the meaning of the suffix. Discuss examples of hardships that colonists faced.
levee	Use this context sentence: "Settlers built levees, or earthen walls, to protect the low-lying town from flood water."

WORD CARDS To help teach the lesson vocabulary, use the Word Cards on pages 251–252.

Build Fluency

Use page 72 and the steps on Procedure Card 2 to reinforce vocabulary and build fluency. Read each vocabulary word aloud and have students repeat it. Then have students work in pairs to reread the words. Follow a similar procedure with the phrases and sentences. Continue to help students build fluency by having them reread "You Are There" in the Student Edition.

Text Comprehension

BEFORE READING

Preview the Lesson Guide students in previewing the lesson using Procedure Card 3. Point out the following features of the lesson on Student Edition pages 170–177.

- **Pages 170–171** Read the "What to Know" question. Review briefly what students have learned about why Spain and England set up colonies. Preview the time line and the illustrations showing French and Huron traders and the statue of Samuel de Champlain, founder of Quebec. Have students examine the map on page 171 and answer the map skill question.
- **Pages 172–173** Have students examine the illustration showing the Dutch settlement of New Amsterdam in the 1640s. Then have them read the Fast Fact. Explain that the site where New Amsterdam was located is today part of New York City.

- **Pages 174–175** Preview the photograph of the statue on page 174 and the illustrated map on page 175. Have students read the captions and trace the explorers' routes shown on the map.
- **Page 176–177** Preview the illustration and map of New Orleans on page 176. Call attention to the table on page 177, and discuss the question in the caption. Then preview the Review questions.

During Reading

Build Comprehension of Expository Text Present the graphic organizer on page 73. Have students preview the organizer by filling in the lesson title and comparing the four main heads in the organizer with the matching subheads in the Student Edition pages 170–177. Tell students that the section subheads provide additional help with identifying important information. Use Procedure Card 4, the Reading Check questions in *Harcourt Social Studies,* and the directed reading suggestions below.

- **Page 170** After students have read "You Are There," discuss the relationship it portrays between the French and the Huron.
- **Page 171** Have students read "New France." Discuss the aims of the French merchants and the king. Then guide students in writing in the organizer facts about New France and the first French settlement. Point out how the section subhead in the text can help students locate important information.
- **Pages 172–173** Have students read about the Dutch colony of New Netherland and fill in information about New Netherland in the organizer.
- **Pages 174–175** After students have read "Exploring New France," encourage them to refer to the section subheads as they add information to the organizer about explorers and what the explorers did.
- **Pages 176–177** Tell students to read "Louisiana" and complete the graphic organizer.

After Reading

Summarize Have students use their completed graphic organizers to summarize the lesson. Then have them compare their summaries to the lesson summary on page 177.

Review and Respond If students need additional help identifying main ideas and details, use Focus Skill Transparency 2.

Draw a Map Tell students to use the chart on page 177 and information and maps from Lessons 2 and 3, as well as from this lesson, to help them create their maps of European land claims in North America.

Leveled Readers Use the Leveled Readers and Procedure Card 5 to build fluency and comprehension.

Name ______________________ Date ______________

DIRECTIONS **Read aloud the words in Part A. Practice reading aloud the phrases and the sentences in Part B.**

Part A

Vocabulary Words	Additional Words	
demand	partnership	levee
supply	warehouse	
ally	mouth	
proprietary colony	hardship	

Part B

1. Jacques Cartier / started a trading partnership / with the Huron people / in the region / that became known as New France.
2. The demand for furs / was high, / so the Dutch / set up the colony / of New Netherland / in order to profit / from the fur trade.
3. Trade with Native Americans / added to the supply of fur.
4. By the 1630s, / the Dutch settlement of New Amsterdam / had about 200 people, / 30 houses, / and warehouses / for storing food and furs.
5. When fighting over the fur trade broke out, / the Huron / were allies with the French.
6. In 1684, / La Salle / tried to start a settlement / near the mouth of the Mississippi River, / but hardships / led to disagreements / among the settlers.
7. In 1712, / the French king / made Louisiana / a proprietary colony.
8. Settlers in New Orleans, / Louisiana's capital, / built levees / to protect the low-lying town / from floodwater.

YOU ARE THERE **Turn to Student Edition page 170. Practice reading aloud "You Are There" three times. Try to improve your reading each time. Record your best time on the line below.**

Number of words 82 My Best Time ________ Words per Minute ________

Name ______________________________ Date ______________

Lesson Title: ______________________________

New France

What French merchants wanted ______________________________

What the French king wanted merchants to do ______________________________

First French settlement in North America ______________ Founder ______________

When it was founded ______________ How New France grew ______________

New Netherland

Where ______________________________

What the Dutch wanted ______________________________

What they believed they had bought ______________________________

Name of settlement ______________ Location good for ______________

Results of conflicts ______________________________

Exploring New France

Explorers ______________ and ______________ found the ______________.

Explorer ______________ claimed the ______________ for ______________.

What he named the region ______________ What happened ______________

Louisiana

The French king made Louisiana a ______________________ in ______________.

Capital ______________ What happened ______________________________

LESSON 1

Settling New England

Vocabulary Strategies

Preteach Additional Vocabulary After teaching the Vocabulary words on Student Edition page 198, explain to students that there are several other important words they will see in this lesson. Use Procedure Card 1, along with the suggestions below, to introduce the words.

pure	Point out that some products, such as bottled water, use the word *pure* in their advertising, meaning the water is clean and not mixed with anything else.
sermon	Explain that a sermon is a speech, often one that is given by a religious leader.
guilty	Students are probably familiar with this word but may not recognize it in print. Point out the similarity in spelling and pronunciation between *guilty, guitar,* and *guinea pig.*
authority	Tell students that a synonym for *authority* is *power*. Someone who has the authority to do something has the power to do it.
fundamental	Tell students that *fundamental* has the same root as *foundation.* Like the foundation of a house, a fundamental principle or idea is one on which other ideas are built.

WORD CARDS To help teach the lesson vocabulary, use the Word Cards on pages 253–254.

Build Fluency

Use page 76 and the steps on Procedure Card 2 to reinforce vocabulary and build fluency. Read each vocabulary word aloud and have students repeat it. Then have students work in pairs to reread the words. Follow a similar procedure with the phrases and sentences. Continue to help students build fluency by having them reread "You Are There" in the Student Edition.

Text Comprehension

BEFORE READING

Preview the Lesson Guide students in previewing the lesson using Procedure Card 3. Point out the following features of the lesson on Student Edition pages 198–205.

- **Pages 198–199** Discuss the "What to Know" question. Review briefly what students have learned about reasons for starting other colonies. Preview the time line and the illustrations of the Plymouth colony, Puritans arriving in New England, and John Winthrop, a Puritan leader.
- **Pages 200–201** Preview the illustrations. Explain that Roger Williams and Anne Hutchinson both started new settlements that later joined to form the colony of Rhode Island.
- **Pages 202–203** Have students examine the map of New England Colonies and answer the map skill question. Then preview the photograph of the Connecticut River and have students identify this river on the map.

- **Pages 204–205** Preview the illustration of a Niantic warrior and the Review questions on page 204. Call attention to the biography of Anne Hutchinson on page 205, and have students recall what they know about Anne Hutchinson from their preview of earlier pages in this lesson.

During Reading

Build Comprehension of Expository Text Present the graphic organizer on page 77. Have students preview the organizer by filling in the lesson title and comparing the four main heads in the organizer with the matching subheads in the Student Edition pages 198–204. Tell students that the section subheads provide additional help with identifying important information. Use Procedure Card 4, the Reading Check questions in *Harcourt Social Studies,* and the directed reading suggestions below.

- **Page 198** After students have read "You Are There," have them recall the challenges faced by the Pilgrims in the early years of the Plymouth Colony.
- **Page 199** Have students read "The Puritans Arrive" and write in the graphic organizer information about the new colony and about the location of settlements in New England.
- **Pages 200–201** Before students read "New Ideas, New Settlements," point out the blanks in the organizer for the names of two people with new ideas and information about the new settlements these people started. Tell students that the section subheads will help them identify this information.
- **Page 202** Before students read "New England Grows," discuss the difference between a settlement and a colony. Point out the blanks in the organizer for the names of new colonies. Then have students fill in the organizer either as they read or after reading the section.
- **Pages 203–204** After students have read "Growth Brings Conflict," point out that there are spaces in the organizer to write about two different wars. Have students complete the organizer.

After Reading

Summarize Have students use their completed graphic organizers to summarize the lesson. Then have them compare their summaries to the lesson summary on page 204.

Review and Respond Work through the Review questions with students. Use Focus Skill Transparency 3, Summarize, to summarize information in the lesson.

Draw a Map Suggest that students reread passages from the lesson and also look at the map on page 202 to help them draw their own maps and find the information they will need to include.

Leveled Readers Use the Leveled Readers and Procedure Card 5 to build fluency and comprehension.

Name ______________________________ Date ______________

DIRECTIONS **Read aloud the words in Part A. Practice reading aloud the phrases and the sentences in Part B.**

Part A

Vocabulary Words		Additional Words	
charter	consent	pure	authority
dissent	sedition	sermon	fundamental
expel	frontier	guilty	

Part B

1. In 1628, / English settlers / arrived in North America / with a charter from the king of England / giving them permission / to start a colony.
2. These settlers / were called Puritans / because they wanted / to make the Church of England / more "pure."
3. In 1630, / John Winthrop / led a second group of Puritans / to build "a city upon a hill" / that he had described / in a sermon.
4. Roger Williams / was found guilty of dissent, / and the leaders of the Massachusetts Bay Colony / voted to expel him.
5. Williams / organized a new settlement / based on / the consent of the people.
6. The leaders of the Massachusetts Bay Colony / faced another challenge to their authority / from a colonist named Anne Hutchinson.
7. She was tried for sedition / and expelled from the colony.
8. In 1639, / the leaders of the Connecticut Colony / wrote the Fundamental Orders, / a plan of government / that let voters / elect their own leaders.
9. After King Philip's War, / settlers pushed the frontier / north and west.

YOU ARE THERE **Turn to Student Edition page 198. Practice reading aloud "You Are There" three times. Try to improve your reading each time. Record your best time on the line below.**

Number of words 79 My Best Time ________ Words per Minute ________

Name ______________________________ Date ______________

Lesson Title: ______________________________

The Puritans Arrive

Leader ______________ Colony ______________

Most early settlements in New England were built ______________.

Why ______________________________

New Ideas, New Settlements

Person with new ideas ______________ New settlement ______________

Based on ______________________________

Person with new ideas ______________ Settlement near ______________

The two settlements joined to form ______________

New England Grows

Why settlers moved south 1. ______________________________

2. ______________ New colony ______________

Why settlers moved north ______________________________

New colony ______________________________

Growth Brings Conflict

Conflict between ______________________ Over ______________

War ______________ When __________ War ______________ When __________

Result ______________________________

LESSON 2

Life in New England

Vocabulary Strategies

Preteach Additional Vocabulary After teaching the Vocabulary words on Student Edition page 208, explain to students that there are several other important words they will see in this lesson. Use Procedure Card 1, along with the suggestions below, to introduce the words.

stocks	Discuss familiar meanings. Then read and discuss this context sentence: "In the stocks, a person's head, hands, and feet were locked into a wooden frame."
grazing	Explain that grazing cattle or livestock means putting them out in a field or meadow to eat grass or other plants.
cooper	Tell students that a cooper is a person who makes or repairs barrels or wooden tubs.
harvest	Discuss what it means to harvest, or gather in, crops.
hornbook	Point out the two shorter words *horn* and *book* in this compound word. Tell students that books covered with thin pieces of animal horn were used in New England schools long ago. Call attention to the illustration on page 212.

WORD CARDS To help teach the lesson vocabulary, use the Word Cards on pages 253–254.

Build Fluency

Use page 80 and the steps on Procedure Card 2 to reinforce vocabulary and build fluency. Read each vocabulary word aloud and have students repeat it. Then have students work in pairs to reread the words. Follow a similar procedure with the phrases and sentences. Continue to help students build fluency by having them reread "You Are There" in the Student Edition.

Text Comprehension

BEFORE READING

Preview the Lesson Guide students in previewing the lesson using Procedure Card 3. Point out the following features of the lesson on Student Edition pages 208–213.

- **Pages 208–209** Read the "What to Know" question, and explain that the Puritans had very strong religious beliefs that affected their lives in many ways. Preview the time line and illustrations. Ask students why they think the colonists carried their weapons everywhere they went.
- **Pages 210–211** Have students examine and discuss the illustration of a New England town. Discuss the activities taking place in the illustration, and have students answer the question in the caption.
- **Pages 212–213** Have students read the Primary Sources feature about hornbooks and discuss the document-based question. Then preview the engraving of Harvard College and the Review questions on page 213.

During Reading

Build Comprehension of Expository Text Present the graphic organizer on page 81. Have students preview the organizer by filling in the lesson title and comparing the three main heads in the organizer with the matching subheads in the Student Edition pages 208–213. Tell students that the section subheads provide additional help with identifying important information. Use Procedure Card 4, the Reading Check questions in *Harcourt Social Studies,* and the directed reading suggestions below.

- **Page 208** After students have read "You Are There," ask whether they would have enjoyed being Puritan children, and why or why not.
- **Page 209** Have students read "A Religious Life" and complete the first box in the organizer. Ask students to give examples of how religious beliefs affected the Puritans' daily lives. Point out the subhead "Church Services" that matches the section subhead in the text. Guide students in summarizing information from this part of the lesson.
- **Pages 210–211** After students have read "Everyday Life," discuss how villages were laid out, the economic system, government, and home life. Then have students fill in the next box in the organizer. Point out the two subheads that match the section subheads in the text.
- **Pages 212–213** Have students read "Childhood in New England" and complete the organizer by summarizing key information under each of the two section subheads. Discuss differences between Puritan schools and schools today.

After Reading

Summarize Have students use their completed graphic organizers to summarize the lesson. Then have them compare their summaries to the lesson summary on page 213.

Review and Respond If students need additional help with summarizing, use Focus Skill Transparency 3.

Write a Narrative Review narrative writing with students, emphasizing that the information about school, materials, and how teachers taught should be in the form of a story. Discuss how students might write an account of a fictional event or events in a New England school that will give readers a picture of what these schools were like.

Leveled Readers Use the Leveled Readers and Procedure Card 5 to build fluency and comprehension.

Name ______________________ Date ______________

DIRECTIONS **Read aloud the words in Part A. Practice reading aloud the phrases and the sentences in Part B.**

Part A

Vocabulary Words	Additional Words
common	stocks
town meeting	grazing
	cooper
	harvest
	hornbook

Part B

1. A punishment / for Puritans who missed church / or spoke out in dissent / was several hours in the town stocks.
2. At the center of each New England town / was a common, / used for grazing sheep, / cattle, / and other livestock.
3. A blacksmith might make iron tools / for the cooper, / who in turn might make barrels / for the blacksmith.
4. At least once a year, / the townspeople gathered / for a town meeting / to vote on laws / and elect leaders.
5. Every fall, / all the colonists / helped harvest the crops.
6. The main subject taught in New England schools / was reading, / and most students learned to read / from a hornbook.

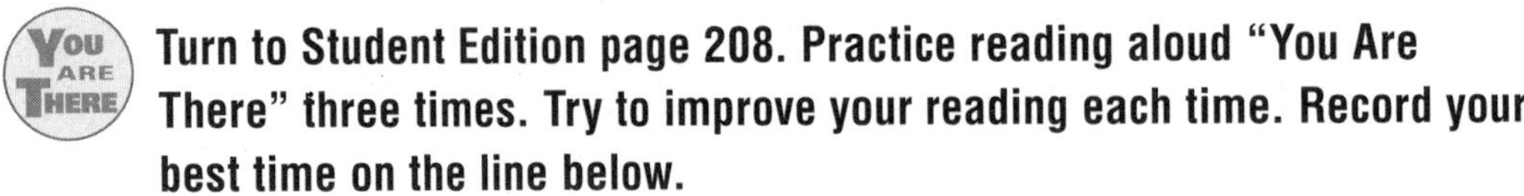

Turn to Student Edition page 208. Practice reading aloud "You Are There" three times. Try to improve your reading each time. Record your best time on the line below.

Number of words 71 My Best Time ______ Words per Minute ______

Name ______________________ Date ______________

Lesson Title: ______________________

A Religious Life

How Puritans lived their lives ______________________

Church Services ______________________

____

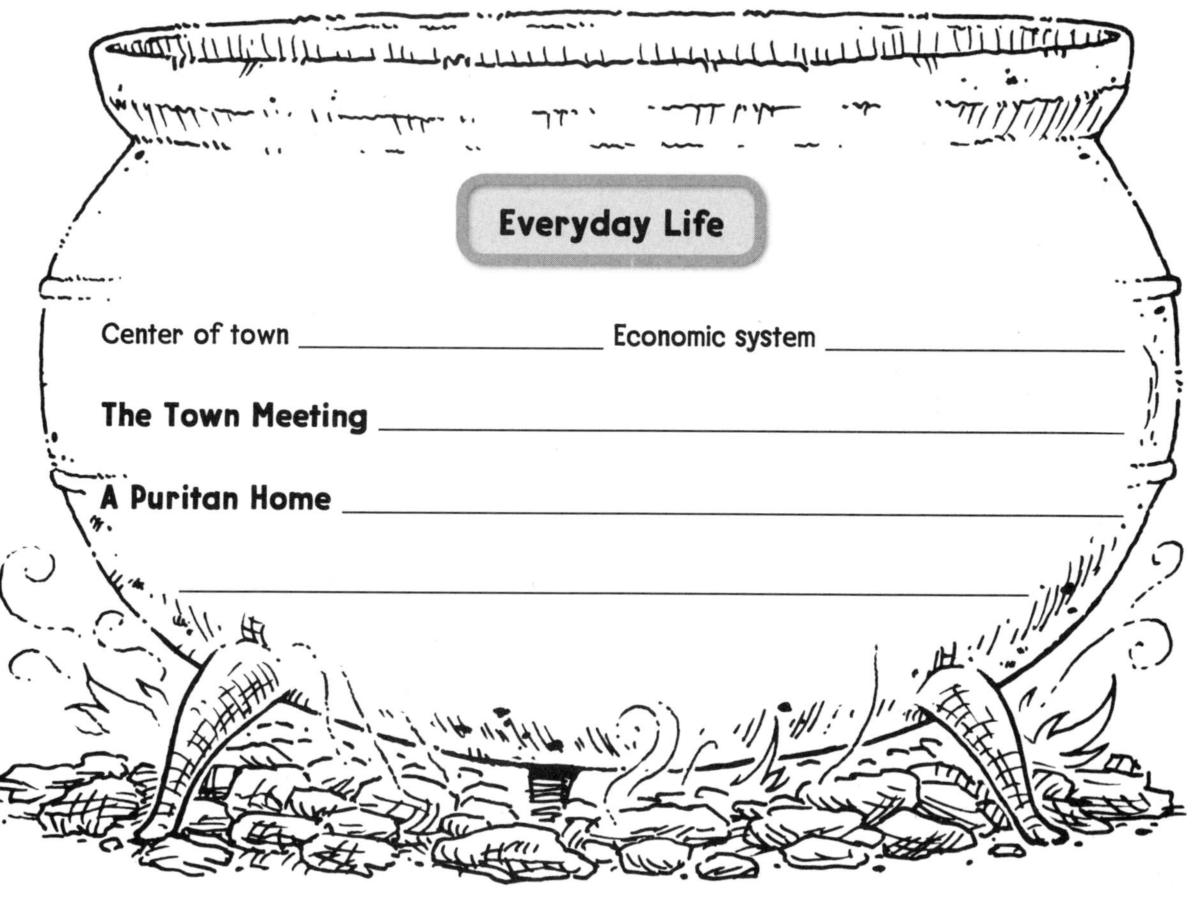

Everyday Life

Center of town ______________ Economic system ______________

The Town Meeting ______________________

A Puritan Home ______________________

____

Childhood in New England

Early Schools ______________________

Learning to Read ______________________

LESSON 3

New England's Economy

Vocabulary Strategies

Preteach Additional Vocabulary After teaching the Vocabulary words on Student Edition page 214, explain to students that there are several other important words they will see in this lesson. Use Procedure Card 1, along with the suggestions below, to introduce the words.

compete	Have students give examples of how people compete, as in games, sports, and contests. Then discuss what it means to compete in business.
turpentine	Tell students that this name for an oily substance obtained from pine trees is from the Greek *terebinthos,* or terebinth, a small European tree that also produces turpentine.
hull	Ask students to draw a sailboat or sailing ship and label the hull, or main body, of the vessel.
mast	Now have students label the masts, the tall poles that hold the sails, on their drawings of sailboats or sailing ships.
cruelty	Point out the word *cruel* and suffix *-ty,* meaning "quality or state of being." Give examples of other words with this suffix, such as *safety* and *loyalty.*

WORD CARDS To help teach the lesson vocabulary, use the Word Cards on pages 253–256.

Build Fluency

Use page 84 and the steps on Procedure Card 2 to reinforce vocabulary and build fluency. Read each vocabulary word aloud and have students repeat it. Then have students work in pairs to reread the words. Follow a similar procedure with the phrases and sentences. Continue to help students build fluency by having them reread "You Are There" in the Student Edition.

Text Comprehension

Before Reading

Preview the Lesson Guide students in previewing the lesson using Procedure Card 3. Point out the following features of the lesson on Student Edition pages 214–219.

- **Pages 214–215** Read the "What to Know" question and discuss in general terms how the natural resources of a region shape its economy. Preview the time line and the illustrations. Ask students why they think most farms had many different types of animals.
- **Pages 216–217** Preview the photograph of the reenactor and carpenter's tools on page 216 and the illustration of whalers on page 217.
- **Pages 218–219** Preview the map of Triangular Trade Routes and discuss the map skill question. Then preview the illustration of the Middle Passage and the Review questions on page 219.

During Reading

Build Comprehension of Expository Text Present the graphic organizer on page 85. Have students preview the organizer by filling in the lesson title and comparing the four main heads in the organizer with the matching subheads in the Student Edition pages 214–219. Tell students that the section subheads provide additional help with identifying important information. Use Procedure Card 4, the Reading Check questions in *Harcourt Social Studies,* and the directed reading suggestions below.

- **Page 214** After students have read "You Are There," call attention to the illustration and caption on this page. Remind students that children in the New England colonies had to do the same jobs their parents did in and around the home.
- **Page 215** Have students read "New England Farming." Then guide them in recording the information in the organizer. Discuss the cause-effect relationship between surpluses and trade.
- **Page 216** After students have read "Logging and Shipbuilding," have them list in the organizer three important industries that colonists developed from New England forests.
- **Page 217** Have students read "Colonial Trade" and fill in the information under that head in the organizer.
- **Pages 218–219** After students have read "Triangular Trade Routes," tell them to complete the organizer by writing the names of the three places the routes connected. Discuss the Middle Passage and why the treatment of enslaved people made some colonists angry.

After Reading

Summarize Have students use their completed graphic organizers to summarize the lesson. Then have them compare their summaries to the lesson summary on page 219.

Review and Respond If students need additional help with summarizing, use Focus Skill Transparency 3.

Write a List of Questions Have students fold a sheet of paper in quarters by first folding it in half lengthwise and then across. Tell them to unfold the paper and label the four boxes "Farmer," "Merchant," and so on. Then as students reread parts of the lesson, they can write their questions in the boxes.

Leveled Readers Use the Leveled Readers and Procedure Card 5 to build fluency and comprehension.

Name ______________________ Date ______________

DIRECTIONS **Read aloud the words in Part A. Practice reading aloud the phrases and the sentences in Part B.**

Part A

Vocabulary Words		Additional Words
free-market	import	compete
naval stores	industry	turpentine
Middle Passage	export	hull
triangular trade route		mast
		cruelty

Part B

1. In a free-market economy, / people are free / to compete in business / and to set whatever prices they choose / for goods and services.
2. The lumber industry / made up a large part / of the colonists' free-market economy.
3. New England forests / supplied the natural resources / needed to make naval stores / such as turpentine and tar.
4. Shipbuilders / formed the ships' hulls / with oak / and used tall pines / to make the masts.
5. The English government / said that the colonists / could only send their exports / to England / or to other English colonies.
6. Colonists could only buy / English-made imports.
7. Some colonial trading ships / followed the triangular trade routes.
8. During the 1700s, / some people in the colonies / grew angry / about the cruelty of the Middle Passage / and slavery.

YOU ARE THERE **Turn to Student Edition page 214. Practice reading aloud "You Are There" three times. Try to improve your reading each time. Record your best time on the line below.**

Number of words 61 My Best Time ________ Words per Minute ________

Name ______________________ Date ____________

Lesson Title: ______________________

New England Farmimg

In time, colonists produced

______________________.

Economic system that developed

____

Logging and Shipbuilding

Important industries

1. ______________________
2. ______________________
3. ______________________

Colonial Trade

Center of New England's economy ______________________

Industries in coastal towns ______________________

Triangular Trade Routes

Places they connected

____

____

____

Lesson 1 Settling the Middle Colonies

Vocabulary Strategies

Preteach Additional Vocabulary After teaching the Vocabulary words on Student Edition page 224, explain to students that there are several other important words they will see in this lesson. Use Procedure Card 1, along with the suggestions below, to introduce the words.

breadbasket	Have students identify the two shorter words, *bread* and *basket*, that make up this compound word. Tell students that bread is sometimes served in a basket called a *breadbasket*.
prosperous	Point out the word *prosper* and suffix *-ous*. Tell students that synonyms include *successful*, *rich*, and *wealthy*.
order	Discuss known meanings of this word. Tell students that one meaning is "a state of peace and respect for law."
expanded	Point out the base word *expand* and ending *-ed*. Have students use hand gestures to show the meaning of *expand*.
outnumbered	Have students identify the elements *out*, *number*, and *-ed*. Divide students into groups containing different numbers of people, and have them tell which is outnumbered by the other.

WORD CARDS To help teach the lesson vocabulary, use the Word Cards on pages 257–258.

Build Fluency

Use page 88 and the steps on Procedure Card 2 to reinforce vocabulary and build fluency. Read each vocabulary word aloud and have students repeat it. Then have students work in pairs to reread the words. Follow a similar procedure with the phrases and sentences. Continue to help students build fluency by having them reread "You Are There" in the Student Edition.

Text Comprehension

Before Reading

Preview the Lesson Guide students in previewing the lesson using Procedure Card 3. Point out the following features of the lesson on Student Edition pages 224–231.

- **Pages 224–225** Read the "What to Know" question and help students identify the Middle Colonies. Preview the time line, the portrait of King Charles II of England, and the illustration of Fort Orange.
- **Pages 226–227** Preview the illustrations of a slave auction and of Peter Stuyvesant in New Netherland. Have students look back at the time line on page 224 to find out when Peter Stuyvesant arrived in New Netherland and when the English took over.

- **Pages 228–229** Preview the illustrated time line on page 228, and have students answer the question in the caption. Have students examine the map of the Middle Colonies on page 229 and answer the map skill question. Preview the portrait of William Penn on page 229, and have students find information about William Penn on the illustrated time line.
- **Pages 230–231** Preview the illustration of William Penn and the Review questions on page 230. Call attention to the biography of the Lenni Lenape leader Tamanend on page 231.

During Reading

Build Comprehension of Expository Text Present the graphic organizer on page 89. Have students preview the organizer by filling in the lesson title and comparing the five main heads in the organizer with the matching subheads in the Student Edition pages 224–230. Tell students that the section subheads provide additional help with identifying important information. Use Procedure Card 4, the Reading Check questions in *Harcourt Social Studies*, and the directed reading suggestions below.

- **Page 224** After students have read "You Are There," discuss what King Charles II wants. Have students predict what the king may do.
- **Page 225** Before students read "The Breadbasket Colonies," have them look at the organizer to set a purpose for reading. They can list resources and crops in the blanks in the organizer either as they read or after reading.
- **Pages 226–227** Have students use the organizer to set a purpose for reading "New Netherland Grows." Tell them to fill in the information as they read or afterwards, using the section subheads to help them. Then have students read "The English Take Over" and summarize what King Charles wanted and what happened.
- **Pages 228–230** Have students read "New York and New Jersey" and record information in the organizer. Then they can read "Pennsylvania and Delaware" and complete the organizer.

After Reading

Summarize Have students use their completed graphic organizers to summarize the lesson. Then have them compare their summaries to the lesson summary on page 230.

Review and Respond If students need additional help with summarizing, use Focus Skill Transparency 3.

Write a Conversation Discuss with students what they have learned about the relationship between William Penn and Tamanend that might help them write their conversations. You may want to have students work with partners to write their conversations and then read them aloud.

Leveled Readers Use the Leveled Readers and Procedure Card 5 to build fluency and comprehension.

Name ______________________________ Date ______________

DIRECTIONS **Read aloud the words in Part A. Practice reading aloud the phrases and the sentences in Part B.**

Part A

Vocabulary Words		Additional Words	
refuge	proprietor	breadbasket	expanded
trial by jury	justice	prosperous	outnumbered
		order	

Part B

1. The Middle Colonies / grew so many crops used in making bread / that they came to be called / the breadbasket colonies.
2. Few Dutch people / came to New Netherland / because their country, / the Netherlands, / was prosperous / and gave its citizens / many freedoms.
3. The Dutch West India Company / sent Peter Stuyvesant to New Netherland / to raise its profits / and bring order.
4. Stuyvesant / expanded New Netherland / into what is now New Jersey / and then pushed south / into what is now Delaware.
5. When the English sent four warships / to take New Netherland, / the Dutch knew they were outnumbered / and surrendered.
6. A group of Quakers, / hoping to find refuge, / founded Salem, New Jersey, / the first Quaker settlement in North America.
7. William Penn, / the proprietor of what is now Pennsylvania, / wrote the Frame of Government / of Pennsylvania.
8. Penn's plan of government / gave citizens / the right to a trial by jury.
9. Penn / also wanted / Native Americans / to be treated with justice.

YOU ARE THERE **Turn to Student Edition page 224. Practice reading aloud "You Are There" three times. Try to improve your reading each time. Record your best time on the line below.**

Number of words 57 My Best Time ________ Words per Minute ________

Name ______________________ Date ____________

Lesson Title ______________________

The Breadbasket Colonies

Resources ____________ ____________

____________ ____________

Crops ____________ ____________ ____________

New Netherland Grows

New leader ____________ When ____________

What he did ____________

New colonists ____________

____

The English Take Over

What King Charles wanted ____________

What happened ____________

New York and New Jersey

New Amsterdam became	New settlers in New Jersey
____________	____________

Pennsylvania and Delaware

Proprietor ____________

How he treated Native Americans

____

LESSON 2 Life in the Middle Colonies

Vocabulary Strategies

Preteach Additional Vocabulary After teaching the Vocabulary words on Student Edition page 234, explain to students that there are several other important words they will see in this lesson. Use Procedure Card 1, along with the suggestions below, to introduce the words.

preach	Tell students that to preach means to give a talk about religious topics or proper behavior. Some religious leaders are called preachers.
revival	Explain that large prayer meetings are often called revivals. The words *revive* and *revival* come from the Latin roots *re-*, meaning "again," and *vivere*, meaning "to live."
participation	Have students define this word from the verb *participate*, "to take part in," and the suffix *-tion*, meaning "act" or "process."
exercise	Discuss familiar meanings of this word. Then talk about the meaning of the phrase "the free exercise of religion."
social	Explain that this word is from the Latin root *socius*, meaning "companion," also the root of *society*. We use *social* to describe things that have to do with human beings as they live and work together in society.

WORD CARDS To help teach the lesson vocabulary, use the Word Cards on pages 257–258.

Build Fluency

Use page 92 and the steps on Procedure Card 2 to reinforce vocabulary and build fluency. Read each vocabulary word aloud and have students repeat it. Then have students work in pairs to reread the words. Follow a similar procedure with the phrases and sentences. Continue to help students build fluency by having them reread "You Are There" in the Student Edition.

Text Comprehension

BEFORE READING

Preview the Lesson Guide students in previewing the lesson using Procedure Card 3. Point out the following features of the lesson on Student Edition pages 234–239.

- **Pages 234–235** Read the "What to Know" question. Discuss why people of different cultures might prefer to settle in places with religious toleration. Preview the time line and the illustration. Ask students why they think buildings in New York had Dutch-style architecture.
- **Pages 236–237** Preview the illustrations, and discuss what students can learn from the picture and caption on page 237 about the lives of African Americans in the Middle Colonies.

- **Pages 238–239** Preview the illustrations of Philadelphia and Benjamin Franklin, and explain that Franklin was the most famous Philadelphian of his time. Then preview the Review questions.

During Reading

Build Comprehension of Expository Text Present the graphic organizer on page 93. Have students preview the organizer by filling in the lesson title and comparing the four main heads in the organizer with the matching subheads in the Student Edition pages 234–239. Tell students that the section subheads provide additional help with identifying important information. Use Procedure Card 4, the Reading Check questions in *Harcourt Social Studies,* and the directed reading suggestions below.

- **Page 234** After students have read "You Are There," ask whether they have heard of Wall Street in New York City. Explain that today it is a famous street where some of the nation's important financial business is done.
- **Page 235** Have students read "A Mix of People" and discuss the diversity of the Middle Colonies. Then have students list in the organizer three reasons that immigrants came to start a new life in the Middle Colonies and what many immigrants found there.
- **Page 236** Use the organizer to have students set a purpose for reading "The Great Awakening." They can fill in the information as they read or afterwards.
- **Page 237** Now have students read "Religion and Social Life" and fill in that box. Tell them to list activities that colonists did in their free time. Point out that the subhead "Free Time" matches the section subhead in the text and will help students locate that information.
- **Page 238** Have students read "Philadelphia Grows" and complete the organizer either as they read or after reading. Point out the dates 1682 and 1770, and tell students to record information that shows how Philadelphia grew in that time. In addition to having students list the roles that Benjamin Franklin played for "What he was," you may want to have them list on a separate sheet of paper ways that he helped improve the city of Philadelphia.

After Reading

Summarize Have students use their completed graphic organizers to summarize the lesson. Then have them compare their summaries to the lesson summary on page 239.

Review and Respond If students need additional help with summarizing, use Focus Skill Transparency 3.

Write a Narrative Suggest that students reread the section of the lesson about Philadelphia to get ideas for the setting of their narratives. Tell them to think about people and events they might write about. Remind students to jot down information about the city's location, people, and businesses to include in their stories.

Leveled Readers Use the Leveled Readers and Procedure Card 5 to build fluency and comprehension.

Name ______________________ Date ______________

DIRECTIONS **Read aloud the words in Part A. Practice reading aloud the phrases and the sentences in Part B.**

Part A

Vocabulary Words		Additional Words	
diversity	militia	preach	exercise
immigrant		revival	social
Great Awakening		participation	
religious tolerance			

Part B

1. The diversity of the Middle Colonies, / where immigrants from many countries / came to make a new life, / made it an interesting place to live.
2. In the 1720s, / a new religious movement / known as the Great Awakening / began in the Middle Colonies.
3. Not only did the ministers / preach new ideas, / they practiced religion differently.
4. The Great Awakening / helped bring people together, / which led to greater religious toleration.
5. Everyone / was welcomed at the revivals, / although such equal participation / was rare at this time in history.
6. The number of church members in the colonies / grew, / as did the free exercise of religion.
7. The social lives of colonists / were as different / as their religious beliefs.
8. Benjamin Franklin / helped improve Philadelphia / in many ways, / including organizing a militia / to protect the city / and the rest of the colony.

YOU ARE THERE **Turn to Student Edition page 234. Practice reading aloud "You Are There" three times. Try to improve your reading each time. Record your best time on the line below.**

Number of words 63 My Best Time ______ Words per Minute ______

Name ______________________ Date ______________

Lesson Title ______________________

A Mix of People

Reasons for immigrating

1. ______________________
2. ______________________
3. ______________________

____

What immigrants found

____

____

The Great Awakening

What it was ______________________

Results

1. ______________________
2. ______________________
3. ______________________
4. ______________________
5. ______________________

Religion and Social Life

Major part of social life in the Middle Colonies ______________________

Free Time Activities ______________________

____

____

____

Philadelphia Grows

Who designed Philadelphia ______________________

1682 ______________ 1770 ______________

Most famous Philadelphian ______________________

What he was ______________________

____

LESSON 3

Busy Farms and Seaports

Vocabulary Strategies

Preteach Additional Vocabulary After teaching the Vocabulary words on Student Edition page 240, explain to students that there are several other important words they will see in this lesson. Use Procedure Card 1, along with the suggestions below, to introduce the words.

gristmill	Point out and discuss the illustration of a gristmill on pages 240–241.
grain	Discuss familiar meanings, such as grains of sand. Explain that grain also means the seeds or fruit of certain plants such as wheat, corn, and rye.
general store	Tell students that general stores were usually found in rural communities. They sold a variety of goods but were not large or divided into departments as modern stores are.
dockhand	Have students identify the two shorter words that make up this compound word. Explain that *hand* sometimes means "worker." A dockhand is someone whose job is loading and unloading ships.
journeyman	Explain that an apprentice who has finished training becomes a journeyman, who works for and is paid by an employer.

WORD CARDS To help teach the lesson vocabulary, use the Word Cards on pages 257–258.

Build Fluency

Use page 96 and the steps on Procedure Card 2 to reinforce vocabulary and build fluency. Read each vocabulary word aloud and have students repeat it. Then have students work in pairs to reread the words. Follow a similar procedure with the phrases and sentences. Continue to help students build fluency by having them reread "You Are There" in the Student Edition.

Text Comprehension

Before Reading

Preview the Lesson Guide students in previewing the lesson using Procedure Card 3. Point out the following features of the lesson on Student Edition pages 240–245.

- **Pages 240–241** Read the "What to Know" question, and review briefly what students have already learned about the geography and the economy of the Middle Colonies. Preview the time line. Have students examine the illustration of a gristmill and answer the question in the caption.
- **Pages 242–243** Preview the graph showing colonial exports, and have students answer the question in the caption. Preview the illustrations of New York City and of English goods that entered the colonies through port cities.

- **Pages 244–245** Have students read Children in History and discuss jobs they would choose if they were apprentices. Preview the illustration of a chandler and the Review questions on page 245.

During Reading

Build Comprehension of Expository Text Present the graphic organizer on page 97. Have students preview the organizer by filling in the lesson title and comparing the three main heads in the organizer with the matching subheads in the Student Edition pages 240–245. Tell students that the section subheads provide additional help with identifying important information. Use Procedure Card 4, the Reading Check questions in *Harcourt Social Studies*, and the directed reading suggestions below.

- **Page 240** After students have read "You Are There," ask what information they learned from it about the lesson topic, busy farms and seaports.
- **Page 241** Have students read "Rich Farmlands." Then guide them in completing the first box of the organizer. Remind students that rereading passages in the lesson can help them recall information.
- **Pages 242–243** After students have read "Port Cities," have them fill in the next section of the organizer. Explain that students should write the names of two different port cities in the Middle Colonies for "An important port" and "The busiest port." Tell them that the section subheads in the text will help them find this information.
- **Pages 244–245** Have students read "Colonial Jobs" and complete the organizer. Explain that for the first item, students should write a general term for the type of work, not the names of specific jobs.

After Reading

Summarize Have students use their completed graphic organizers to summarize the lesson. Then have them compare their summaries to the lesson summary on page 245.

Review and Respond If students need additional help with summarizing, use Focus Skill Transparency 3.

Make a Chart Discuss with students how to set up their charts. You may want to show an example of a two-column chart for students to use as a model. Some students might prefer the option of using the chart function in a computer word processing program to set up and print their charts.

Leveled Readers Use the Leveled Readers and Procedure Card 5 to build fluency and comprehension.

Name ______________________ Date ____________

DIRECTIONS **Read aloud the words in Part A. Practice reading aloud the phrases and the sentences in Part B.**

Part A

Vocabulary Words	Additional Words	
prosperity	gristmill	dockhand
artisan	grain	journeyman
apprentice	general store	

Part B

1. Wheat fields / stretched across the Middle Colonies, / and every market town/ had a gristmill, / which ground grain into flour.
2. During visits to market towns, / farm families / shopped at the general store / for things they could not make/ or grow themselves.
3. The colonies' prosperity / depended largely on the ports, / which were major trade centers.
4. Port cities / were busy places / where merchants talked over prices / as dockhands moved goods.
5. In addition to farming and shipping, / many colonists / worked as artisans / in skilled trades.
6. Young people / learned skills needed by artisans / by becoming apprentices.
7. An apprentice / lived and worked with an artisan / for several years / before he could go on / to earn a living as a journeyman.

YOU ARE THERE **Turn to Student Edition page 240. Practice reading aloud "You Are There" three times. Try to improve your reading each time. Record your best time on the line below.**

Number of words 73 My Best Time ______ Words per Minute ______

Name ______________________ Date ____________

Lesson Title ______________________

Rich Farmlands

The Middle Colonies had plenty of ______________________

How most people made their living ______________________

What farmers traded or sold ______________________

Port Cities

What largely depended on the ports

____

An important port ______________________

The busiest port ______________________

Almost all trade was with ______________________

______________________.

Colonial Jobs

Type of work besides farming and shipping

____

What most artisans used to make goods

____

How artisans learned their skills

____

LESSON 1 Settling the South

Vocabulary Strategies

Preteach Additional Vocabulary After teaching the Vocabulary words on Student Edition page 252, explain to students that there are several other important words they will see in this lesson. Use Procedure Card 1, along with the suggestions below, to introduce the words.

founded	Discuss familiar meanings for *found*. Explain that to found means to establish, create, or set up something such as a company, an organization, or a colony.
assembly	Have students define the word in this context: "Both colonies had governors and elected assemblies." Point out that the plural is formed by changing *y* to *i* and adding *-es*.
limited	Have students identify the base word *limit* and *-ed* ending that shows action in the past. Explain that *limit* can be a noun, as in the phrase "speed limit" and can also be a verb, as in "The law limited the speed on city streets to 30 miles per hour."
labor	Tell students that synonyms include *work* and *effort*.
sugarcane	Point out the two shorter words that make up this compound word. Explain that sugarcane is a plant from which sugar is made. A cane is a hollow stem.

WORD CARDS To help teach the lesson vocabulary, use the Word Cards on pages 259–260.

Build Fluency

Use page 100 and the steps on Procedure Card 2 to reinforce vocabulary and build fluency. Read each vocabulary word aloud and have students repeat it. Then have students work in pairs to reread the words. Follow a similar procedure with the phrases and sentences. Continue to help students build fluency by having them reread "You Are There" in the Student Edition.

Text Comprehension

BEFORE READING

Preview the Lesson Guide students in previewing the lesson using Procedure Card 3. Point out the following features of the lesson on Student Edition pages 252–259.

- **Pages 252–253** Read the "What to Know" question and discuss briefly what students know about how geography affects people's lives. Preview the time line and the illustration of Chesapeake Bay, and have students read the Fast Fact. On page 253, preview the painting and have students discuss the question in the caption. Explain that Maryland was founded in part as a refuge for Catholics.
- **Pages 254–255** Preview the illustrations and the map of the Southern Colonies. Have students name the colonies shown on the map and answer the map skill question.
- **Pages 256–257** Preview the portrait of James Oglethorpe, the founder of the Georgia Colony, and the illustration showing settlers heading to the backcountry. Have students examine the map and trace the route of the Great Wagon Road.

- **Pages 258–259** Have students read the Primary Sources feature, examine the drawing, and discuss the document-based question. Then preview the illustration of Town Creek Indian Mound and the Review questions on page 259.

During Reading

Build Comprehension of Expository Text Present the graphic organizer on page 101. Have students preview the organizer by filling in the lesson title and comparing the six main heads in the organizer with the matching subheads in the Student Edition pages 252–259. Tell students that the section subheads provide additional help with identifying important information. Use Procedure Card 4, the Reading Check questions in *Harcourt Social Studies*, and the directed reading suggestions below.

- **Page 252** After students have read "You Are There," have them tell what they learned from it about the Maryland Colony.
- **Page 253** Have students read and discuss "Maryland." Tell them to write in the organizer the name of the family that founded the colony and their reasons for building a colony in North America.
- **Page 254** After students have read "Life in Maryland and Virginia," discuss the information briefly and have them fill in the next box in the organizer. Point out that the section subheads in the text will be helpful in completing items in the organizer.
- **Pages 255–256** Have students read "The Carolina Colonies" and complete the next section of the organizer. Then students can read "Georgia" and fill in that information.
- **Pages 257–259** After students have read "Heading West," tell them to write the time when settlers were moving west and the region to which they moved for "When" and "Where" in the organizer. Point out that the section subhead in the text can help students with the last item, the name of the trail that settlers followed. Then have students read "Conflicts with Native Americans" and complete the organizer by writing a brief summary of what happened to Native Americans in the Southern Colonies.

After Reading

Summarize Have students use their completed graphic organizers to summarize the lesson. Then have them compare their summaries to the lesson summary on page 259.

Review and Respond If students need additional help with summarizing, use Focus Skill Transparency 3.

Make an Illustrated Time Line Suggest that students go back to the lesson and jot down dates of important events to include in their time lines. You may want to have students work with partners. Provide art materials, and encourage students to make their time lines colorful and interesting. Display completed time lines so students can compare and contrast.

Leveled Readers Use the Leveled Readers and Procedure Card 5 to build fluency and comprehension.

Name ______________________________ Date ______________

DIRECTIONS **Read aloud the words in Part A. Practice reading aloud the phrases and the sentences in Part B.**

Part A

Vocabulary Words	Additional Words	
constitution	founded	labor
debtor	assembly	sugarcane
backcountry	limited	

Part B

1. The Maryland Colony / was founded by the Calverts, / a family of wealthy English landowners.
2. Both Virginia and Maryland / had governors / and elected assemblies.
3. In 1669, / the leaders of the Carolina Colony / adopted a constitution, / but the colony / soon became hard to govern.
4. James Oglethorpe / brought English debtors / to settle the colony of Georgia.
5. The leaders of Georgia / limited the size of farms / and did not allow slavery.
6. When leaders / decided to allow slavery, / Georgia's economy grew / as a result of plantations / and the labor of enslaved Africans.
7. Settlers used a trail / known as the Great Wagon Road / to reach the backcountry / in the Piedmont of Virginia and the Carolinas.
8. Some Native Americans / in the Southern Colonies / were captured / and sent to the West Indies / to work on sugarcane plantations.

You Are There **Turn to Student Edition page 252. Practice reading aloud "You Are There" three times. Try to improve your reading each time. Record your best time on the line below.**

Number of words 84 My Best Time ________ Words per Minute ________

Name ______________________ Date ______________

Lesson Title ______________________

Maryland

Founded by ______________________

Reasons

1. ______________________

2. ______________________

Life in Maryland and Virginia

________ climate ________ soil

Crop ______________________

Similar ______________________

Maryland passed ______________________

The Carolina Colonies

Split into ______________________

and ______________________

North Carolina crops ______________________

South Carolina's most important crop ________

Large part of population ______________________

Georgia

Founder ______________________

Settlers were ______________________

Economy grew as a result of

______________________ and

______________________.

Conflicts with Native Americans

What happened to Native Americans

____

____

____

____

Heading West

When ______________________

Where ______________________

____

Trail ______________________

LESSON 2 Life in the South

Vocabulary Strategies

Preteach Additional Vocabulary After teaching the Vocabulary words on Student Edition page 262, explain to students that there are several other important words they will see in this lesson. Use Procedure Card 1, along with the suggestions below, to introduce the words.

legal	Tell students that *legal* is from the Latin root *lex,* meaning "law." Something that is legal is allowed or permitted by law. Another word from this root is *legislature.*
abused	Discuss the meaning, using this context sentence from the lesson: "Enslaved people were often beaten and abused, and the law did not protect them."
illegal	Have students identify the word *legal* and prefix *il-*. Explain that *il-* means "not," so *illegal* is an antonym of *legal.*
former	Give an example, such as a former President, meaning someone who was President in the past. Encourage students to offer other examples.
runaway	Divide the compound word between the shorter words *run* and *away.* Have students use the meanings of the shorter words to determine that a runaway is someone who has left, or escaped from somewhere.

WORD CARDS To help teach the lesson vocabulary, use the Word Cards on pages 259–260.

Build Fluency

Use page 104 and the steps on Procedure Card 2 to reinforce vocabulary and build fluency. Read each vocabulary word aloud and have students repeat it. Then have students work in pairs to reread the words. Follow a similar procedure with the phrases and sentences. Continue to help students build fluency by having them reread "You Are There" in the Student Edition.

Text Comprehension

BEFORE READING

Preview the Lesson Guide students in previewing the lesson using Procedure Card 3. Point out the following features of the lesson on Student Edition pages 262–267.

- **Pages 262–263** Read the "What to Know" question and have students recall what they have learned about plantations. Preview the time line and illustrations. Discuss students' responses to the information about enslaved people.
- **Pages 264–265** Have students examine the illustration of a Southern plantation, read the labels, and discuss the question in the caption.

- **Pages 266–267** Preview the illustration of an enslaved person seeking freedom, and the Review questions on page 266. On page 267, call attention to the biography of Olaudah Equiano, an enslaved person who earned his freedom and wrote his autobiography.

During Reading

Build Comprehension of Expository Text Present the graphic organizer on page 105. Have students preview the organizer by filling in the lesson title and comparing the three main heads in the organizer with the matching subheads in the Student Edition pages 262–266. Tell students that the section subheads provide additional help with identifying important information. Use Procedure Card 4, the Reading Check questions in *Harcourt Social Studies*, and the directed reading suggestions below.

- **Page 262** After students have read "You Are There," explain that plantation owners in the Southern Colonies depended on enslaved people to do the work on the plantations. Point out the illustration of people bound in shackles, about to be sold.
- **Page 263** Have students read "Slavery and Society." Then guide them in filling in the information in the first box of the organizer. Point out the subhead in the organizer that matches the section subhead in the text.
- **Pages 264–265** After students have read "A Farming Economy," discuss the information briefly and have them fill in the next box in the organizer. Point out the subheads that can help students locate information in the text.
- **Pages 265–266** After students have read "Free Africans," have them complete the organizer. Point out the two subheads that match the section subheads in the text.

After Reading

Summarize Have students use their completed graphic organizers to summarize the lesson. Then have them compare their summaries to the lesson summary on page 266.

Review and Respond If students need additional help with summarizing, use Focus Skill Transparency 3.

Draw a Scene Have students as a group suggest possible scenes that they might draw. List their ideas on the board or on chart paper. Then students may choose a scene from the list or draw another scene, if they wish. Tell them to reread passages from the lesson to locate details so their drawings and captions will be accurate.

Leveled Readers Use the Leveled Readers and Procedure Card 5 to build fluency and comprehension.

Name ______________________________ Date ______________

DIRECTIONS **Read aloud the words in Part A. Practice reading aloud the phrases and the sentences in Part B.**

Part A

Vocabulary Words	Additional Words	
planter	legal	former
overseer	abused	runaway
	illegal	

Part B

1. By the mid-1700s, / slavery was legal / in every colony.
2. Enslaved people / were often beaten and abused.
3. The cash crops produced by enslaved workers / made some planters / the richest people in the Southern Colonies.
4. Plantation owners / often hired an overseer / to watch enslaved people / as they worked.
5. It was illegal / for enslaved people / to learn to read or write.
6. Former indentured servants / often owned small farms, / but few became rich.
7. Enslaved people who ran away / were often caught, / but some runaways / found safety in Spanish Florida / or were helped by Native American tribes.

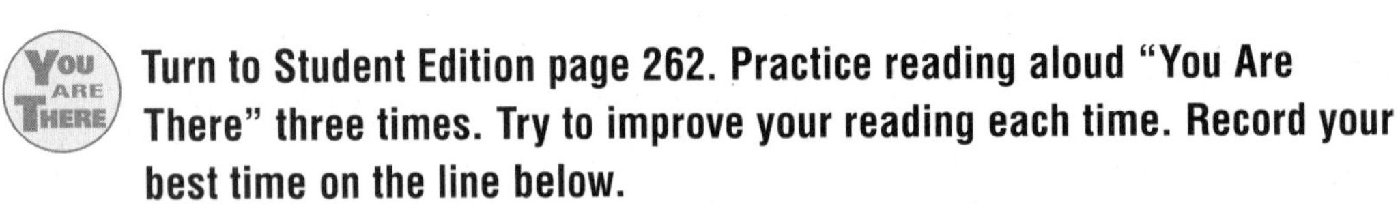

Turn to Student Edition page 262. Practice reading aloud "You Are There" three times. Try to improve your reading each time. Record your best time on the line below.

Number of words 64 My Best Time ________ Words per Minute ________

Name ______________________ Date ______________

Lesson Title ______________________

Slavery and Society

Treatment of Enslaved People

The way slaves were treated depended on ______________________.

How enslaved people kept their culture alive

____

A Farming Economy

Economy based mostly on ______________________

What made owners rich ______________________

____

The Plantation System

What some plantations looked like ______________________

Life on Small Farms

Most owners did not

______________________.

Free Africans

What a few were able to do ______________________

Where some runaways found safety ______________________

The Black Seminoles Who they were ______________________

____

Fort Mose What it was ______________________

LESSON 3 The Southern Economy

Vocabulary Strategies

Preteach Additional Vocabulary After teaching the Vocabulary words on Student Edition page 268, explain to students that there are several other important words they will see in this lesson. Use Procedure Card 1, along with the suggestions below, to introduce the words.

ton	Point out that *ton* is spelled with *o,* although it rhymes with *fun* and *run.* Have students look up *ton* on a table of weights and measures.
nutrient	Explain that nutrients are substances in food that help our bodies grow and be healthy. Fertile soil contains nutrients that help plants grow and be healthy.
experimented	Tell students that *experiment* is from the Latin root *experiri,* meaning "to try." Other words from the same root are *experience* and *expert.*
dye	Point out that this word, which means "a substance that causes a change in color," is a homophone of *die.*
clipper	Explain that a clipper was a type of fast sailing ship. Clippers were usually long and slender with tall masts and large sails.

WORD CARDS To help teach the lesson vocabulary, use the Word Cards on pages 259–260.

Build Fluency

Use page 108 and the steps on Procedure Card 2 to reinforce vocabulary and build fluency. Read each vocabulary word aloud and have students repeat it. Then have students work in pairs to reread the words. Follow a similar procedure with the phrases and sentences. Continue to help students build fluency by having them reread "You Are There" in the Student Edition.

Text Comprehension

BEFORE READING

Preview the Lesson Guide students in previewing the lesson using Procedure Card 3. Point out the following features of the lesson on Student Edition pages 268–271.

- **Pages 268–269** Read the "What to Know" question and have students recall what they have learned about natural resources in the Southern Colonies. Preview the time line and the illustration of Charles Town. Have students read the Children in History feature about Eliza Lucas Pinckney and discuss the Make It Relevant question.
- **Pages 270–271** Preview the illustrations of Baltimore and of workers on a dock, and discuss what these pictures show about the Southern economy. Then preview the Review questions on page 271.

During Reading

Build Comprehension of Expository Text Present the graphic organizer on page 109. Have students preview the organizer by filling in the lesson title and comparing the two main heads in the organizer with the matching subheads in the Student Edition pages 268–271. Tell students that the section subheads provide additional help with identifying important information. Use Procedure Card 4, the Reading Check questions in *Harcourt Social Studies*, and the directed reading suggestions below.

- **Page 268** After students have read "You Are There," ask what they think will happen to the barrels of rice after they are loaded onto the ship. Be sure students understand that the rice will be sent to England or to another English colony to be sold.
- **Page 269** Before students read "Cash Crops," have them look at the graphic organizer to set a purpose for reading. Point out the subhead "Adapting to the Climate" that matches the section subhead in the text. As students read, or after reading, they can fill in the names of the three main cash crops and where each crop was grown.
- **Pages 270–271** Have students read "The Economy Grows" and discuss why and how the Southern economy grew. Then have students record the information in the organizer. Point out the two subheads that match the section subheads in the text and can help students locate information.

After Reading

Summarize Have students use their completed graphic organizers to summarize the lesson. Then have them compare their summaries to the lesson summary on page 271.

Review and Respond If students need additional help with summarizing, use Focus Skill Transparency 3.

Make a Table Tell students to locate and list on scrap paper the names of the colonies and the crops grown there. This will give them a better idea of how to set up their tables to display the information. Suggest using rulers to set up straight columns. Students might also use computer programs to generate tables.

Leveled Readers Use the Leveled Readers and Procedure Card 5 to build fluency and comprehension.

Name ______________________ Date ______________

DIRECTIONS **Read aloud the words in Part A. Practice reading aloud the phrases and the sentences in Part B.**

Part A

Vocabulary Words	Additional Words
indigo	ton
interdependence	nutrient
broker	experimented
	dye
	clipper

Part B

1. Plantations / produced tons of cash crops each year, / and those crops needed to be shipped / to markets in England and the West Indies / to be sold.

2. In Maryland, / Virginia, / and northern North Carolina, / tobacco was the main cash crop, / but it used up the nutrients / in the soil.

3. Eliza Lucas Pinckney / experimented with indigo plants / that produced a blue dye.

4. By the 1740s, / indigo was a major cash crop / throughout South Carolina.

5. Interdependence / between plantation owners and merchants / was part of the Southern economy.

6. Brokers / took the crops to market / and bought the goods / the planters wanted.

7. Shipbuilders in Baltimore, Maryland, / developed the Baltimore clipper, / one of the world's fastest sailing ships.

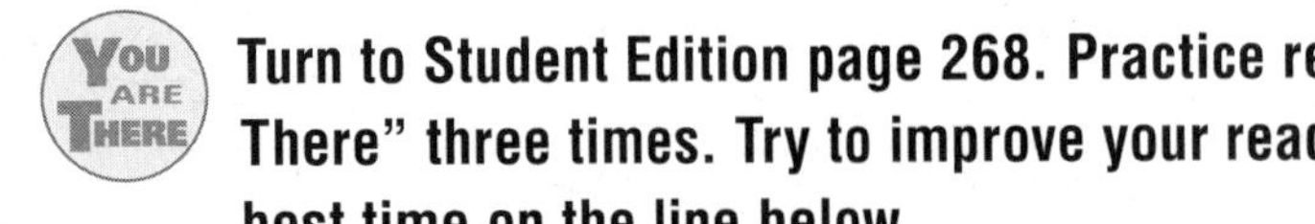

YOU ARE THERE **Turn to Student Edition page 268. Practice reading aloud "You Are There" three times. Try to improve your reading each time. Record your best time on the line below.**

Number of words ___78___ My Best Time ________ Words per Minute ________

Name ______________________ Date ____________

Lesson Title ______________________

Cash Crops

Adapting to the Climate

Crop ______________ Where ______________

____

____

Crop ______________ Where ______________

____

____

Crop ______________ Where ______________

____

The Economy Grows

Exporting Goods

How plantation owners sold crops ______________

Where most successful plantations were ______________

Why ______________

What Baltimore became ______________

Other Industries

Important natural resources ______________

Products ______________

UNIT 4
Chapter 8

LESSON 1 Fighting for Control

Vocabulary Strategies

Preteach Additional Vocabulary After teaching the Vocabulary words on Student Edition page 294, explain to students that there are several other important words they will see in this lesson. Use Procedure Card 1, along with the suggestions below, to introduce the words.

conflicting	Point out the head "Conflicting Claims" on page 295. Explain that the base word *conflict* is a verb accented on the second syllable. It is a homograph of the noun *conflict*, accented on the first syllable. Two countries that claim the same land have conflicting claims.
union	Discuss the relationship between this word and the known words *united* and *unity*.
favor	Discuss familiar meanings. Then discuss this context: "Britain sent more troops and supplies to the colonies, and the war slowly turned in its favor."
molasses	Explain that molasses is a kind of brown syrup that comes from sugar during processing. It is used for cooking.
objected	Tell students that synonyms for this word are *opposed* and *disagreed*. Point out the base word *object*, accented on the second syllable, a homograph of the noun *object*.

WORD CARDS To help teach the lesson vocabulary, use the Word Cards on pages 261–262.

Build Fluency

Use page 112 and the steps on Procedure Card 2 to reinforce vocabulary and build fluency. Read each vocabulary word aloud and have students repeat it. Then have students work in pairs to reread the words. Follow a similar procedure with the phrases and sentences. Continue to help students build fluency by having them reread "You Are There" in the Student Edition.

Text Comprehension

BEFORE READING

Preview the Lesson Guide students in previewing the lesson using Procedure Card 3. Point out the following features of the lesson on Student Edition pages 294–299.

- **Pages 294–295** Read the "What to Know" question. Explain that the French and Indian War was not between the French and Native Americans but between Britain and France, with Native Americans fighting for both sides. Preview the time line and the map of North America, and have students answer the map skill question. Then have students look at the illustration of Fort Necessity, read the Fast Fact, and locate the date of the Battle of Fort Necessity on the time line.
- **Pages 296–297** Preview the illustration and the map of the French and Indian War. Have students answer the map skill question.

- **Pages 298–299** Preview the illustration of a frontier settlement and the portrait of Pontiac. Then preview the Review questions on page 299.

During Reading

Build Comprehension of Expository Text Present the graphic organizer on page 113. Have students preview the organizer by filling in the lesson title and comparing the four main heads in the organizer with the matching subheads in the Student Edition pages 294–299. Tell students that the section subheads provide additional help with identifying important information. Use Procedure Card 4, the Reading Check questions in *Harcourt Social Studies,* and the directed reading suggestions below.

- **Page 294** After students have read "You Are There," have them look at the illustration on pages 294 and 295 and describe in their own words the events taking place at Fort Necessity.
- **Page 295** Have students read "Conflicting Claims." Ask them to identify the region claimed by two different countries. Then guide students in filling in the first box of the organizer. Point out that the organizer is a sequence chart. The events described in the chart are in time order.
- **Page 296** After students have read "The French and Indian War Begins," they can fill in the information in the next part of the organizer. On the first line, they should explain briefly who formed alliances.
- **Pages 297–299** Have students read "The War Expands." Discuss and have students summarize orally the information in the subsections "Early Defeats for Britain" and "Britain Wins Control." Tell students to add information from the subsection "The Treaty of Paris" to the organizer. Then they can read "More Troubles" and list in the organizer two reasons for more troubles in the colonies.

After Reading

Summarize Have students use their completed graphic organizers to summarize the lesson. Then have them compare their summaries to the lesson summary on page 299.

Review and Respond Work through the Review questions with students. Use Focus Skill Transparency 4, Cause and Effect, to identify causes and effects in the lesson.

Write a Newspaper Story Remind students that a newspaper story answers the questions When, Where, Who, What, and Why. Suggest that students write these five questions as headings on scrap paper and jot down information under each heading as they skim or reread passages in the lesson. Then they can use their notes as a basis for writing their articles.

Leveled Readers Use the Leveled Readers and Procedure Card 5 to build fluency and comprehension.

Name ______________________________ Date ______________

DIRECTIONS **Read aloud the words in Part A. Practice reading aloud the phrases and the sentences in Part B.**

Part A

Vocabulary Words		Additional Words	
alliance	proclamation	conflicting	molasses
delegate	budget	union	objected
Parliament		favor	

Part B

1. Conflicting claims / to the Ohio Valley region / were made by Britain and France.
2. By the mid-1700s, / both France and Britain / had formed alliances / with many of the Native American tribes / in the Ohio Valley.
3. Seven colonies / sent delegates to Albany in 1754, / but they did not approve / Benjamin Franklin's / Albany Plan of Union.
4. Parliament / sent an army to the colonies / to help fight the French / and their Native American allies.
5. After early defeats, / Britain sent more troops and supplies / to the colonies, / and the war / slowly turned in its favor.
6. After the French and Indian War, / Britain's king / made a proclamation / that all lands west of the Appalachian Mountains / belonged to Native Americans.
7. British leaders / looked at their budget / and decided that the colonists / should help pay off / the cost of the war.
8. Many merchants / objected to the Sugar Act, / which taxed the sugar and molasses / brought into the colonies from the West Indies.

You ARE THERE **Turn to Student Edition page 294. Practice reading aloud "You Are There" three times. Try to improve your reading each time. Record your best time on the line below.**

Number of words 72 My Best Time _______ Words per Minute _______

Name ______________________ Date ____________

Lesson Title ______________________

Conflicting Claims

Region ______________ Who claimed it ______________

What France did ______________________

What the British decided ______________________

The French and Indian War Begins

Alliances ______________________

Meeting When ____________ Where ____________ Who ____________

What they talked about ______________________

Start of French and Indian War When ________ Where ____________

The War Expands

When war ended ____________ Treaty of Paris gave Britain ______________

____

More Troubles

Why

1. ______________________

2. ______________________

LESSON 2 Colonists Speak Out

Vocabulary Strategies

Preteach Additional Vocabulary After teaching the Vocabulary words on Student Edition page 302, explain to students that there are several other important words they will see in this lesson. Use Procedure Card 1, along with the suggestions below, to introduce the words.

document	Tell students that a document is a formal piece of writing. Other kinds of documents may include computer files, photographs, videos, and audio recordings. Ask students which kind of documents their text most likely refers to when telling about events that took place in 1765.
taxation	Point out the root word *tax* and suffix *-ation,* meaning "act or process." Have students define *taxation* in their own words.
liberty	Give *freedom* and *independence* as synonyms for *liberty.*
massacre	Point out that authors sometimes give definitions to help readers understand a text. Use this sentence from the lesson as an example: "A massacre is the killing of many people who cannot defend themselves."

WORD CARDS To help teach the lesson vocabulary, use the Word Cards on pages 261–262.

Build Fluency

Use page 116 and the steps on Procedure Card 2 to reinforce vocabulary and build fluency. Read each vocabulary word aloud and have students repeat it. Then have students work in pairs to reread the words. Follow a similar procedure with the phrases and sentences. Continue to help students build fluency by having them reread "You Are There" in the Student Edition.

Text Comprehension

BEFORE READING

Preview the Lesson Guide students in previewing the lesson using Procedure Card 3. Point out the following features of the lesson on Student Edition pages 302–309.

- **Pages 302–303** Read the "What to Know" question. Have students recall how colonists felt about the Sugar Act. Preview the time line and explain that the Stamp Act and Townshend Acts were new taxes on the colonists. After previewing the illustration of the British Parliament on page 302, have students read the Primary Sources feature about the Stamp Act Cartoon and discuss the document-based question.
- **Pages 304–305** Have students examine the diagram and answer the questions in the captions. Discuss methods that people use today to exchange information rapidly, such as e-mail and instant messaging.

- **Pages 306–307** Have students read Children In History and discuss the Make It Relevant question. Preview the paintings and captions on page 307.
- **Pages 308–309** Preview the engraving on page 308. Ask students if they have heard of Paul Revere and what they know about him. Preview the Review questions. Call attention to the biography of Patrick Henry on page 309. Explain that Henry was one of the leaders of the colonists who protested against British rule.

During Reading

Build Comprehension of Expository Text Present the graphic organizer on page 117. Have students preview the organizer by filling in the lesson title and comparing the four main heads in the organizer with the matching subheads in the Student Edition pages 302–308. Tell students that the section subheads provide additional help with identifying important information. Use Procedure Card 4, the Reading Check questions in *Harcourt Social Studies,* and the directed reading suggestions below.

- **Page 302** After students have read "You Are There," have them predict what Parliament will do and why.
- **Page 303** Have students read about the Stamp Act. Discuss the colonists' reactions, including Patrick Henry's speech to the House of Burgesses, and the Stamp Act Congress. Then guide students in filling in the first box of the organizer.
- **Pages 304–305** After students have read "Colonists Work Together," have them write information in the organizer. Tell students that the section subheads will help them identify important information.
- **Page 306–308** Have students read about the Townshend Acts and add to the organizer. Then they can read "The Boston Massacre" and complete the organizer by writing a brief summary of the events that took place.

After Reading

Summarize Have students use their completed graphic organizers to summarize the lesson. Then have them compare their summaries to the lesson summary on page 308.

Review and Respond Work through the Review questions with students. If students need additional help with causes and effects, use Focus Skill Transparency 4.

Draw a Cartoon Discuss the use of political cartoons to try to persuade people to believe or act in a certain way. You may want to display and discuss examples of political cartoons, pointing out symbolism, the use of caricatures, and labels or other text that helps viewers understand the cartoonist's point of view. Provide appropriate art materials for students to use in creating their own cartoons.

Leveled Readers Use the Leveled Readers and Procedure Card 5 to build fluency and comprehension.

Name ______________________________ Date ______________

DIRECTIONS **Read aloud the words in Part A. Practice reading aloud the phrases and the sentences in Part B.**

Part A

Vocabulary Words		Additional Words
representation	repeal	document
imperial policy	treason	taxation
congress	protest	liberty
boycott		massacre

Part B

1. In 1765, / Parliament approved / the Stamp Act, / which put a tax on paper documents / in the colonies.
2. Some members of the Virginia House of Burgesses / accused Patrick Henry of treason / when he said that Parliament / did not represent the colonies.
3. After the Stamp Act Congress / met in New York City / in 1765, / people began to repeat these words /—no taxation / without representation.
4. Some colonists / began to boycott / all British goods.
5. Groups called the Sons of Liberty / and the Daughters of Liberty / took action / against the Stamp Act.
6. By 1766, / so many colonists / opposed the Stamp Act / that Parliament voted to repeal it.
7. Committees of Correspondence / were organized to protest / British imperial policies.
8. In 1770, / British soldiers / killed five colonists / in a fight / that became known as the Boston Massacre.

YOU ARE THERE **Turn to Student Edition page 302. Practice reading aloud "You Are There" three times. Try to improve your reading each time. Record your best time on the line below.**

Number of words 87 My Best Time ________ Words per Minute ________

Name ______________________ Date ______________

Lesson Title ______________________

The Stamp Act

When ________ What it was ______________________

What people said about it ______________________

Colonists Work Together

What colonists wanted ______________________

Groups who took action ______________________

What happened as a result ______________________

What the colonists formed ______________________

Why ______________________

What they asked people to do ______________________

The Townshend Acts

When passed ________ What they were ______________________

What colonists did ______________________

What Parliament did ______________________

____

The Boston Massacre

When ________ What happened ______________________

____

Lesson 3 Disagreements Grow

Vocabulary Strategies

Preteach Additional Vocabulary After teaching the Vocabulary words on Student Edition page 310, explain to students that there are several other important words they will see in this lesson. Use Procedure Card 1, along with the suggestions below, to introduce the words.

competition	Have students use the meanings of the base word *compete* and suffix *-ition* ("act or process") to define *competition.*
set	Discuss known meanings for this multiple-meaning word. Point out the phrases *set sail* on page 311 and *set of laws* on page 312 in the text.
coercive	Explain that a law or action that is coercive forces people to do something they do not want to do.
intolerable	Give these synonyms: *unacceptable, unbearable.*
weapon	Students may know the meaning of this word but not recognize the word in print. Give examples of other words in which *ea* has the short *e* sound, such as *bread, threat,* and *feather.*

WORD CARDS To help teach the lesson vocabulary, use the Word Cards on pages 263–264.

Build Fluency

Use page 120 and the steps on Procedure Card 2 to reinforce vocabulary and build fluency. Read each vocabulary word aloud and have students repeat it. Then have students work in pairs to reread the words. Follow a similar procedure with the phrases and sentences. Continue to help students build fluency by having them reread "You Are There" in the Student Edition.

Text Comprehension

Before Reading

Preview the Lesson Guide students in previewing the lesson using Procedure Card 3. Point out the following features of the lesson on Student Edition pages 310–315.

- **Pages 310–311** Read the "What to Know" question. Have students recall what the colonists did to protest the Stamp Act and the Townshend Acts. Preview the time line and the illustration of the Boston Tea Party. Have students read the Fast Fact and locate the date of the Boston Tea Party on the time line.
- **Pages 312–313** Have students look at the illustration on page 312 and read the caption. Explain that colonists were forced to give food and housing to British soldiers. Discuss how students and their families might feel if they were in the colonists' position. Then have students examine the illustrated time line on page 313 and answer the Time Line question.

- **Pages 314–315** Call attention to the map of Lexington and Concord, and have students answer the map skill question. Preview the photograph of the statue of Paul Revere in Boston, and the Review questions.

During Reading

Build Comprehension of Expository Text Present the graphic organizer on page 121. Have students preview the organizer by filling in the lesson title and comparing the four main heads in the organizer with the matching subheads in the Student Edition pages 310–315. Tell students that the section subheads provide additional help with identifying important information. Use Procedure Card 4, the Reading Check questions in *Harcourt Social Studies,* and the directed reading suggestions below.

- **Page 310** After students have read "You Are There," ask why they think colonists might want to protest British rule.
- **Page 311** Have students read about the Boston Tea Party and then turn to the graphic organizer. Point out that the organizer is a sequence diagram. Guide students in writing information in the first box. Explain that the date they should write in the organizer is the date that the Boston Tea Party took place.
- **Pages 312–313** After students have read "The Coercive Acts," have them record information in the organizer. Then do the same with "The First Continental Congress." Point out that students should list three actions taken by the First Continental Congress.
- **Pages 314–315** Have students read "Lexington and Concord" and complete the organizer by writing the date and a brief summary of the events that took place.

After Reading

Summarize Have students use their completed graphic organizers to summarize the lesson. Then have them compare their summaries to the lesson summary on page 315.

Review and Respond Work through the Review questions with students. If students need additional help with causes and effects, use Focus Skill Transparency 4.

Write a Poem Remind students that poems do not have to rhyme but should use colorful language and images to describe the battle scenes. You may want to read aloud to students the first verse of Ralph Waldo Emerson's poem "Concord Hymn" and discuss Emerson's use of poetic language to create an image of the scene in readers' minds.

Leveled Readers Use the Leveled Readers and Procedure Card 5 to build fluency and comprehension.

Name ______________________ Date ____________

DIRECTIONS **Read aloud the words in Part A. Practice reading aloud the phrases and the sentences in Part B.**

Part A

Vocabulary Words		Additional Words	
monopoly	petition	competition	intolerable
blockade	Minutemen	set	weapon
quarter	revolution	coercive	

Part B

1. In 1773, / Parliament passed the Tea Act, / giving Britain's East India Company / a monopoly on tea.
2. Because there was no competition, / colonists had to buy their tea / from the East India Company / and pay the tax.
3. After colonists / threw more than 300 chests of tea / into Boston Harbor, / Parliament / passed a new set of laws.
4. To enforce these laws, / which colonists called / the Coercive Acts, / Parliament / ordered the British navy / to blockade Boston Harbor.
5. Britain / also ordered the colonists / to quarter British soldiers.
6. Many colonists / said the new laws / were intolerable.
7. In 1774, / the First Continental Congress / sent a petition to the king / to remind him / of the colonists' basic rights / as British citizens.
8. In April 1775, / the British General Gage / sent over 700 soldiers / to arrest the leaders of the Sons of Liberty / and take their weapons.
9. Fighting between British soldiers and the Minutemen / was the beginning of a long war / called the American Revolution.

YOU ARE THERE **Turn to Student Edition page 310. Practice reading aloud "You Are There" three times. Try to improve your reading each time. Record your best time on the line below.**

Number of words 73 My Best Time ______ Words per Minute ______

Name ______________________________ Date ______________

Lesson Title ______________________________

The Boston Tea Party

Date ______________ Reason ______________

Who did it ______________ What they did ______________

____

The Coercive Acts

Date ______________ What they were ______________

Purpose ______________

These laws united colonists ______________.

The First Continental Congress

Date of meeting ______________ Place ______________

Who ______________

What they did

1. ______________

2. ______________

3. ______________

Lexington and Concord

Date ______________ What happened ______________

____

____

LESSON 4 The Road to War

Vocabulary Strategies

Preteach Additional Vocabulary After teaching the Vocabulary words on Student Edition page 318, explain to students that there are several other important words they will see in this lesson. Use Procedure Card 1, along with the suggestions below, to introduce the words.

currency	Have students use this context clue from page 319: "Congress also decided to print its own paper money, which became known as Continental currency."
bill	Discuss known meanings for this multiple-meaning word, including its use as a name for paper money, such as a one-dollar bill or a ten-dollar bill.
cannon	Have students point out the cannon in the picture of George Washington on page 318.
retreat	Tell students that an antonym of *retreat* is *advance*. Ask volunteers to demonstrate advancing and retreating.
rebellion	Explain that a rebellion is an attempt to overthrow a government by the use of force. Discuss related words such as *rebel* (noun accented on first syllable), *rebel* (verb accented on second syllable) and *rebellious*.

WORD CARDS To help teach the lesson vocabulary, use the Word Cards on pages 263–264.

Build Fluency

Use page 124 and the steps on Procedure Card 2 to reinforce vocabulary and build fluency. Read each vocabulary word aloud and have students repeat it. Then have students work in pairs to reread the words. Follow a similar procedure with the phrases and sentences. Continue to help students build fluency by having them reread "You Are There" in the Student Edition.

Text Comprehension

BEFORE READING

Preview the Lesson Guide students in previewing the lesson using Procedure Card 3. Point out the following features of the lesson on Student Edition pages 318–323.

- **Pages 318–319** Read the "What to Know" question. Explain that Britain was a nation with a powerful army and navy, while the colonists lived in separate colonies with only part-time militias. Ask students to predict how the colonists may have prepared for war with Britain. Preview the time line and the illustrations. Have students locate the date of the Second Continental Congress on the time line.
- **Pages 320–321** Have students examine the illustration of the Battle of Bunker Hill and read the labels. Then have them examine the inset map and discuss the Illustration question.

- **Pages 322–323** Preview the portrait of King George III and the Review questions on page 322. Call attention to the biography of the poet Phillis Wheatley on page 323.

During Reading

Build Comprehension of Expository Text Present the graphic organizer on page 125. Have students preview the organizer by filling in the lesson title and comparing the three main heads in the organizer with the matching subheads in the Student Edition pages 318–322. Tell students that the section subheads provide additional help with identifying important information. Use Procedure Card 4, the Reading Check questions in *Harcourt Social Studies,* and the directed reading suggestions below.

- **Page 318** After students have read "You Are There," have them tell what they know about the kind of person Washington was.
- **Page 319** Have students look at the organizer to set a purpose for reading "The Second Continental Congress." Point out that they will need to list four actions taken by Congress. Students can fill in the information as they read or after reading.
- **Pages 320–321** Have students use the organizer to set a purpose for reading "The Battle of Bunker Hill." Point out that they will need to locate and record information about when and where the battle was fought, the names of the colonial commanders, and the outcome of the battle.
- **Page 322** Have students read "Trying for Peace" and complete the organizer by writing the date and a brief summary of the events that took place.

After Reading

Summarize Have students use their completed graphic organizers to summarize the lesson. Then have them compare their summaries to the lesson summary on page 322.

Review and Respond Work through the Review questions with students. If students need additional help with causes and effects, use Focus Skill Transparency 4.

Conduct an Interview Suggest that students reread passages in the lesson to find information that can help them write good questions and accurate answers. Remind students that Washington was chosen as the army's commander in chief partly because he had served in the French and Indian War. An interviewer might ask questions about his background and experience.

Leveled Readers Use the Leveled Readers and Procedure Card 5 to build fluency and comprehension.

Name ______________________________ Date ______________

DIRECTIONS **Read aloud the words in Part A. Practice reading aloud the phrases and the sentences in Part B.**

Part A

Vocabulary Words	Additional Words
commander in chief	currency
earthwork	bill
olive branch	cannon
	retreat
	rebellion

Part B

1. The Second Continental Congress / formed an army / and chose George Washington / as the army's commander in chief.
2. Congress / also printed its own paper money, / which became known as / Continental currency.
3. Congress paid the soldiers / in bills called Continentals.
4. After sunset on June 16, 1775, / colonial commanders / ordered their soldiers / to build earthworks on Breed's Hill / near Boston.
5. The nearby city of Charlestown / was hit and set on fire / by cannons shooting from British ships / in the harbor.
6. On Breed's Hill, / the colonists / ran out of ammunition / and had to retreat.
7. Congress / sent King George III another petition, / which became known as the Olive Branch Petition / because it asked for peace.
8. King George III / promised to do / whatever was necessary / to crush the rebellion.

You Are There **Turn to Student Edition page 318. Practice reading aloud "You Are There" three times. Try to improve your reading each time. Record your best time on the line below.**

Number of words ___70___ My Best Time ________ Words per Minute ________

Name ______________________ Date __________

Lesson Title: ______________________

The Second Continental Congress

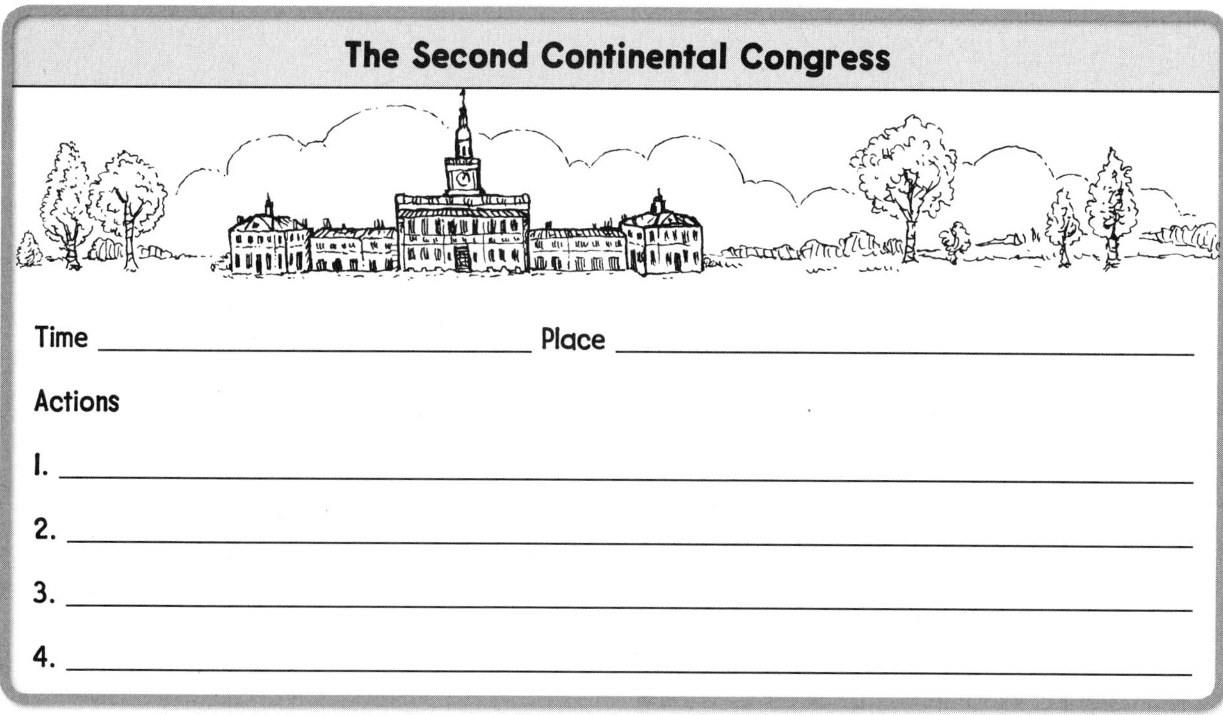

Time ______________ Place ______________

Actions

1. ______________________
2. ______________________
3. ______________________
4. ______________________

The Battle of Bunker Hill

Time ______________ Actual place ______________

Colonial commanders ______________________

Outcome ______________________

Trying for Peace

Time ______________ Events ______________

____

LESSON 5 Declaring Independence

Vocabulary Strategies

Preteach Additional Vocabulary After teaching the Vocabulary words on Student Edition page 324, explain to students that there are several other important words they will see in this lesson. Use Procedure Card 1, along with the suggestions below, to introduce the words.

pamphlet	Display an example of a pamphlet. Explain that this word comes from the title of a Latin poem of the 12th century, *Pamphilus seu De Amore.*
self-evident	Tell students that synonyms for *self-evident* are *clear* and *obvious.*
unalienable	Point out the prefix *un-*, which means "not," and the suffix *-able,* which means "able." Tell students that *unalienable* means "not able to be changed or taken away."
pursuit	Students may know the word *pursue.* Explain that pursuit is the act of pursuing, or seeking, something.
confederation	Remind students that the Iroquois League, which they learned about in Chapter 2, was a confederation. Have them recall the meaning of *confederation.*

WORD CARDS To help teach the lesson vocabulary, use the Word Cards on pages 263–266.

Build Fluency

Use page 128 and the steps on Procedure Card 2 to reinforce vocabulary and build fluency. Read each vocabulary word aloud and have students repeat it. Then have students work in pairs to reread the words. Follow a similar procedure with the phrases and sentences. Continue to help students build fluency by having them reread "You Are There" in the Student Edition.

Text Comprehension

BEFORE READING

Preview the Lesson Guide students in previewing the lesson using Procedure Card 3. Point out the following features of the lesson on Student Edition pages 324–331.

- **Pages 324–325** Read the "What to Know" question and have students predict how the colonies will cut their ties with Britain. Preview the time line and the illustration of Thomas Paine and *Common Sense.* Have students locate on the time line the date that the pamphlet was published. Preview the illustration on page 325 and explain that Thomas Jefferson was chosen to write the words of the Declaration of Independence.
- **Pages 326–327** Preview the mural on page 326. Then have students examine the Primary Sources feature about the Declaration of Independence on page 327 and discuss the document-based question.

- **Pages 328–329** Preview and discuss the paintings of historic events. Point out that photography had not yet been invented in the 1700s, so works of art such as drawings and paintings are the only way for people today to see how people, places, and events may have looked.
- **Pages 330–331** Preview the illustrations of John Dickinson and the Articles of Confederation and of early money. Then preview the Review questions.

During Reading

Build Comprehension of Expository Text Present the graphic organizer on page 129. Have students preview the organizer by filling in the lesson title and comparing the four main heads in the organizer with the matching subheads in the Student Edition pages 324–331. Tell students that the section subheads provide additional help with identifying important information. Use Procedure Card 4, the Reading Check questions in *Harcourt Social Studies,* and the directed reading suggestions below.

- **Page 324** After students have read "You Are There," discuss reasons the pamphlet might have given to make colonists want to be free of Britain.
- **Page 325** Have students read "Moving Toward Independence." Then guide them in filling in the information in the first box in the organizer.
- **Pages 326–327** After students have read "The Declaration of Independence," have them record information about the Declaration in the graphic organizer. Point out the key words *rights* and *grievances* in the section subhead on page 326.
- **Pages 328–331** Have students read "Congress Approves the Declaration" and fill in the next box in the organizer. Then they can read "Forming a New Government" and complete the organizer. Explain that students should write a brief summary of the weaknesses of the new plan of government. Point out the section subhead "Weaknesses of the Article" in the text.

After Reading

Summarize Have students use their completed graphic organizers to summarize the lesson. Then have them compare their summaries to the lesson summary on page 331.

Review and Respond Work through the Review questions with students. If students need additional help with causes and effects, use Focus Skill Transparency 4.

Write a Persuasive Letter Have students discuss the reasons that colonists had for wanting to become independent. Remind students of the difference between fact and opinion. Tell them to be sure and support their opinions with facts, including information and examples. Provide a model of the correct format for a business letter.

Leveled Readers Use the Leveled Readers and Procedure Card 5 to build fluency and comprehension.

Name ______________________________ Date ______________

DIRECTIONS **Read aloud the words in Part A. Practice reading aloud the phrases and the sentences in Part B.**

Part A

Vocabulary Words	Additional Words
independence	pamphlet
resolution	self-evident
grievance	unalienable
declaration	pursuit
preamble	confederation

Part B

1. In his pamphlet *Common Sense,* / Thomas Paine wrote / that the colonists should rule themselves.
2. Many colonists / began to call for independence.
3. At the Second Continental Congress / on June 7, 1776, / Richard Henry Lee of Virginia / called for a resolution of independence.
4. In the preamble / to the Declaration of Independence, / Thomas Jefferson / explained why the colonies / had the right to form a new nation.
5. The next part of the Declaration / describes the colonists' main ideas about government / and says that certain truths / are self-evident.
6. Jefferson wrote / that people have / "certain unalienable Rights," / including "Life, / Liberty, / and the pursuit of Happiness."
7. The longest part of the Declaration / lists the colonists' grievances / against King George III and Parliament.
8. A committee headed by John Dickinson / wrote the country's first plan of government, / the Articles of Confederation.

YOU ARE THERE **Turn to Student Edition page 324. Practice reading aloud "You Are There" three times. Try to improve your reading each time. Record your best time on the line below.**

Number of words ___73___ My Best Time _______ Words per Minute _______

Name ______________________ Date ______________

Lesson Title: ______________________

Moving Toward Independence

Pamphlet title ______________________

Author ______________________

What people began to call for ______________________

What Lee called for ______________________

COMMON SENSE;
INHABITANTS
AMERICA,
SUBJECTS

The Declaration of Independence

States that all people have certain

______________________.

Longest part lists the colonists'

____

States that the colonies were

______________________ states

Congress Approves the Declaration

Accepted on ______________________

Signed by ______________________

____

The Declaration has inspired people around the world to work for

______________ and ______________.

Forming a New Government

Committee head ______________ Plan ______________

National legislature ______________________

Weaknesses ______________________

______________________.

UNIT 4

Chapter 9

Lesson 1 Americans and the Revolution

Vocabulary Strategies

Preteach Additional Vocabulary After teaching the Vocabulary words on Student Edition page 338, explain to students that there are several other important words they will see in this lesson. Use Procedure Card 1, along with the suggestions below, to introduce the words.

personal	Tell students that *personal* and related words such as *person, impersonate,* and *personality* are from the Latin word *persona,* which means "person" and also "an actor's mask" or "a character in a play."
shortage	Students may be familiar with the concept of a water shortage due to a lack of rain. Explain that a shortage occurs when people run short of, or lack, something.
hoard	Discuss the idea that during a shortage, people may try to hoard, or save up and hide away, items that are in short supply.
recognized	Have students offer a familiar meaning or meanings. Then discuss the meaning in this context: "She became the first woman veteran to be recognized by Congress."
reward	Ask students to give examples of how people earn rewards, such as returning a lost wallet or rescuing someone from danger.
divided	Point out that things can be divided by cutting or breaking them into parts. Discuss how groups of people can be divided by having different ideas or opinions.

WORD CARDS To help teach the lesson vocabulary, use the Word Cards on pages 267–268.

Build Fluency

Use page 132 and the steps on Procedure Card 2 to reinforce vocabulary and build fluency. Read each vocabulary word aloud and have students repeat it. Then have students work in pairs to reread the words. Follow a similar procedure with the phrases and sentences. Continue to help students build fluency by having them reread "You Are There" in the Student Edition.

Text Comprehension

Before Reading

Preview the Lesson Guide students in previewing the lesson using Procedure Card 3. Point out the following features of the lesson on Student Edition pages 338–343.

- **Pages 338–339** Read the "What to Know" question. Ask students to imagine what it was like for American colonists to live with a war going on around them. Preview the time line and the illustration of British soldiers below the text, and have students read the Fast Fact. Preview the illustration of British soldiers burning a home, and discuss how the war affected the lives of these colonists.

- **Pages 340–341** Have students examine the graph of American imports from Britain and answer the question in the caption. Then preview the illustrations. Tell students that the women pictured on page 341 were some of the women they will read about who played important roles in the war.
- **Pages 342–343** Preview the illustrations of African American soldiers and of Thayendanegea. Explain that different groups of people had their own reasons for supporting either the Patriots or the British. Then preview the Review questions.

During Reading

Build Comprehension of Expository Text Present the graphic organizer on page 133. Have students preview the organizer by filling in the lesson title and comparing the five main heads in the organizer with the matching subheads in the Student Edition pages 338–343. Tell students that the section subheads provide additional help with identifying important information. Use Procedure Card 4, the Reading Check questions in *Harcourt Social Studies,* and the directed reading suggestions below.

- **Page 338** After students have read "You Are There," discuss how the war has affected the lives of the people in the family it describes.
- **Pages 339–340** Have students read "Personal Hardships." Discuss and identify the main idea. Then have students write a main idea sentence for this section in the organizer. Tell students that the section subhead can help them identify an important personal hardship. Follow the same procedure for "Economic Hardships." Point out the arrows showing how these two sections of the lesson are related.
- **Pages 341–343** Point out in the organizer that the next three sections of the lesson are about particular groups of people and how each group was affected by the war. Have students read "Women and the War" and write a main idea sentence in the organizer. Follow the same procedure for "African Americans, Free and Enslaved," and for "People in the West."

After Reading

Summarize Have students use their completed graphic organizers to summarize the lesson. Then have them compare their summaries to the lesson summary on page 343.

Review and Respond Work through the Review questions with students. If students need additional help with causes and effects, use Focus Skill Transparency 4.

Write a Conversation Tell students that each speaker in the conversation should express an opinion and use facts to support that opinion. Explain that students can use information from this lesson and from previous lessons to support the speakers' opinions. Help students set up their written conversations in a script format. Students might like to take turns with a classmate reading aloud their completed conversations.

Leveled Readers Use the Leveled Readers and Procedure Card 5 to build fluency and comprehension.

Name ________________________________ Date ______________

DIRECTIONS **Read aloud the words in Part A. Practice reading aloud the phrases and the sentences in Part B.**

Part A

Vocabulary Words		Additional Words	
Patriot	inflation	personal	recognized
Loyalist	profiteering	shortage	reward
neutral	veteran	hoard	divided

Part B

1. Colonists who supported independence / called themselves Patriots, / while those who remained loyal to the king / were called Loyalists.
2. About one-third of the colonists / stayed neutral.
3. Colonists / faced personal and economic hardships / during the war.
4. British ships / set up blockades, / causing a shortage / of imported goods.
5. As the shortage of goods grew worse, / Americans also faced inflation.
6. Laws were passed / to limit profiteering / and to make it illegal / for people to hoard large amounts of goods.
7. Women / such as Margaret Corbin, / the first woman veteran to be recognized by Congress, / took on new roles.
8. Some enslaved African Americans / fought for the Continental Army, / and many were promised / their freedom as a reward.
9. Native Americans / were divided by the war.

YOU ARE THERE **Turn to Student Edition page 338. Practice reading aloud "You Are There" three times. Try to improve your reading each time. Record your best time on the line below.**

Number of words 94 My Best Time _______ Words per Minute _______

Name ______________________ Date ____________

Lesson Title ______________________

Hardships

Personal Hardships

Main Idea ______________________

Economic Hardships

Main Idea ______________________

Groups of people affected by the war

Women and the War

Main Idea ______________________

People in the West

Main Idea ______________________

African Americans, Free and Enslaved

Main Idea ______________________

LESSON 2

Fighting for Independence

Vocabulary Strategies

Preteach Additional Vocabulary After teaching the Vocabulary words on Student Edition page 346, explain to students that there are several other important words they will see in this lesson. Use Procedure Card 1, along with the suggestions below, to introduce the words.

everyday	Explain that the compound word *everyday* is an adjective, used to describe a noun, as in the phrase "his everyday clothes." However, in the phrase "the clothes he wears every day," *every* and *day* are written as two separate words.
experienced	Discuss the kinds of knowledge and skills an experienced soldier might have, and how a soldier would acquire them.
loss	Have students offer known meanings for *loss,* such as a win or loss in a game, or a loss of appetite. Then discuss this context: "The Americans suffered great losses at the Battle of Long Island."
rowboat	Have students identify the two shorter words *row* and *boat*. Point out the rowboat in the illustration on page 348 and have students describe how it moves through the water.

WORD CARDS To help teach the lesson vocabulary, use the Word Cards on pages 267–268.

Build Fluency

Use page 136 and the steps on Procedure Card 2 to reinforce vocabulary and build fluency. Read each vocabulary word aloud and have students repeat it. Then have students work in pairs to reread the words. Follow a similar procedure with the phrases and sentences. Continue to help students build fluency by having them reread "You Are There" in the Student Edition.

Text Comprehension

BEFORE READING

Preview the Lesson Guide students in previewing the lesson using Procedure Card 3. Point out the following features of the lesson on Student Edition pages 346–353.

- **Pages 346–347** Read the "What to Know" question. Have students recall important events that led up to the Revolutionary War. Preview the time line and illustrations. Have students compare the British soldier and American soldier and answer the question in the caption.
- **Pages 348–349** Preview the paintings and the illustration of the medal. Tell students that the battle that followed the crossing of the Delaware was the Battle of Trenton, an American victory. Have students determine from the caption on page 349 the outcome of the Battle of Saratoga. Then have them locate the dates for both of these battles on the time line on page 346.

- **Pages 350–353** Preview the illustration of the march to Valley Forge and the portrait of von Steuben. On page 352, preview the portrait of Jorge Farragut and the Review questions. Call attention to the biography of Bernardo de Gálvez on page 353. Tell students that Gálvez was a leader who helped the Americans during the American Revolution.

During Reading

Build Comprehension of Expository Text Present the graphic organizer on page 137. Have students preview the organizer by filling in the lesson title and comparing the five main heads in the organizer with the matching subheads in the Student Edition pages 346–352. Tell students that the section subheads provide additional help with identifying important information. Use Procedure Card 4, the Reading Check questions in *Harcourt Social Studies,* and the directed reading suggestions below.

- **Page 346** After students read "You Are There," discuss the hardships that Washington's army faced. Tell students that they will read more about the Marquis de Lafayette in the lesson.
- **Page 347** Have students read "Comparing Armies." Then guide them in writing four details about each army in the graphic organizer.
- **Pages 348–349** After students have read "Early Battles in the North," have them discuss and fill in the information in the organizer. Follow the same procedure for "An Important Victory."
- **Pages 350–352** Have students read "Winter at Valley Forge." Tell them to write in the organizer a brief description of conditions at Valley Forge and the names of two people from other countries who helped Washington and the Continental Army. Point out that the section subheads can help students locate this information. Then have students read "Contributions from Other Nations" and complete the organizer by listing four contributions.

After Reading

Summarize Have students use their completed graphic organizers to summarize the lesson. Then have them compare their summaries to the lesson summary on page 352.

Review and Respond Work through the Review questions with students. If students need additional help with causes and effects, use Focus Skill Transparency 4.

Write a Speech Suggest that students reread sections of the lesson and make notes about events that might have cheered the soldiers at Valley Forge, such as battles they had already won, and help they were receiving. Students can practice their speeches by reading to a partner or by making and playing back a recording.

Leveled Readers Use the Leveled Readers and Procedure Card 5 to build fluency and comprehension.

Name ______________________ Date __________

DIRECTIONS **Read aloud the words in Part A. Practice reading aloud the phrases and the sentences in Part B.**

Part A

Vocabulary Words		Additional Words
enlist	turning point	everyday
mercenary	negotiate	experienced
campaign		loss
		rowboat

Part B

1. When George Washington / took command of the Continental Army, / the soldiers had no uniforms / —only their everyday clothes.
2. Many of the soldiers / were farmers / who had enlisted in the army.
3. The British army, / one of the most powerful armies in the world, / was made up of experienced soldiers / and mercenaries.
4. The Americans / suffered great losses / at the Battle of Long Island / in the spring of 1776.
5. On Christmas night, / 1776, / Patriot troops / crossed the icy Delaware River in rowboats / and won a victory / that gave them hope for the future.
6. In 1777, / the British army / planned a new campaign, / but the British loss at Saratoga / was a turning point in the war.
7. While the war raged on / in North America, / Benjamin Franklin / was in France, / negotiating with the French government.

YOU ARE THERE **Turn to Student Edition page 346. Practice reading aloud "You Are There" three times. Try to improve your reading each time. Record your best time on the line below.**

Number of words 60 My Best Time _______ Words per Minute _______

Name ______________________ Date ____________

Lesson Title ______________________

Comparing Armies

Continental Army	British Army
______	______
______	______
______	______
______	______

Early Battles in the North

Where	Outcome
______	______
______	______

An Important Victory

Where ______

Why it was important

______

Winter at Valley Forge

What it was like ______

Who helped ______, ______

Contributions from Other Nations

1. ______
2. ______
3. ______
4. ______

LESSON 3 Winning Independence

Vocabulary Strategies

Preteach Additional Vocabulary After teaching the Vocabulary words on Student Edition page 356, explain to students that there are several other important words they will see in this lesson. Use Procedure Card 1, along with the suggestions below, to introduce the words.

hanged	Tell students that *hanged* is often used as the past tense of *hang* in the context of executing a human being by hanging. In other contexts, we often use *hung*, as in "We hung up our jackets."
volunteer	Explain that a volunteer is a person who offers to do a job that he or she is not required to do.
betrayed	Tell students that *betray* comes from the Latin *tradere*, "to hand over." The words *traitor* and *treason* are from the same root.
surrounded	Explain that *surround* means "to encircle." Ask what the *-ed* ending shows.
accept	Students may know this word in the context of accepting a gift. Explain that it can also mean to allow or approve of something.
retired	Ask whether students know of an older family member or acquaintance who has retired from his or her job.

WORD CARDS To help teach the lesson vocabulary, use the Word Cards on pages 267–270.

Build Fluency

Use page 140 and the steps on Procedure Card 2 to reinforce vocabulary and build fluency. Read each vocabulary word aloud and have students repeat it. Then have students work in pairs to reread the words. Follow a similar procedure with the phrases and sentences. Continue to help students build fluency by having them reread "You Are There" in the Student Edition.

Text Comprehension

BEFORE READING

Preview the Lesson Guide students in previewing the lesson using Procedure Card 3. Point out the following features of the lesson on Student Edition pages 356–361.

- **Pages 356–357** Read the "What to Know" question. Have students recall what they learned in Lesson 2 about the fight for independence, and ask them to predict how the Americans will win the war. Preview the time line and the illustrations of a naval battle and of Mary McCauley, who carried water to American troops during a battle.

- **Pages 358–359** Have students examine the map of major battles and answer the map skill question. Then preview the illustration of the Battle of Cowpens and have students locate Cowpens on the map.
- **Pages 360–361** Preview the illustrations of the surrender at Yorktown and of Washington retiring. Have students use their prior knowledge to predict what Washington will do after the war. Then preview the Review questions.

During Reading

Build Comprehension of Expository Text Present the graphic organizer on page 141. Have students preview the organizer by filling in the lesson title and comparing the three main heads in the organizer with the matching subheads in the Student Edition pages 356–361. Tell students that the section subheads provide additional help with identifying important information. Use Procedure Card 4, the Reading Check questions in *Harcourt Social Studies,* and the directed reading suggestions below.

- **Page 356** After students have read "You Are There," explain that John Paul Jones was a hero of the Revolution. Have students tell why he might have been called a hero.
- **Page 357** Have students look at the graphic organizer to set a purpose for reading "Revolutionary Heroes." Either as they read or after reading the section, students can fill in the names of four heroes and tell what each did.
- **Pages 358–359** Follow a similar procedure for "The War Moves" as for the previous section, having students record in the chart the places where four battles took place in the South and the outcome of each battle. Point out that the section subhead "Battles in the South" in the text matches a subhead in the organizer. Tell students that if they are not sure from the text which side won a battle, they can also refer to the map on page 358.
- **Pages 360–361** Have students read "The War Ends" and complete the organizer. Point out that the three subheads in the organizer match the section subheads in the text and can help students locate information.

After Reading

Summarize Have students use their completed graphic organizers to summarize the lesson. Then have them compare their summaries to the lesson summary on page 361.

Review and Respond Work through the Review questions with students. If students need additional help with causes and effects, use Focus Skill Transparency 4.

Draw a Medal Tell students to choose one of the Patriot heroes they read about in this lesson. Explain that students will then need to choose a symbol that represents the hero's contribution and will also make an attractive design for a medal. Tell students they may include words on their medals.

Leveled Readers Use the Leveled Readers and Procedure Card 5 to build fluency and comprehension.

Name ______________________ Date ____________

DIRECTIONS **Read aloud the words in Part A. Practice reading aloud the phrases and the sentences in Part B.**

Part A

Vocabulary Words	Additional Words	
civilian	hanged	surrounded
traitor	volunteer	accept
	betrayed	retired

Part B

1. During the Revolutionary War, / the Continental Army and Navy / received help / from many civilians.
2. Nathan Hale / was a teacher / who served as an American spy / and was hanged by the British.
3. As word of the fight for freedom spread, / more volunteers came.
4. Benedict Arnold, / a former Continental Army officer / who had become a traitor, / led British attacks on Virginia towns.
5. He betrayed his country / because he was not happy / with his rank and salary.
6. At the Battle of Yorktown, / in 1781, / British General Charles Cornwallis / finally gave up / after being surrounded for weeks.
7. The Americans who went to Paris / to negotiate a peace treaty / wanted Britain to accept / American independence.
8. After British troops left the country, / George Washington / retired as leader of the army, / telling Congress / that his work was done.

YOU ARE THERE **Turn to Student Edition page 356. Practice reading aloud "You Are There" three times. Try to improve your reading each time. Record your best time on the line below.**

Number of words 57 My Best Time ________ Words per Minute ________

Name ______________________ Date ____________

Lesson Title ______________________

Revolutionary Heroes

Hero	What he or she did

The War Moves

Battles in the South	Outcome

The War Ends

Victory at Yorktown

When ______________ What happened ______________

The Treaty of Paris

When it was signed ______________ What it did ______________

After the War

What happened ______________

LESSON 4

Effects of the War

Vocabulary Strategies

Preteach Additional Vocabulary After teaching the Vocabulary words on Student Edition page 364, explain to students that there are several other important words they will see in this lesson. Use Procedure Card 1, along with the suggestions below, to introduce the words.

press	Discuss the phrase "freedom of the press." Explain that this meaning for *press* developed from the name of the printing press, which made it possible to publish newspapers.
antislavery	Identify the familiar word *slavery* and the prefix *anti-*, which means "against." Students may know other words with this prefix, such as *antiwar* or *antibacterial*.
sued	Point out the *-ed* ending. Tell students that to sue is to seek justice in a court of law. The word *sue* is from the Latin root *sequi*, meaning "to follow." Other words with this root include *sequence* and *sequel*.
acre	Tell students that an acre is a unit of area that is used to measure land. Students may want to look up the number of square feet in an acre.

WORD CARDS To help teach the lesson vocabulary, use the Word Cards on pages 269–270.

Build Fluency

Use page 144 and the steps on Procedure Card 2 to reinforce vocabulary and build fluency. Read each vocabulary word aloud and have students repeat it. Then have students work in pairs to reread the words. Follow a similar procedure with the phrases and sentences. Continue to help students build fluency by having them reread "You Are There" in the Student Edition.

Text Comprehension

BEFORE READING

Preview the Lesson Guide students in previewing the lesson using Procedure Card 3. Point out the following features of the lesson on Student Edition pages 364–369.

- **Pages 364–365** Read the "What to Know" question. Explain that one immediate effect of the war was freedom from Britain, but becoming a new nation brought about many other changes as well. Preview the time line and the illustrations of antislavery artifacts. Tell students that a stronger antislavery movement was one result of the American Revolution.
- **Pages 366–367** Preview the illustration of settlers moving west and the map of the Northwest Territory. Have students answer the map skill question.
- **Pages 368–369** Have students examine the illustrated time line on these pages. Explain that Native Americans' lives changed greatly after the Revolution. Preview the Review questions on page 369.

During Reading

Build Comprehension of Expository Text Present the graphic organizer on page 145. Have students preview the organizer by filling in the lesson title and comparing the four main heads in the organizer with the matching subheads in the Student Edition pages 364–369. Tell students that the section subheads provide additional help with identifying important information. Use Procedure Card 4, the Reading Check questions in *Harcourt Social Studies,* and the directed reading suggestions below.

- **Page 364** After students have read "You Are There," have them state in their own words the viewpoints expressed by the speakers. Discuss the reasons that these people give to support their opinions.
- **Page 365** Have students look at the organizer to set a purpose for reading "New Ideas." Either as they read or after reading the section, students can write in the organizer what the states began doing by 1776, what the Declaration of Independence said about people's rights, and what some people believed should happen.
- **Pages 366–367** Have students read "Western Settlements" and fill in the next section of the organizer. Help students see how the section subheads in the text can help them locate information. Then students can read "The Northwest Territory" and fill in that section of the organizer.
- **Pages 368–369** After students have read "Battles for Land" they can complete the graphic organizer by writing the names of the two groups who fought for land in the Northwest Territory and what happened as a result.

After Reading

Summarize Have students use their completed graphic organizers to summarize the lesson. Then have them compare their summaries to the lesson summary on page 369.

Review and Respond Work through the Review questions with students. If students need additional help with causes and effects, use Focus Skill Transparency 4.

Write a News Article Remind students that newspaper articles tell Who, When, Where, What, and Why. Suggest that they reread the section of the lesson about Elizabeth Freeman's court case and make notes for each of the five W's. Then students can write articles based on their notes.

Leveled Readers Use the Leveled Readers and Procedure Card 5 to build fluency and comprehension.

Name ______________________ Date ____________

DIRECTIONS **Read aloud the words in Part A. Practice reading aloud the phrases and the sentences in Part B.**

Part A

Vocabulary Words	Additional Words
abolitionist	press
abolish	antislavery
territory	sued
ordinance	acre

Part B

1. By 1776, / the states had begun to write / their own constitutions, / giving people basic freedoms, / including freedom of the press.
2. In 1775, / Quakers in Philadelphia / had started the country's first abolitionist group.
3. Antislavery feelings grew / after the Declaration was approved.
4. In Massachusetts, / an enslaved woman named Elizabeth Freeman / sued to be free.
5. Massachusetts / abolished slavery in 1783, / and over time, / other northern states / also abolished slavery.
6. After the Revolutionary war ended, / the United States / paid soldiers with land, / and some soldiers / were given hundreds of acres.
7. In 1787, / Congress passed the Northwest Ordinance, / a plan for governing the Northwest Territory / and for forming new states from its lands.
8. Native American forces / soundly defeated United States soldiers / but later gave up most of their land / in the Northwest Territory.

YOU ARE THERE **Turn to Student Edition page 364. Practice reading aloud "You Are There" three times. Try to improve your reading each time. Record your best time on the line below.**

Number of words 61 My Best Time ________ Words per Minute ________

Name ______________________ Date __________

Lesson Title: ______________________

New Ideas

What states did ______________________

What the Declaration said ______________________

What some people believed ______________________

Western Settlements

What the United States had won ______________________

Who moved west ______________________

Who lived in the west ______________________

Fast growing areas ______________________

The Northwest Territory

Where it was ______________________

When __________ What happened ______________________

When __________ What happened ______________________

Battles for Land

Who fought for land ______________________

What happened ______________________

____

UNIT 5 Chapter 10

Lesson 1 The Constitutional Convention

Vocabulary Strategies

Preteach Additional Vocabulary After teaching the Vocabulary words on Student Edition page 388, explain to students that there are several other important words they will see in this lesson. Use Procedure Card 1, along with the suggestions below, to introduce the words.

debt	Explain that a debt is an amount of money that someone owes. We say that someone goes into debt when he or she owes money. Point out that the letter *b* is silent in this word.
convention	Tell students that this word is from the Latin *convenire,* "to come together." One kind of convention is a meeting of delegates to discuss important issues. A related word is *convene.*
supreme	Have students substitute the synonym *highest* for *supreme* in this sentence: "The Constitution of the United States is the supreme law of the land."
house	Explain that a special meaning for the word *house* is "a part of a government." The house can be the group of people who make up that part of the government, or the building where they meet.
approve	Discuss the meaning of *approve* in this context: "Both houses had to approve a bill before it became a law."

WORD CARDS To help teach the lesson vocabulary, use the Word Cards on pages 271–272.

Build Fluency

Use page 148 and the steps on Procedure Card 2 to reinforce vocabulary and build fluency. Read each vocabulary word aloud and have students repeat it. Then have students work in pairs to reread the words. Follow a similar procedure with the phrases and sentences. Continue to help students build fluency by having them reread "You Are There" in the Student Edition.

Text Comprehension

Before Reading

Preview the Lesson Guide students in previewing the lesson using Procedure Card 3. Point out the following features of the lesson on Student Edition pages 388–395.

- **Pages 388–389** Read the "What to Know" question. Have students recall what they have learned about the first government of the United States, formed under the Articles of Confederation. Preview the time line and the illustrations. Explain that Shays's Rebellion made some people think that the national government was not strong enough to keep order.
- **Pages 390–391** Have students examine the map on page 390 and use the distance scale to answer the map skill question. Discuss how long it must have taken delegates from various states to get to Philadelphia. Then preview the illustration of the Pennsylvania State House on page 391.

- **Pages 392–393** Preview the illustration of the Constitutional Convention, and have students identify delegates. Discuss the question in the caption. Then preview the illustration of an African American woman on page 393.
- **Pages 394–395** Have students examine the graph and answer the question in the caption. Preview the Review questions on page 394, and the biography of Gouverneur Morris on page 395.

During Reading

Build Comprehension of Expository Text Present the graphic organizer on page 149. Have students preview the organizer by filling in the lesson title and comparing the five main heads in the organizer with the matching subheads in the Student Edition pages 388–394. Tell students that the section subheads provide additional help with identifying important information. Use Procedure Card 4, the Reading Check questions in *Harcourt Social Studies*, and the directed reading suggestions below.

- **Page 388** After students have read "You Are There," discuss why this meeting in 1787 was so important.
- **Pages 389–390** Have students read "Reasons for Change" and write information in the first box of the organizer. Point out the subhead "Ideas for Change" that matches the section subhead in the text. Next, have students read "The Work Begins" and fill in the second box. Point out that students will need to identify two major decisions that delegates made.
- **Pages 391–392** After students have read "A Major Debate," point out that the subheads "The Virginia Plan" and "The New Jersey Plan" match the section subheads in the text and can help students locate information they need as they fill in the organizer. Then have students read "Working Together" and write information about the Great Compromise in the next box of the organizer.
- **Pages 393–394** Students should read "Compromises on Slavery" and complete the last box of the organizer. Tell them to name the areas of the country that had different points of view on slavery, write a very brief description of the Three-Fifths Compromise, and write the year that was agreed upon for banning states from bringing in slaves from other countries.

After Reading

Summarize Have students use their completed graphic organizers to summarize the lesson. Then have them compare their summaries to the lesson summary on page 394.

Review and Respond Work through the Review questions with students. Use Focus Skill Transparency 5, Draw Conclusions, to help students draw conclusions based on information in the lesson.

Write a Persuasive Letter Discuss what students might tell their families about how and why the delegates reached compromises on important issues. Have students identify a point of view that they would want to persuade their family to accept. Remind students to use the correct form for a friendly letter.

Leveled Readers Use the Leveled Readers and Procedure Card 5 to build fluency and comprehension.

Name ______________________ Date ______________

DIRECTIONS **Read aloud the words in Part A. Practice reading aloud the phrases and the sentences in Part B.**

Part A

Vocabulary Words	Additional Words
arsenal	debt
federal system	convention
republic	supreme
compromise	house
bill	approve

Part B

1. During the 1780s, / state courts took away people's farms / or sent people to prison / when the people could not repay / their debts.

2. Because there was no national army, / the governor / had to send the state militia / when farmers tried to take over / a Massachusetts arsenal.

3. The Constitutional Convention / met in Philadelphia / in 1787 / to try to improve the Articles of Confederation.

4. The delegates / finally agreed / to strengthen the existing federal system.

5. The Constitution of the United States / became the supreme law of the land / and helped found / the American republic.

6. After arguing for weeks / about how the states / should be represented in Congress, / the delegates realized that each side / would have to compromise.

7. A committee of delegates / suggested a two-house Congress, / in which either house / could present a bill.

8. On July 16, 1787, / the delegates approved / the Great Compromise.

YOU ARE THERE **Turn to Student Edition page 388. Practice reading aloud "You Are There" three times. Try to improve your reading each time. Record your best time on the line below.**

Number of words 72 My Best Time ________ Words per Minute ________

Name ______________________________ Date ______________

Lesson Title ______________________________

Reasons for Change

What people thought ______________

____

____

Ideas for Change

Date of convention ______________

Goal ______________________________

The Work Begins

Creating the Constitution

Major decisions

1. ______________________________
2. ______________________________

Helped found the

____

A Major Debate

Disagreement about ______________________________

The Virginia Plan Number of representatives based on ______________

The New Jersey Plan Each state would be ______________ .

Working Together

The Great Compromise

One house based on ______________________________

In the other house ______________________________

Compromises on Slavery

Different Points of View Between ______________________________

The Three-Fifths Compromise ______________________________

A Continuing Issue Slave trade with other countries banned after ______________

Lesson 2 Three Branches of Government

Vocabulary Strategies

Preteach Additional Vocabulary After teaching the Vocabulary words on Student Edition page 398, explain to students that there are several other important words they will see in this lesson. Use Procedure Card 1, along with the suggestions below, to introduce the words.

propose	Tell students that synonyms for *propose* include *suggest* and *recommend.*
majority	Call attention to the root word *major,* which means "greater" in Latin. Divide students into two groups of unequal size. Identify the larger group as the majority because it contains more than half the total number of students.
elector	Point out the root word *elect* and suffix *-or.* Explain that *-or* means "person or thing that does," so electors are people who elect. Other words with this suffix include *actor* and *inventor.*
override	Have students identify the two shorter words, *over* and *ride,* that make up this compound word. Discuss situations in which a teacher might override a decision made by students.

WORD CARDS To help teach the lesson vocabulary, use the Word Cards on pages 271–274.

Build Fluency

Use page 152 and the steps on Procedure Card 2 to reinforce vocabulary and build fluency. Read each vocabulary word aloud and have students repeat it. Then have students work in pairs to reread the words. Follow a similar procedure with the phrases and sentences. Continue to help students build fluency by having them reread "You Are There" in the Student Edition.

Text Comprehension

Before Reading

Preview the Lesson Guide students in previewing the lesson using Procedure Card 3. Point out the following features of the lesson on Student Edition pages 398–403.

- **Pages 398–399** Read the "What to Know" question. Have students use the question to set a purpose for reading the lesson. Preview the illustration of delegates at the Constitutional Convention on page 398, and the illustration of the National Archives on page 399.
- **Pages 400–401** Have students examine the illustration of Washington, D.C., and discuss the question about monuments and memorials in the caption.
- **Pages 402–403** Preview the illustration of the Supreme Court building on page 402, and have students locate this building in the illustration on pages 400–401. Preview the illustration and the Review questions on page 403.

During Reading

Build Comprehension of Expository Text Present the graphic organizer on page 153. Have students preview the organizer by filling in the lesson title and comparing the four main heads in the organizer with the matching subheads in the Student Edition pages 398–403. Tell students that the section subheads provide additional help with identifying important information. Use Procedure Card 4, the Reading Check questions in *Harcourt Social Studies,* and the directed reading suggestions below.

- **Page 398** After students have read "You Are There," have them recall briefly what they learned about Gouverneur Morris from his biography in Lesson 1.
- **Page 399** Have students read "The Preamble" and record in the graphic organizer the opening words of the Preamble, the purpose of the Constitution as stated in the Preamble, and the basic principles on which the new government would be based. Point out that the section subhead in the text, "The Purpose of the Constitution," can help students locate some of this information.
- **Pages 400–403** Point out the subheads ARTICLE I, ARTICLE II, and ARTICLE III in the organizer that show which article of the Constitution describes each branch of government. Have students read "The Legislative Branch," discuss what this branch is and does, and then write the information in the organizer. Follow a similar procedure for "The Executive Branch" and "The Judicial Branch."

After Reading

Summarize Have students use their completed graphic organizers to summarize the lesson. Then have them compare their summaries to the lesson summary on page 403.

Review and Respond If students need additional help with drawing conclusions, use Focus Skill Transparency 5.

Write a Set of Rules In a group discussion, help students identify some ideas in the Constitution that could apply to the classroom, such as fairness to all and protecting the rights of individuals. Then have students work with partners or in small groups to write their classroom rules. Students can share their rules with other groups and explain how each rule illustrates an idea or ideas in the Constitution.

Leveled Readers Use the Leveled Readers and Procedure Card 5 to build fluency and comprehension.

Name ______________________________ Date ______________

DIRECTIONS **Read aloud the words in Part A. Practice reading aloud the phrases and the sentences in Part B.**

Part A

Vocabulary Words		Additional Words
separation of powers	impeach	propose
legislative branch	judicial branch	majority
executive branch	justice	elector
electoral college	amendment	override
veto	rule of law	

Part B

1. The delegates to the Constitutional Convention / created a separation of powers / to keep any one branch / from controlling the government.
2. Article I of the Constitution / explains the legislative branch.
3. Either house of Congress / could propose most bills.
4. For a bill to become law, / a majority in each house /must vote for it.
5. Article II / gives the executive branch / the power to enforce laws.
6. Citizens vote / for a group of electors, / called the electoral college, / who vote for the President.
7. The President / can veto bills passed by Congress, / but Congress can then override the President's veto / with a two-thirds vote.
8. Congress / can impeach a President / who does not take care / that the laws are faithfully executed.
9. The Supreme Court justices / and the judicial branch of government / help make sure / we have rule of law.
10. The delegates agreed / on how to add amendments / to the Constitution.

YOU ARE THERE **Turn to Student Edition page 398. Practice reading aloud "You Are There" three times. Try to improve your reading each time. Record your best time on the line below.**

Number of words 74 My Best Time ________ Words per Minute ________

Name ______________________ Date ____________

Lesson Title ______________________

The Preamble

First words ______________________ . . .

Purpose of the Constitution ______________________

Principles ______________________

ARTICLE I

The Legislative Branch

Reason for three branches ______________________

Two houses

1. ______________________

2. ______________________

ARTICLE II

The Executive Branch

Chief executive ______________________

Powers

1. ______________________

2. ______________________

3. ______________________

ARTICLE III

The Judicial Branch

Created a ____________ Highest court ____________

Has the power to ______________________

____

Citizens could add ______________________ to the Constitution.

UNIT 5 Chapter 10

Lesson 3 The Bill of Rights

Vocabulary Strategies

Preteach Additional Vocabulary After teaching the Vocabulary words on Student Edition page 404, explain to students that there are several other important words they will see in this lesson. Use Procedure Card 1, along with the suggestions below, to introduce the words.

press	Discuss known meanings. Explain that *press* is often used as a name for the news media, including newspapers, magazines, radio and TV news.
house	Tell students that this word is a verb and a homograph of the familiar word *house*, meaning "home." This word, pronounced *howz*, means "to provide with living quarters or shelter."
minority	Have students recall the meaning of *majority*. Then discuss these sentences: "The Bill of Rights protects the rights of people in the minority. The majority cannot take their rights away."

WORD CARDS To help teach the lesson vocabulary, use the Word Cards on pages 273–274.

Build Fluency

Use page 156 and the steps on Procedure Card 2 to reinforce vocabulary and build fluency. Read each vocabulary word aloud and have students repeat it. Then have students work in pairs to reread the words. Follow a similar procedure with the phrases and sentences. Continue to help students build fluency by having them reread "You Are There" in the Student Edition.

Text Comprehension

Before Reading

Preview the Lesson Guide students in previewing the lesson using Procedure Card 3. Point out the following features of the lesson on Student Edition pages 404–409.

- **Pages 404–405** Read the "What to Know" question. Preview the time line and the illustration. Help students identify some of the delegates pictured in the illustration, such as George Washington and Benjamin Franklin. Have students read the Fast Fact.
- **Pages 406–407** Have students examine the table showing votes to ratify the Constitution, and look at the illustration of Alexander Hamilton on page 406. Discuss the question in the caption. Then preview the illustration on page 407.
- **Pages 408–409** Preview the illustrations of the postage stamp honoring Benjamin Banneker and the national capital at Washington, D.C., under construction. On page 409, preview the portrait of John Adams and the Review questions.

During Reading

Build Comprehension of Expository Text Present the graphic organizer on page 157. Have students preview the organizer by filling in the lesson title and comparing the four main heads in the organizer with the matching subheads in the Student Edition pages 404–409. Tell students that the section subheads provide additional help with identifying important information. Use Procedure Card 4, the Reading Check questions in *Harcourt Social Studies,* and the directed reading suggestions below.

- **Page 404** After students have read "You Are There," have them note the date and place of the conversation with Benjamin Franklin. Be sure they understand that Franklin is talking about the new Constitution.
- **Page 405** Have students read and discuss "The Struggle to Ratify" and identify the issues that created arguments at the state conventions. Then have students write the information in the first box of the organizer.
- **Page 406** After students have read "The Vote of Approval," be sure they understand that only nine states needed to ratify the Constitution but that all thirteen states eventually did approve it. Then have students record information in the organizer.
- **Pages 407–409** Have students read "The Bill of Rights." Discuss how each of the amendments helps protect the rights of the people. Then have students write information in the organizer. After reading "The New Government," students can complete the final box in the organizer.

After Reading

Summarize Have students use their completed graphic organizers to summarize the lesson. Then have them compare their summaries to the lesson summary on page 409.

Review and Respond If students need additional help with drawing conclusions, use Focus Skill Transparency 5.

Make a Poster Provide or help students locate a copy of the Bill of Rights that lists all ten amendments. Suggest that students design their posters on scrap paper and plan carefully so that everything will fit and look attractive. Provide posterboard and markers or other appropriate art materials.

Leveled Readers Use the Leveled Readers and Procedure Card 5 to build fluency and comprehension.

Name ______________________________ Date ______________

DIRECTIONS **Read aloud the words in Part A. Practice reading aloud the phrases and the sentences in Part B.**

Part A

Vocabulary Words		Additional Words
ratify	Cabinet	press
Federalists	political party	house
Anti-Federalists		minority
due process of law		
reserved powers		

Part B

1. Before the Constitution could become / the law of the land, / 9 of the 13 states / had to ratify it.
2. Those citizens who favored the Constitution / were called Federalists.
3. The Anti-Federalists / feared that the national government / would have too much power.
4. The First Amendment / protects freedom of the press.
5. The government / cannot make people house soldiers / in peacetime.
6. The Fifth through Eighth Amendments / deal with due process of law.
7. The Tenth Amendment / says that the reserved powers / belong to the states / or to the people.
8. The Bill of Rights / protects the rights / of people in the minority.
9. An argument / between two members of George Washington's Cabinet / led to / the rise of political parties.

YOU ARE THERE **Turn to Student Edition page 404. Practice reading aloud "You Are There" three times. Try to improve your reading each time. Record your best time on the line below.**

Number of words 72 My Best Time ________ Words per Minute ________

Name ______________________ Date ______________

Lesson Title ______________________

The Struggle to Ratify

What some delegates wanted

1. ______________________

2. ______________________

What supporters promised

____

____

____

The Vote of Approval

First state to ratify ______________________

What Federalists wanted ______________________

____

What Anti-Federalists feared

____

____

When ninth state ratified ______________________

The Bill of Rights

How many amendments ______________________

Purpose of the Bill of Rights

____

____

Added to Constitution in ______________________

Reserved powers belong to

____

The New Government

First President ______________________

Became President in ______________________

Federal government moved to

____

When ______________________

Second President

____

LESSON 4 A Constitutional Government

Vocabulary Strategies

Preteach Additional Vocabulary After teaching the Vocabulary words on Student Edition page 412, explain to students that there are several other important words they will see in this lesson. Use Procedure Card 1, along with the suggestions below, to introduce the words.

empower	Point out the familiar word *power*. Discuss this context sentence: "The Constitution had to empower the federal government, or give it enough power to govern the nation."
misusing	Have students identify the elements of this word: prefix *mis-*, meaning "wrong" or "wrongly," base word *use*, and ending *-ing*. Other words with the same prefix include *misspell* and *misbehave*.
unconstitutional	Identify the word *constitution*, the prefix *un-*, and suffix *-al*. Explain that something that is not allowed by the constitution is unconstitutional.
preserve	Tell students that *preserve* is from the Latin root *servare*, "to keep or guard." To preserve something is to protect it or to keep it safe. Other words with this root include *reserve* and *conserve*.

WORD CARDS To help teach the lesson vocabulary, use the Word Cards on pages 273–276.

Build Fluency

Use page 160 and the steps on Procedure Card 2 to reinforce vocabulary and build fluency. Read each vocabulary word aloud and have students repeat it. Then have students work in pairs to reread the words. Follow a similar procedure with the phrases and sentences. Continue to help students build fluency by having them reread "You Are There" in the Student Edition.

Text Comprehension

BEFORE READING

Preview the Lesson Guide students in previewing the lesson using Procedure Card 3. Point out the following features of the lesson on Student Edition pages 412–419.

- **Pages 412–413** Read the "What to Know" question. Explain that the Constitution empowers the federal government but also limits that power so that the states have power, too. Preview the time line and illustration on page 412 and the photograph of the President and other leaders on page 413.
- **Pages 414–415** Have students examine the diagram of checks and balances on page 414 and answer the question in the caption. Then have students examine the chart on page 415. Explain that the shared powers belong to both the federal and state governments. For instance, the federal government collects taxes, but state governments can collect their own taxes. Discuss the caption question.

- **Pages 416–419** Preview the photographs on pages 416 and 417. On page 418, have students read Children in History and discuss the Make It Relevant question. Then preview the photograph and the Review questions on page 419.

During Reading

Build Comprehension of Expository Text Present the graphic organizer on page 161. Have students preview the organizer by filling in the lesson title and comparing the six main heads in the organizer with the matching subheads in the Student Edition pages 412–419. Tell students that the section subheads provide additional help with identifying important information. Use Procedure Card 4, the Reading Check questions in *Harcourt Social Studies*, and the directed reading suggestions below.

- **Page 412** After students have read "You Are There," have them tell whether they would like to live in a place with no government and why or why not.
- **Page 413** Have students read and discuss "Sharing Powers." Guide them in writing in the first box of the organizer how the Constitution allows the branches of government to share powers and the reason for doing so.
- **Page 414** After students have read "Checks and Balances," discuss how the system works and have students give examples. Then have students record information in the organizer.
- **Pages 415–417** Have students read "State Powers" and write in the organizer a general statement about the powers that the Constitution gives to the states or the people. Then have students read "State and Local Governments" and record information in the organizer. Follow the same procedure for "Rights and Responsibilities."
- **Pages 418–419** After students have read "Being a Citizen," they can complete the organizer by writing two other responsibilities of citizens, in addition to voting.

After Reading

Summarize Have students use their completed graphic organizers to summarize the lesson. Then have them compare their summaries to the lesson summary on page 419.

Review and Respond If students need additional help with drawing conclusions, use Focus Skill Transparency 5.

Write a Persuasive Letter Discuss with students some issues that are important to your community. You may want to provide articles from your local newspaper that address specific issues. You will also want to help students decide what official to write to and how to locate that person's name and address. Remind students of rules for persuasive writing and of proper form for a business letter.

Leveled Readers Use the Leveled Readers and Procedure Card 5 to build fluency and comprehension.

Name ______________________________ Date ______________

DIRECTIONS **Read aloud the words in Part A. Practice reading aloud the phrases and the sentences in Part B.**

Part A

Vocabulary Words		Additional Words
union	suffrage	empower
democracy	civic virtue	misusing
public agenda	naturalization	unconstitutional
checks and balances		preserve
popular sovereignty		

Part B

1. The Constitution / had to empower / the federal government.
2. The system of checks and balances / keeps any one branch / from becoming too powerful / or misusing its authority.
3. The Supreme Court / can declare new laws / or government actions / unconstitutional.
4. The system of checks and balances / was developed / in the hope that it would allow the nation / to form "a more perfect union."
5. The writers of the Constitution / were careful to preserve / the powers of the states.
6. Our democracy / is based on the principle / of popular sovereignty.
7. Writing one's leaders / helps the leaders / keep track of a public agenda.
8. Women / were not given suffrage / in national elections / until 1920.
9. One responsibility of citizens / is to act with civic virtue.
10. Immigrants / can become legal citizens / through naturalization.

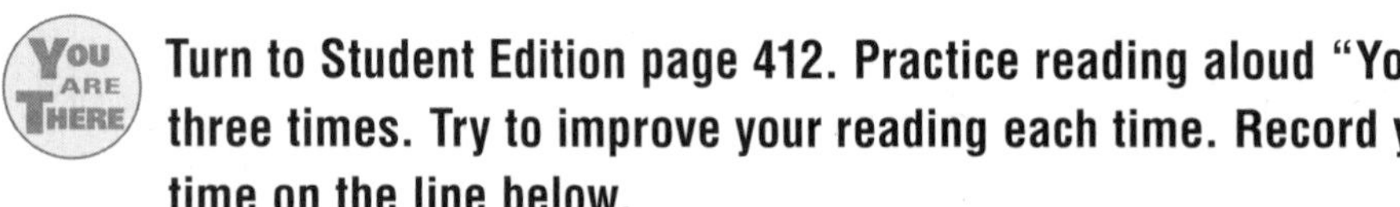

Turn to Student Edition page 412. Practice reading aloud "You Are There" three times. Try to improve your reading each time. Record your best time on the line below.

Number of words 91 My Best Time ______ Words per Minute ______

Name ________________________ Date ____________

Lesson Title: ________________________

Sharing Powers

How the federal government's power is shared ________________________

____

Why ________________________

Checks and Balances

What the system does ________________________

____

What each branch has ________________________

____

State Powers

Powers of the states or the people ________________________

____

State and Local Governments

Three levels of government ________________________

Something they have in common ________________________

Rights and Responsibilities

How government gets its power

____

One responsibility ________________________

Being a Citizen

Two other responsibilities

____

____

LESSON 1 Exploring the West

Vocabulary Strategies

Preteach Additional Vocabulary After teaching the Vocabulary words on Student Edition page 426, explain to students that there are several other important words they will see in this lesson. Use Procedure Card 1, along with the suggestions below, to introduce the words.

widen	Point out the familiar word *wide* and suffix *-en*, added after dropping the final *e*. To widen a road means to make it wider. Other words with the same suffix include *sharpen*, *tighten*, and *shorten*.
wilderness	Tell students that this word comes from an Old English word *wilddeoren*, which means "of wild beasts."
purchase	Tell students that to purchase something is to buy it. A purchase is the thing that has been bought. Discuss examples of purchases such as a carton of milk, a TV, or a piece of land.
corps	Explain that a corps is a team or group of people who are working together or carrying out a duty. Point out that *p* and *s* are silent, so this word is a homophone of *core*.
unknowingly	Have students identify the base word *know*, prefix *-un*, ending *-ing*, and suffix *-ly*. Discuss this context sentence: "Pike and his men unknowingly entered Spanish territory."

WORD CARDS To help teach the lesson vocabulary, use the Word Cards on pages 277–278.

Build Fluency

Use page 164 and the steps on Procedure Card 2 to reinforce vocabulary and build fluency. Read each vocabulary word aloud and have students repeat it. Then have students work in pairs to reread the words. Follow a similar procedure with the phrases and sentences. Continue to help students build fluency by having them reread "You Are There" in the Student Edition.

Text Comprehension

BEFORE READING

Preview the Lesson Guide students in previewing the lesson using Procedure Card 3. Point out the following features of the lesson on Student Edition pages 426–433.

- **Pages 426–427** Read the "What to Know" question. Explain to students that the United States bought a huge amount of land in the Louisiana Purchase. Preview the time line and the illustrations of frontier life and pioneers.
- **Pages 428–429** Have students read the Children in History feature and discuss the Make It Relevant question. Then preview the map of the Louisiana Purchase on page 429 and have students answer the map skill question.

- **Pages 430–431** Tell students that Lewis and Clark explored the lands that the United States gained from the Louisiana Purchase. Have students examine and discuss the illustrated time line of Lewis and Clark's journey.
- **Pages 432–433** Preview the illustration on page 432, and explain that Zebulon Pike explored part of the Louisiana Purchase. Preview the Review questions on page 432 and the biography of Sacagawea on page 433.

During Reading

Build Comprehension of Expository Text Present the graphic organizer on page 165. Have students preview the organizer by filling in the lesson title and comparing the five main heads in the organizer with the matching subheads in the Student Edition pages 426–432. Tell students that the section subheads provide additional help with identifying important information. Use Procedure Card 4, the Reading Check questions in *Harcourt Social Studies,* and the directed reading suggestions below.

- **Page 426** After students have read "You Are There," have them locate Kentucky on the map on page 429.
- **Pages 427–428** Have students read "Immigrants and Pioneers." Guide them in listing briefly in the first box of the organizer reasons that immigrants came to the United States. Point out the subhead "The Cumberland Gap" that matches the section subhead in the text, and have students write the name of the main route through the gap. Then have students read "Americans Continue West" and list the three new states named in the text under the section subhead "New States."
- **Pages 429–431** After students have read "The Louisiana Purchase," have them write the information in the organizer. Point out that the subhead matches the section subhead in the text and can help students locate information. Follow a similar procedure for the next section, "Lewis and Clark."
- **Page 432** Have students read "Pike in the Southwest" and complete the organizer.

After Reading

Summarize Have students use their completed graphic organizers to summarize the lesson. Then have them compare their summaries to the lesson summary on page 432.

Review and Respond If students need additional help with drawing conclusions, use Focus Skill Transparency 5.

Write a Journal Entry Suggest that students reread the section of the lesson that tells about the expedition of the Corps of Discovery. As they read, students can jot down ideas to use in their journal entries. Call attention to the entry that Clark wrote in his journal, quoted on page 431. Remind students that someone writing in a journal may record both observations and feelings.

Leveled Readers Use the Leveled Readers and Procedure Card 5 to build fluency and comprehension.

Name ______________________________ Date ______________

DIRECTIONS **Read aloud the words in Part A. Practice reading aloud the phrases and the sentences in Part B.**

Part A

Vocabulary Words	Additional Words	
gap	widen	corps
pioneer	wilderness	unknowingly
consequence	purchase	

Part B

1. A company / hired Daniel Boone / and about thirty others / to widen an old Native American trail / through the Cumberland Gap.
2. The group / built the Wilderness Road, / which became the main route for pioneers / going to the West.
3. Pioneers / formed the new states / of Kentucky, Tennessee, and Ohio.
4. In 1803, / France sold all of Louisiana / to the United States / in a deal called the Louisiana Purchase.
5. The Corps of Discovery, / led by Lewis and Clark, / set out to learn about the land / in the Louisiana Purchase.
6. Lewis and Clark / had to make many hard decisions / that had important consequences / for the expedition.
7. In 1806, / Captain Zebulon Pike / led an expedition / to explore the southwestern area / of the Louisiana Purchase.
8. After unknowingly entering Spanish territory, / Pike reported / that people there / needed manufactured goods.

YOU ARE THERE **Turn to Student Edition page 426. Practice reading aloud "You Are There" three times. Try to improve your reading each time. Record your best time on the line below.**

Number of words 75 My Best Time ________ Words per Minute ________

Name ______________________ Date ______________

Lesson Title ______________________

Immigrants and Pioneers

Why immigrants came ______________________

____

The Cumberland Gap

Main route ______________________

Americans Continue West

New States

1. ______________________
2. ______________________
3. ______________________

The Louisiana Purchase

President of the United States ______________________

Problem ______________________

A Very Big Purchase

Date of final deal ______________________

Result ______________________

Lewis and Clark

The Corps of Discovery Set out from ______________________ in ______________

The Expedition Succeeds Reached ______________________ in ______________

What their work did ______________________

____

Pike in the Southwest

What he reported ______________________

Result ______________________

LESSON 2 Expanding Borders

Vocabulary Strategies

Preteach Additional Vocabulary After teaching the Vocabulary words on Student Edition page 436, explain to students that there are several other important words they will see in this lesson. Use Procedure Card 1, along with the suggestions below, to introduce the words.

threatened	Give *endangered* as a synonym for *threatened.* Point out the base words *danger* and *threat*, which are also synonyms.
naval	Explain that this word is from the Latin *navis*, which means "ship." Related words include *navy*, *navigation*, and *navigable*.
doctrine	Tell students that a doctrine is a statement of principles that may be put forth by a government.
colonization	Point out the relationship of this word to *colony* and *colonize*. Explain that colonization is the act of colonizing, or establishing a colony.
removal	Have students identify the familiar word *remove* and suffix *-al*. Removal is the action of removing something.

WORD CARDS To help teach the lesson vocabulary, use the Word Cards on pages 277–278.

Build Fluency

Use page 168 and the steps on Procedure Card 2 to reinforce vocabulary and build fluency. Read each vocabulary word aloud and have students repeat it. Then have students work in pairs to reread the words. Follow a similar procedure with the phrases and sentences. Continue to help students build fluency by having them reread "You Are There" in the Student Edition.

Text Comprehension

BEFORE READING

Preview the Lesson Guide students in previewing the lesson using Procedure Card 3. Point out the following features of the lesson on Student Edition pages 436–441.

- **Pages 436–437** Read the "What to Know" question. Remind students that the United States more than doubled in size with the Louisiana Purchase in 1803. Explain that Native Americans were the only people living on much of that land at that time. Preview the time line, the portrait of Chief Tecumseh and the illustration of trading ships.
- **Pages 438–439** Have students examine the map of major battles of the War of 1812 on page 438 and answer the map skill question. Preview the illustration of Francis Scott Key on page 439, and have students read the words of the "Star-Spangled Banner."

- **Pages 440–441** Preview the painting on page 440. Ask students why they think the walk shown here and described in the caption was called the Trail of Tears. Have students examine the map on page 441 and answer the map skill question. Then preview the Review questions.

During Reading

Build Comprehension of Expository Text Present the graphic organizer on page 169. Have students preview the organizer by filling in the lesson title and comparing the four main heads in the organizer with the matching subheads in the Student Edition pages 436–441. Tell students that the section subheads provide additional help with identifying important information. Use Procedure Card 4, the Reading Check questions in *Harcourt Social Studies,* and the directed reading suggestions below.

- **Page 436** After students have read "You Are There," tell them that in this lesson they will learn more about Chief Tecumseh and why the Shawnee needed to defend their lands.
- **Page 437** Have students read "Troubles Grow" and write information in the first box of the organizer. Point out the subhead "Conflicts with Britain" that matches the section subhead in the text. Call attention also to the fact that the organizer is a sequence chart or time line with arrows indicating the sequence of events.
- **Pages 438–439** After students have read "The War of 1812," have them fill in the next box of the organizer, using the section subheads to locate information. Then students can read "Extending Democracy" and fill in that box.
- **Pages 440–441** Have students read "The Indian Removal Act" and complete the organizer. Point out that they will need to write a brief summary of the Trail of Tears. After students have completed the organizer, have them look at all the dates shown in it to confirm that the events are in time order.

After Reading

Summarize Have students use their completed graphic organizers to summarize the lesson. Then have them compare their summaries to the lesson summary on page 441.

Review and Respond If students need additional help with drawing conclusions, use Focus Skill Transparency 5.

Write an Article Suggest that students reread passages from the lesson that tell about Fort McHenry and Francis Scott Key. Remind them that a newspaper article tells When, Where, Who, What, and Why. Students might like to print their articles in a newspaper column format on the computer.

Leveled Readers Use the Leveled Readers and Procedure Card 5 to build fluency and comprehension.

Name ______________________ Date ____________

DIRECTIONS **Read aloud the words in Part A. Practice reading aloud the phrases and the sentences in Part B.**

Part A

Vocabulary Words	Additional Words	
impressment	threatened	colonization
national anthem	naval	removal
nationalism	doctrine	
assimilate		

Part B

1. In the early 1800s, / many Americans / believed that British actions / in both the West and the East / threatened the United States.
2. The impressment of American sailors / by the British navy / angered many Americans / and led to the War of 1812.
3. Britain / had the strongest navy / in the world, / but the United States / won several important naval battles.
4. During the British attack / on Fort McHenry, / Francis Scott Key / wrote "The Star-Spangled Banner," / which became the national anthem.
5. After the war ended, / many Americans / felt a sense of nationalism.
6. In 1823, / President James Monroe / announced the Monroe Doctrine.
7. It said / that the American continents / were "not to be considered as subjects / for future colonization / by any European powers."
8. Unlike most other Native American tribes, / the Cherokee / assimilated to the ways of life / of white settlers.
9. In 1830, / President Jackson / signed the Indian Removal Act.

You Are There

Turn to Student Edition page 436. Practice reading aloud "You Are There" three times. Try to improve your reading each time. Record your best time on the line below.

Number of words 66 My Best Time ________ Words per Minute ________

Name ______________________ Date ______________

Lesson Title ______________________

Troubles Grow

Where pioneers often settled ______________________

What Britain encouraged Native Americans to do ______________________

Conflicts with Britain What angered Americans ______________________

The War of 1812

Important American victories ______________________

British Attacks on Cities When ______________ Events ______________

____

The Growth of Nationalism When ______________ Plan ______________

Extending Democracy

Who could vote in 1828 ______________________

New President ______________ New Ideas ______________

The Indian Removal Act

Purpose ______________________

The Trail of Tears

When it started ______________ What happened ______________

____

____

Lesson 3 From Ocean to Ocean

Vocabulary Strategies

Preteach Additional Vocabulary After teaching the Vocabulary words on Student Edition page 444, explain to students that there are several other important words they will see in this lesson. Use Procedure Card 1, along with the suggestions below, to introduce the words.

mission	Remind students that they learned in Chapter 4 that Spanish missionaries built religious settlements, or missions, in the region of North America called New Spain.
lone	Discuss this sentence: "Texas was called the Lone Star Republic because its flag had one star." Point out that *lone* is a homophone of *loan*. Noticing that *lone* without *l* spells *one* can help students distinguish between the two words.
schooner	Tell students that a schooner is a type of sailing ship. Pioneers went west in covered wagons that they called prairie schooners. Point out the picture of a prairie schooner on page 447.
nugget	Students probably recognize this word as a food term. Explain that a small lump of metal, such as gold, is also called a nugget.

WORD CARDS To help teach the lesson vocabulary, use the Word Cards on pages 277–280.

Build Fluency

Use page 172 and the steps on Procedure Card 2 to reinforce vocabulary and build fluency. Read each vocabulary word aloud and have students repeat it. Then have students work in pairs to reread the words. Follow a similar procedure with the phrases and sentences. Continue to help students build fluency by having them reread "You Are There" in the Student Edition.

Text Comprehension

Before Reading

Preview the Lesson Guide students in previewing the lesson using Procedure Card 3. Point out the following features of the lesson on Student Edition pages 444–451.

- **Pages 444–445** Read the "What to Know" question. Remind students that even after the Louisiana Purchase, there were large parts of the present-day United States that were still claimed by other countries. Preview the time line, the illustration showing the battle of the Alamo, and the map of battles in the Texas War of Independence. Have students locate the Alamo on the map and answer the map skill question.
- **Pages 446–447** Have students examine the map showing trails to the West and answer the map skill question. Preview the illustration of a covered wagon on page 447. Have students compare traveling in a wagon like this to traveling in a camper or recreational vehicle today.

- **Pages 448–451** Preview the illustration of the Mexican-American War on page 448 and the map on page 449 showing the growth of the United States. Have students answer the map skill question. Then have students examine the illustration of gold mining on pages 450–451 and discuss the question in the caption. Preview the Review questions on page 451.

During Reading

Build Comprehension of Expository Text Present the graphic organizer on page 173. Have students preview the organizer by filling in the lesson title and comparing the five main heads in the organizer with the matching subheads in the Student Edition pages 444–451. Tell students that the section subheads provide additional help with identifying important information. Use Procedure Card 4, the Reading Check questions in *Harcourt Social Studies*, and the directed reading suggestions below.

- **Page 444** After students have read "You Are There," tell them that in 1836 Texas was not yet part of the United States. Mexico had won its independence from Spain, so the Southwest region that had once belonged to Spain now belonged to Mexico.
- **Pages 445–446** Have students read "Texas Independence." Then they can write information in the first box of the organizer, after identifying the two subheads that match the section subheads in the text. Next, have students read "The Lone Star Republic" and fill in that box. Point out that students will need to summarize briefly what happened and the result.
- **Pages 446–449** After students have read "Trails West," have them fill in the next box of the organizer, using the section subheads to locate information. Then students can read "Expanding Borders" and fill in that box. Point out that following the subhead "New Borders," there are spaces to list three ways that the United States acquired new borders.
- **Pages 450–451** Have students read "The California Gold Rush" and complete the organizer. Point out that there are spaces after the subhead "Changing California" to write two ways that California changed as a result of the gold rush.

After Reading

Summarize Have students use their completed graphic organizers to summarize the lesson. Then have them compare their summaries to the lesson summary on page 451.

Review and Respond If students need additional help with drawing conclusions, use Focus Skill Transparency 5.

Write a Journal Entry Have students recall what they have learned about how to write a journal entry. Point out that forty-niners who traveled to California from other parts of the United States to find gold used the same overland trails as pioneers who went west for other reasons.

Leveled Readers Use the Leveled Readers and Procedure Card 5 to build fluency and comprehension.

Name ______________________________ Date ____________

DIRECTIONS **Read aloud the words in Part A. Practice reading aloud the phrases and the sentences in Part B.**

Part A

Vocabulary Words		Additional Words
dictator	cession	mission
annex	gold rush	lone
ford	forty-niners	schooner
manifest destiny		nugget

Part B

1. Fighting broke out / between American settlers in Mexico / and troops sent by the dictator of Mexico, / General Santa Anna.
2. American defenders / fought Santa Anna's army / at the Alamo, / a mission / they had turned into a fort.
3. Texas gained its independence / and was called the Lone Star Republic / until it was annexed by the United States / in 1845.
4. Pioneers / traveled in covered wagons / called prairie schooners / on the Oregon Trail / to the Pacific Northwest.
5. Wagons faced danger / when they had to ford rivers.
6. Many people in the United States / believed in manifest destiny, / even if it meant / going to war.
7. After the Mexican-American War, / Mexico sold the United States / a large area / known as the Mexican Cession.
8. The news / that workers in California / had found a small nugget / and then more gold / caused a gold rush.

YOU ARE THERE **Turn to Student Edition page 444. Practice reading aloud "You Are There" three times. Try to improve your reading each time. Record your best time on the line below.**

Number of words 59 My Best Time ________ Words per Minute ________

Name ______________________________ Date ______________

Lesson Title ______________________________

Texas Independence

Americans in Texas Angered by

____

The Alamo Year ______________

Who won ______________

The Lone Star Republic

Date ______________

What happened ______________

____

Result ______________

Trails West

The Oregon Trail From ______________ to ______________

How pioneers traveled ______________

The Mormon Trail Mormon leader ______________

Route from ______________ to ______________

Expanding Borders

New Conflicts Solution ______________

The Mexican-American War Cause ______________

New Borders How 1. ______________

2. ______________ 3. ______________

The California Gold Rush

The Forty-Niners Came from ______________

Changing California How ______________ ______________

New Ideas and Inventions

LESSON 4

Vocabulary Strategies

Preteach Additional Vocabulary After teaching the Vocabulary words on Student Edition page 452, explain to students that there are several other important words they will see in this lesson. Use Procedure Card 1, along with the suggestions below, to introduce the words.

obstacle	Tell students that this word is from the Latin *ob-*, "in the way," and *stare*, "stand." An obstacle is something that blocks the way or prevents progress.
current	Point out that this word has multiple meanings. A current in a river or stream is a swift flow of water in one direction. Have students pantomime what happens to objects in a current.
quantity	Give *amount* and *number* as synonyms for *quantity*. Point out final *y* that changes to *i* before adding *-es* to form the plural.
mass production	Explain that mass production is the manufacture of large numbers of goods at one time by machine instead of making them one at a time by hand.
reaper	Have student use this context sentence to figure out the meaning of *reaper*: "In 1832, Cyrus McCormick invented a mechanical reaper for harvesting grain."

WORD CARDS To help teach the lesson vocabulary, use the Word Cards on pages 279–280.

Build Fluency

Use page 176 and the steps on Procedure Card 2 to reinforce vocabulary and build fluency. Read each vocabulary word aloud and have students repeat it. Then have students work in pairs to reread the words. Follow a similar procedure with the phrases and sentences. Continue to help students build fluency by having them reread "You Are There" in the Student Edition.

Text Comprehension

BEFORE READING

Preview the Lesson Guide students in previewing the lesson using Procedure Card 3. Point out the following features of the lesson on Student Edition pages 452–457.

- **Pages 452–453** Read the "What to Know" question, and invite students to suggest possible answers. Preview the time line and the illustration of how boats use locks to move through different elevations in a canal. Discuss the Illustration question.
- **Pages 454–455** Have students examine the map showing roads and railroads in the United States in 1850 and answer the map skill question. Preview the illustration and the graph on page 455, and have students answer the question in the caption.

- **Pages 456–457** Preview the Primary Sources feature on page 456 and discuss the document-based question. Then preview the photograph of factory workers and the Review questions on page 457.

During Reading

Build Comprehension of Expository Text Present the graphic organizer on page 177. Have students preview the organizer by filling in the lesson title and comparing the four main heads in the organizer with the matching subheads in the Student Edition pages 452–457. Tell students that the section subheads provide additional help with identifying important information. Use Procedure Card 4, the Reading Check questions in *Harcourt Social Studies,* and the directed reading suggestions below.

- **Page 452** After students have read "You Are There," have them identify the waterway that connected Lake Erie to the Hudson River. Call attention to the illustration of the canal on this page, and discuss how building canals changed transportation by boat.
- **Page 453** Have students read "Transportation" and fill in the information about an important road and an important canal mentioned under the section subhead "Roads and Canals" in the text.
- **Page 454** Then students can read "Steamboats and Railroads" and write information about these two forms of transportation in the next box of the organizer. Point out that the first two boxes are linked because both tell about developments in transportation.
- **Page 455** After students have read "The Industrial Revolution," have them fill in the next box of the organizer. Point out the subhead that matches the section subhead in the lesson and can help students locate information.
- **Pages 456–457** Have students read "More Inventions" and complete the organizer.

After Reading

Summarize Have students use their completed graphic organizers to summarize the lesson. Then have them compare their summaries to the lesson summary on page 457.

Review and Respond If students need additional help with drawing conclusions, use Focus Skill Transparency 5.

Make an Advertisement Discuss with the group what makes an advertisement effective. Then have students work individually or with partners to go back through the lesson and list the inventions they read about. Tell students to choose one of these inventions for their advertisement. Suggest that students also look back at the advertisement for the McCormick reaper on page 456 to recall what advertisements were like at the time of the Industrial Revolution.

Leveled Readers Use the Leveled Readers and Procedure Card 5 to build fluency and comprehension.

Name ______________________ Date ____________

DIRECTIONS **Read aloud the words in Part A. Practice reading aloud the phrases and the sentences in Part B.**

Part A

Vocabulary Words		Additional Words	
Industrial Revolution	canal	obstacle	mass production
interchangeable parts	lock	current	reaper
	locomotive	quantity	
	cotton gin		

Part B

1. Canals could avoid obstacles / and extend natural waterways.
2. The Erie Canal, / which was 363 miles long / and had 83 locks, / linked the Great Lakes / to the Atlantic.
3. Steamboats, / which could travel upstream / against the current, / became the main form of travel / on large rivers / across the nation.
4. Peter Cooper / built the first American locomotive / in 1830.
5. During the 1800s, / new inventions / allowed people to use machines / instead of hand tools / to make large quantities of goods.
6. This change / came to be called / the Industrial Revolution.
7. Eli Whitney / invented the cotton gin / and also a system of interchangeable parts / for making guns.
8. One result / of Whitney's invention of interchangeable parts / was a system called mass production.
9. With the mechanical reaper / that Cyrus McCormick / invented in 1832, / farmers / could cut wheat much faster / than they had with hand tools.

YOU ARE THERE **Turn to Student Edition page 452. Practice reading aloud "You Are There" three times. Try to improve your reading each time. Record your best time on the line below.**

Number of words 66 My Best Time ________ Words per Minute ________

Name ______________________ Date ______________

Lesson Title: ______________________

Transportation

Roads and Canals Road ______________ Across ______________

Canal ______________ Linked ______________

Effect on New York City ______________

Steamboats and Railroads

What steamboats became ______________

Effect of railroads ______________

The Industrial Revolution

When it began ______________ What it was ______________

____

Mills in the North British mill worker ______________

What he did ______________

What it marked ______________

More Inventions

Inventor ______________ Invention ______________ Result ______________

Another invention ______________ Result ______________

Farm Machinery Inventor ______________ Invention ______________

Inventor ______________ Invention ______________

Lesson 1 The North and the South

Vocabulary Strategies

Preteach Additional Vocabulary After teaching the Vocabulary words on Student Edition page 476, explain to students that there are several other important words they will see in this lesson. Use Procedure Card 1, along with the suggestions below, to introduce the words.

strengthened	Point out the word *strength,* suffix *-en,* and ending *-ed.* Have students use these elements to determine the meaning.
outlawed	Have students identify the parts of this compound word: *out, law,* and ending *-ed.* Explain that to outlaw something is to pass a law against it.
debated	Tell students that *debate* is from the Latin root *battuere,* meaning "to beat." The word *battle* is from the same root. People who debate take part in a "battle of words," a formal argument or discussion.
objection	Have students recall that *object* with the second syllable stressed means "to oppose, or to disagree." To have an objection is to have an opposing, or opposite, opinion.
advantage	Discuss the idea that having an advantage means being in a better position or having a better chance than someone else. Have students offer examples, such as older students having the advantage in some games against younger students.

WORD CARDS To help teach the lesson vocabulary, use the Word Cards on pages 281–282.

Build Fluency

Use page 180 and the steps on Procedure Card 2 to reinforce vocabulary and build fluency. Read each vocabulary word aloud and have students repeat it. Then have students work in pairs to reread the words. Follow a similar procedure with the phrases and sentences. Continue to help students build fluency by having them reread "You Are There" in the Student Edition.

Text Comprehension

Before Reading

Preview the Lesson Guide students in previewing the lesson using Procedure Card 3. Point out the following features of the lesson on Student Edition pages 476–481.

- **Pages 476–477** Read the "What to Know" question. Preview the time line and the paintings. Discuss how the information about differences between the Southern economy and the Northern economy might offer clues about what caused conflicts.

- **Pages 478–479** Have students examine the map that shows the Missouri Compromise and answer the question in the caption. Preview the illustration and the portrait Andrew Jackson on page 479. Have students recall that Andrew Jackson was the President of the United States.
- **Pages 480–481** Preview the map on page 480, and have students answer the map skill question. Preview the painting and flyer, and the Review questions on page 481.

During Reading

Build Comprehension of Expository Text Present the graphic organizer on page 181. Have students preview the organizer by filling in the lesson title and comparing the four main heads in the organizer with the matching subheads in the Student Edition pages 476–481. Tell students that the section subheads provide additional help with identifying important information. Use Procedure Card 4, the Reading Check questions in *Harcourt Social Studies,* and the directed reading suggestions below.

- **Page 476** After students have read "You Are There," have them compare the observations in the paragraph with the scenes shown in the two paintings on pages 476 and 477.
- **Page 477** Have students read "Different Regions." In the organizer, point out the subhead "Different Ways of Life " that matches the section subhead in the text. In the two boxes below that, have students write briefly about ways of life in the Northern states and in the Southern states.
- **Pages 478–479** After students have read "Division Over Slavery," have them write the information in the organizer. Point out that the subhead matches the section subhead in the text and can help students locate information. Follow a similar procedure for the next section, "Different Ideas."
- **Pages 480–481** Have students read "More Divisions" and complete the organizer, using the section subheads to help them locate information.

After Reading

Summarize Have students use their completed graphic organizers to summarize the lesson. Then have them compare their summaries to the lesson summary on page 481.

Review and Respond Work through the Review questions with students. Use Focus Skill Transparency 6, Generalize, to help students make generalizations about information in the lesson.

Make a Chart Discuss how to set up a two-column chart, and what title and headings students might use. Suggest that they reread the lesson and jot down information about the North and the South, either on two separate sheets of paper or by dividing a sheet of paper in half. Then students can use that information to create the chart.

Leveled Readers Use the Leveled Readers and Procedure Card 5 to build fluency and comprehension.

Name ______________________________ Date ____________

DIRECTIONS **Read aloud the words in Part A. Practice reading aloud the phrases and the sentences in Part B.**

Part A

Vocabulary Words		Additional Words	
sectionalism	tariff	strengthened	objection
states' rights	industry	outlawed	advantage
free state	fugitive	debated	
slave state			

Part B

1. By the mid-1800s, / national leaders / often decided issues / based on sectionalism.
2. The Northern states / had more industries / than the Southern states.
3. In Southern states, / the money brought in by cash crops / strengthened the system of slavery.
4. By 1804, / all the Northern states / had outlawed slavery.
5. In 1819, / Congress debated / admitting Missouri / as a slave state.
6. Henry Clay of Kentucky / suggested the Missouri Compromise, / under which / the number of free states and slave states / remained equal.
7. In 1828, / sectionalism and states' rights / became serious issues / when Congress / passed a high tariff.
8. Despite the objections of Southerners, / Congress passed a new tariff.
9. If California joined the Union / as a free state / that would give the free states / an advantage in the Senate.

YOU ARE THERE **Turn to Student Edition page 476. Practice reading aloud "You Are There" three times. Try to improve your reading each time. Record your best time on the line below.**

Number of words 66 My Best Time ________ Words per Minute ________

Name ______________________ Date ______________

Lesson Title ______________________

Different Regions

Different Ways of Life

Northern States

Southern States

Division Over Slavery

The Missouri Compromise

When ________ Issue ______________

____

____

Who suggested a plan ______________

Result ______________________

____

Different Ideas

Arguing Over Trade

Why ______________________

____

Ideas About Government

What people disagreed about

____

____

More Divisions

Why ______________________

The Compromise of 1850 Law that was part of it ______________

Reaction in the North ______________________

Bleeding Kansas Why ______________________

What happened ______________________

LESSON 2 Resisting Slavery

Vocabulary Strategies

Preteach Additional Vocabulary After teaching the Vocabulary words on Student Edition page 482, explain to students that there are several other important words they will see in this lesson. Use Procedure Card 1, along with the suggestions below, to introduce the words.

privilege	Explain that a privilege is a right that is allowed only to certain people or under certain conditions. Have students give examples.
property	Point out items belonging to different students, such as pencils or notebooks, and have students tell whose property each item is. Be sure students understand that anything that someone owns is that person's property.
limb	Discuss known meanings, such as a large tree branch. Tell students that their arms and legs are also sometimes called limbs.
mistreated	Have students identify the word *treat*, prefix *mis-*, and ending *-ed*. Remind them that *mis-* means "wrongly," as in *misuse, misspell,* and *misbehave*.
conductor	Ask students to describe the job of a conductor on a train. Explain that although the Underground Railroad was not an actual railroad, the people who helped runaways along the way were called conductors.

WORD CARDS To help teach the lesson vocabulary, use the Word Cards on pages 281–282.

Build Fluency

Use page 184 and the steps on Procedure Card 2 to reinforce vocabulary and build fluency. Read each vocabulary word aloud and have students repeat it. Then have students work in pairs to reread the words. Follow a similar procedure with the phrases and sentences. Continue to help students build fluency by having them reread "You Are There" in the Student Edition.

Text Comprehension

BEFORE READING

Preview the Lesson Guide students in previewing the lesson using Procedure Card 3. Point out the following features of the lesson on Student Edition pages 482–487.

- **Pages 482–483** Read the "What to Know" question and have students use information they have already learned to predict the answer. Preview the time line and the portrait of Dred Scott. Have students examine the Primary Sources feature and discuss the Document-Based Question.
- **Pages 484–485** Preview the illustrated time line of events in the fight to end slavery. Tell students that they will learn more about these people and events

when they read the lesson. Have students study the map of Underground Railroad routes on page 485 and discuss the map skill question.

- **Pages 486–487** Have students read "Follow the Drinking Gourd" and discuss how the secret message in this song might have helped runaways find their way on the Underground Railroad. Preview the Review questions on page 486 and the biography of the famous Underground Railroad conductor Harriet Tubman on page 487.

During Reading

Build Comprehension of Expository Text Present the graphic organizer on page 185. Have students preview the organizer by filling in the lesson title and comparing the two main heads in the organizer with the matching subheads in the Student Edition pages 482–486. Tell students that the section subheads provide additional help with identifying important information. Use Procedure Card 4, the Reading Check questions in *Harcourt Social Studies*, and the directed reading suggestions below.

- **Page 482** After students have read "You Are There," tell them that the Quakers were one of the groups of people who strongly resisted slavery.
- **Page 483** Have students read "The Dred Scott Decision." Guide them in summarizing important information from this section of the lesson in the organizer. Point out the subhead "Disagreements Over Scott" that matches the section subhead in the text.
- **Pages 484–486** Before students read "Challenging Slavery," have them use the organizer to set a purpose for reading. As students read, they can write in the chart the names of people who challenged slavery and what these people did. Tell students that if two people worked together, their names should be written together on the same line in the chart. Point out the subhead "Women Fight for Change," and tell students they should add to the chart the names of women they read about under this section subhead in the text. Point out the two additional section subheads that are not included in the chart but are also related to the topic of challenging slavery.

After Reading

Summarize Have students use their completed graphic organizers to summarize the lesson. Then have them compare their summaries to the lesson summary on page 486.

Review and Respond Work through the Review questions with students. If students need additional help with generalizing, use Focus Skill Transparency 6.

Make a Poster Suggest that students reread the section of the lesson that tells about the Underground Railroad to get information and ideas for their posters. Remind students that a poster may include both art and text. Provide appropriate art materials and a space to display students' work.

Leveled Readers Use the Leveled Readers and Procedure Card 5 to build fluency and comprehension.

Name ______________________________ Date ______________

DIRECTIONS **Read aloud the words in Part A. Practice reading aloud the phrases and the sentences in Part B.**

Part A

Vocabulary Words	Additional Words
Underground Railroad	privilege property limb mistreated conductor

Part B

1. In 1857, / Supreme Court Chief Justice Roger B. Taney / wrote that Dred Scott, / an enslaved man, / had "none of the rights and privileges / of an American citizen."

2. Taney also wrote / that enslaved people were property, / a ruling / that troubled many people.

3. Frederick Douglass, / who escaped slavery and became famous, / often told audiences / that he had stolen his head, / limbs, / and body / from his master.

4. Harriet Beecher Stowe / wrote a book called *Uncle Tom's Cabin* / that told the story / of how enslaved workers / were mistreated.

5. Some enslaved people who ran away to gain their freedom / found helpers / —the brave men and women / of the Underground Railroad.

6. Harriet Tubman, / an African American / who had escaped from slavery herself, / was one of the best-known conductors / of the Underground Railroad.

Turn to Student Edition page 482. Practice reading aloud "You Are There" three times. Try to improve your reading each time. Record your best time on the line below.

Number of words 78 My Best Time ________ Words per Minute ________

Name ______________________ Date ____________

Lesson Title ______________________

The Dred Scott Decision

Why Scott went to court ______________________

Disagreements Over Scott

How the Supreme Court ruled ______________________

What this decision did ______________________

Challenging Slavery

Who	What they did

The Underground Railroad

What it was ______________________

One of the best-known conductors ______________________

Facing Dangers A constant danger ______________________

LESSON 3

The Nation Divides

Vocabulary Strategies

Preteach Additional Vocabulary After teaching the Vocabulary words on Student Edition page 488, explain to students that there are several other important words they will see in this lesson. Use Procedure Card 1, along with the suggestions below, to introduce the words.

opponent	Give *ally* as an antonym of *opponent*. Discuss how the words *opponent, oppose, opposite,* and *opposition* are related.
raid	Tell students that a raid is a surprise attack.
secession	Have students write and compare the words *secede* and *secession*. Explain that secession is the act of seceding.
torn	Ask students to describe what happens when paper or cloth is torn. Then discuss the use of *torn* in this context: "People in the border states—Delaware, Maryland, Kentucky, and Missouri—were torn between the two sides."
resign	Have students role play resigning from a job. Encourage them to use synonyms, such as *quit* and *leave*, in their role play.

WORD CARDS To help teach the lesson vocabulary, use the Word Cards on pages 281–282.

Build Fluency

Use page 188 and the steps on Procedure Card 2 to reinforce vocabulary and build fluency. Read each vocabulary word aloud and have students repeat it. Then have students work in pairs to reread the words. Follow a similar procedure with the phrases and sentences. Continue to help students build fluency by having them reread "You Are There" in the Student Edition.

Text Comprehension

BEFORE READING

Preview the Lesson Guide students in previewing the lesson using Procedure Card 3. Point out the following features of the lesson on Student Edition pages 488–493.

- **Pages 488–489** Read the "What to Know" question and have students discuss events and issues they have read about so far that created tension and disagreement in the nation. Preview the time line and the paintings, along with the meeting notice and poster.
- **Pages 490–491** Preview the photograph and the notice of Lincoln's election on page 490. Explain that John Brown's raid helped to divide the nation, and the election of Abraham Lincoln caused some states to secede. Have students examine the map on page 491, identify Union and Confederate states, and answer the map skill question.

- **Pages 492–493** Preview the painting of Fort Sumter and the South Carolina state flag on page 492. Have students examine the graph on page 493 and answer the question in the caption. Then preview the Review questions.

During Reading

Build Comprehension of Expository Text Present the graphic organizer on page 189. Have students preview the organizer by filling in the lesson title and comparing the four main heads in the organizer with the matching subheads in the Student Edition pages 488–493. Tell students that the section subheads provide additional help with identifying important information. Use Procedure Card 4, the Reading Check questions in *Harcourt Social Studies,* and the directed reading suggestions below.

- **Page 488** After students have read "You Are There," invite them to share their prior knowledge about Abraham Lincoln.
- **Pages 489–490** Have students read "Abraham Lincoln" and fill in the first box in the organizer. Point out the two subheads that match the section subheads in the text. Then follow the same procedure for the next section of the lesson, "Events Further Divide the Nation."
- **Pages 491–493** After students have read "The Nation Separates," they can write information in the next box in the organizer. Point out the subhead that matches the section subhead in the text. Then have students read "Fort Sumter" and complete the organizer.

After Reading

Summarize Have students use their completed graphic organizers to summarize the lesson. Then have them compare their summaries to the lesson summary on page 493.

Review and Respond Work through the Review questions with students. If students need additional help with generalizing, use Focus Skill Transparency 6.

Write a Newspaper Headline Provide examples of newspaper headlines and discuss how headline writers try to give the maximum amount of information in a limited space. Discuss how most people in the North and in the South probably reacted to the election of 1860. Point out that the headlines students write should reflect those viewpoints.

Leveled Readers Use the Leveled Readers and Procedure Card 5 to build fluency and comprehension.

Name ______________________________ Date ______________

DIRECTIONS **Read aloud the words in Part A. Practice reading aloud the phrases and the sentences in Part B.**

Part A

Vocabulary Words	Additional Words
secede	opponent
Confederacy	raid
border state	secession
artillery	torn
civil war	resign

Part B

1. Stephen A. Douglas / was Abraham Lincoln's opponent / in debates about slavery.
2. A raid on a government storehouse, / led by abolitionist John Brown, / divided the nation even more.
3. After Abraham Lincoln was elected President / in 1860, / some states seceded from the Union / and formed their own government, / the Confederacy.
4. President Lincoln / told the Southern states / that he opposed secession / but that he would not use / military force against them.
5. People in the border states / —Delaware, Maryland, Kentucky, and Missouri / —were torn between the two sides.
6. On April 12, 1861, / Confederate troops / fired their artillery / at Fort Sumter, / starting a civil war.
7. When Virginia seceded, / Union officer Robert E. Lee / resigned from the Union army / and later led the Southern army.

YOU ARE THERE **Turn to Student Edition page 488. Practice reading aloud "You Are There" three times. Try to improve your reading each time. Record your best time on the line below.**

Number of words 68 My Best Time _______ Words per Minute _______

Name ______________________ Date ______________

Lesson Title ______________________

Abraham Lincoln

Lincoln's Early Political Life

Elected to ______________________

and ______________________

New political party formed to

____

Called ______________________

The Lincoln-Douglas Debates

What the debates did ______________________

____

Events Further Divide the Nation

John Brown's Raid

Result ______________________

The Election of 1860

Main issue ______________________

What some Southerners said

____

____

Who won the election

____

The Nation Separates

What some Southern states did ______________________

What they formed ______________________

The Border States How people there felt ______________________

Fort Sumter

Date __________ What happened ______________________

The Civil War Begins Effects ______________________

____

Lesson 4 The War Begins

Vocabulary Strategies

Preteach Additional Vocabulary After teaching the Vocabulary words on Student Edition page 498, explain to students that there are several other important words they will see in this lesson. Use Procedure Card 1, along with the suggestions below, to introduce the words.

invade	Discuss what happens when an army invades. Be sure students understand that the invading army comes into an area that belongs to the other side.
prey	Have students use this context sentence to determine the meaning of *prey*: "An anaconda is a snake that squeezes its prey to death." Point out that *prey* is a homophone of *pray.*
battlefield	Have students identify the two shorter words that make up this compound word. Then have them define the compound word.
regiment	Explain that armies are organized into units of different sizes. One such unit, or group of soldiers, is called a regiment. Some students may be interested in researching how armies are organized.
heavy	Discuss familiar usages for *heavy,* such as a heavy load, heavy rain, a heavy coat, a heavy schedule, a heavy line, a heavy heart. Have students use other words to describe heavy fire in a battle.

WORD CARDS To help teach the lesson vocabulary, use the Word Cards on pages 283–284.

Build Fluency

Use page 192 and the steps on Procedure Card 2 to reinforce vocabulary and build fluency. Read each vocabulary word aloud and have students repeat it. Then have students work in pairs to reread the words. Follow a similar procedure with the phrases and sentences. Continue to help students build fluency by having them reread "You Are There" in the Student Edition.

Text Comprehension

Before Reading

Preview the Lesson Guide students in previewing the lesson using Procedure Card 3. Point out the following features of the lesson on Student Edition pages 498–503.

- **Pages 498–499** Read the "What to Know" question, and have students identify key events shown on the time line. Preview the photograph on page 498 and the graph and illustrations on page 499. Have students answer the question in the caption.

- **Pages 500–501** Preview the painting of the Battle of Bull Run on page 500 and the painting of Abraham Lincoln and his cabinet on page 501. Have students locate the dates of the Battle of Bull Run and the Emancipation Proclamation on the time line on page 498.
- **Pages 502–503** Preview the portraits of three women on page 502, and tell students that they will read in the lesson about each woman's contribution to the war effort. On page 503, preview the painting and poster. Tell students that the 54th regiment, which led the attack on Fort Wagner, was one of the best-known African American regiments. Preview the Review questions.

During Reading

Build Comprehension of Expository Text Present the graphic organizer on page 193. Have students preview the organizer by filling in the lesson title and comparing the four main heads in the organizer with the matching subheads in the Student Edition pages 498–503. Tell students that the section subheads provide additional help with identifying important information. Use Procedure Card 4, the Reading Check questions in *Harcourt Social Studies,* and the directed reading suggestions below.

- **Page 498** After students have read "You Are There," discuss the feelings that people in both the North and South may have had about the war at that point.
- **Pages 499–500** Have students read "War Plans." Point out the two boxes with subheads that match the section subheads in the text. Guide students in writing key ideas of the Union plans and Confederate plans. Follow a similar procedure for the next section of the lesson, "Early Battles."
- **Pages 501–503** After students have read "The Emancipation Proclamation," have them write a brief summary of this section of the lesson in the organizer. Then have students read "Americans at War" and complete the organizer by writing important information under the two subheads that match the section subheads in the text.

After Reading

Summarize Have students use their completed graphic organizers to summarize the lesson. Then have them compare their summaries to the lesson summary on page 503.

Review and Respond Work through the Review questions with students. If students need additional help with generalizing, use Focus Skill Transparency 6.

Write a Letter Discuss with students the kind of information they might include in their letters, such as who is running the farm while the father is away in the army and how the family feels about events such as major battles and the Emancipation Proclamation. Remind students to use the correct form for a friendly letter.

Leveled Readers Use the Leveled Readers and Procedure Card 5 to build fluency and comprehension.

Name ________________________________ Date ______________

DIRECTIONS **Read aloud the words in Part A. Practice reading aloud the phrases and the sentences in Part B.**

Part A

Vocabulary Words	Additional Words
strategy	invade
emancipate	prey
prejudice	battlefield
	regiment
	heavy

Part B

1. The Union strategy for winning the war / was first to weaken the South / and then to invade it.
2. Lincoln's plan to blockade Southern ports / was called the Anaconda Plan / because an anaconda / squeezes its prey to death.
3. The Confederates / won the first major battle, / which was fought on a battlefield near Manassas Junction, Virginia, / on July 21, 1861.
4. On January 1, 1863, / President Lincoln / issued a proclamation / to emancipate enslaved people / in areas still fighting against the Union.
5. African American soldiers who served in the Union army / faced prejudice / from people in the North / and the South.
6. One of the best-known African American regiments / was the Fifty-fourth Massachusetts, / led by Robert Gould Shaw.
7. In 1863, / the Fifty-fourth / led an attack on Fort Wagner, / in South Carolina, / fighting their way into the fort, / despite heavy fire.

YOU ARE THERE **Turn to Student Edition page 498. Practice reading aloud "You Are There" three times. Try to improve your reading each time. Record your best time on the line below.**

Number of words 59 My Best Time ________ Words per Minute ________

Name ______________________ Date ____________

Lesson Title: ______________________

War Plans

Union Plans

Confederate Plans

Early Battles

The Battle of Bull Run

The Battle of Antietam

The Emancipation Proclamation

Americans At War

Women Help the War Effort

African American Soldiers

LESSON 5 Toward a Union Victory

Vocabulary Strategies

Preteach Additional Vocabulary After teaching the Vocabulary words on Student Edition page 506, explain to students that there are several other important words they will see in this lesson. Use Procedure Card 1, along with the suggestions below, to introduce the words.

effective	Explain that *effective* is often used to describe a person or action that brings about the results that were wanted or hoped for.
siege	Tell students that this word is from the Latin word *sedere,* "to sit." During a siege, an army blockades a city or fort so that no supplies can reach it, and then waits for it to surrender.
deadliest	Help students see that this word is formed by adding the suffix *-ly* and ending *-est* to the word *dead.* Discuss the difference between a deadly battle or accident, in which many die, and the deadliest battle or accident.
evacuate	Tell students that *evacuate* is from the Latin word *vacuus,* meaning "empty." Other words from this root include *vacant* and *vacuum.*
short-lived	Have students use the shorter words that make up this hyphenated word to determine its meaning. Explain that some people pronounce the second syllable with the short *i* sound and others with the long *i* sound.

WORD CARDS To help teach the lesson vocabulary, use the Word Cards on pages 283–284.

Build Fluency

Use page 196 and the steps on Procedure Card 2 to reinforce vocabulary and build fluency. Read each vocabulary word aloud and have students repeat it. Then have students work in pairs to reread the words. Follow a similar procedure with the phrases and sentences. Continue to help students build fluency by having them reread "You Are There" in the Student Edition.

Text Comprehension

BEFORE READING

Preview the Lesson Guide students in previewing the lesson using Procedure Card 3. Point out the following features of the lesson on Student Edition pages 506–511.

- **Pages 506–507** Read the "What to Know" question, and have students locate the end of the Civil War on the time line. Preview the painting of Vicksburg on page 506, and have students locate Vicksburg in the state of Mississippi on the map on page 507. Then have them answer the map skill question.
- **Pages 508–509** Have students examine and discuss the illustration of the Battle of Gettysburg.

- **Pages 510–511** Preview the painting on page 510 that shows the surrender of General Lee. Explain that this surrender marked the end of the Civil War. Preview the photograph of the city of Richmond, Virginia, left in ruins when the war ended. Then preview the Review questions.

During Reading

Build Comprehension of Expository Text Present the graphic organizer on page 197. Have students preview the organizer by filling in the lesson title and comparing the three main heads in the organizer with the matching subheads in the Student Edition pages 506–511. Tell students that the section subheads provide additional help with identifying important information. Use Procedure Card 4, the Reading Check questions in *Harcourt Social Studies,* and the directed reading suggestions below.

- **Page 506** After students have read "You Are There," discuss what it must have felt like to know that a great battle would take place so close to home.
- **Page 507** Have students read "Two Major Battles" and fill in the first box in the organizer. Point out the subhead in the organizer that is the same as the section subhead in the text.
- **Pages 508–509** After students have read "Union Victories," have them write information in the next box in the organizer. Point out that the section subheads can help students locate information in the text.
- **Pages 510–511** Have students read "The War Ends" and complete the organizer.

After Reading

Summarize Have students use their completed graphic organizers to summarize the lesson. Then have them compare their summaries to the lesson summary on page 511.

Review and Respond Work through the Review questions with students. If students need additional help with generalizing, use Focus Skill Transparency 6.

Write a Poem Review with students what they have learned about writing poetry, including the use of rhythm, imagery, and figurative language. Possible extensions of this activity include having students combine their individual poems to create an anthology or researching famous Civil War poems.

Leveled Readers Use the Leveled Readers and Procedure Card 5 to build fluency and comprehension.

Name ______________________________ Date ______________

DIRECTIONS **Read aloud the words in Part A. Practice reading aloud the phrases and the sentences in Part B.**

Part A

Vocabulary Words	Additional Words
address	effective
assassinate	siege
	deadliest
	evacuate
	short-lived

Part B

1. By May 1863, / the Union army / finally had a general as effective / as Confederate General Robert E. Lee.
2. This general, / Ulysses S. Grant, / laid siege to the city of Vicksburg, Mississippi / and won a major victory for the Union.
3. The Union victory at the Battle of Gettysburg, / one of the deadliest battles of the war, / marked a turning point.
4. On November 19, 1863, / President Lincoln went to Gettysburg / and gave an address / that is one of the most famous speeches / in American history.
5. In April 1865, / Confederate troops / evacuated Richmond, Virginia.
6. The Civil War / was soon over, / but in the North / the joy at the victory / was short-lived.
7. On April 14, 1865, / just five days after the war ended, / President Lincoln was assassinated.

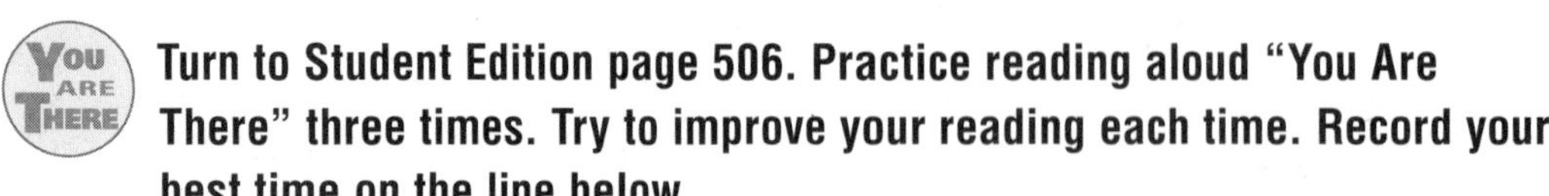

Turn to Student Edition page 506. Practice reading aloud "You Are There" three times. Try to improve your reading each time. Record your best time on the line below.

Number of words ___69___ My Best Time ________ Words per Minute ________

Name ______________________ Date ______________

Lesson Title: ______________________

Two Major Battles

Effective Union general ______________________

Vicksburg and Chancellorsville

Outcome at Vicksburg ______________________

Outcome at Chancellorsville ______________________

Union Victories

The Battle of Gettysburg When ____________ How long ______________

Outcome ______________________

The Gettysburg Address When ____________ Who ______________

What it is ______________________

Sherman's March When ____________ Who ______________

What happened ______________________

The War Ends

Appomattox Courthouse When ______________________

What happened ______________________

Bitter Victory Why ______________________

____

LESSON 1 Reconstruction

Vocabulary Strategies

Preteach Additional Vocabulary After teaching the Vocabulary words on Student Edition page 516, explain to students that there are several other important words they will see in this lesson. Use Procedure Card 1, along with the suggestions below, to introduce the words.

rejoin	Have students identify the word *join* and prefix *re-*, which means "again." Other words with this prefix include *rebuild*, *reconstruct*, and *regain*.
corrupt	Give *dishonest* as a synonym for *corrupt*. Related words include *corruption* and *corruptible*.
society	Tell students that one meaning of *society* is "an organized group with common interests or beliefs."
trade school	Explain that skilled occupations are sometimes called trades. A trade school teaches skills that prepare students for work in these occupations.

WORD CARDS To help teach the lesson vocabulary, use the Word Cards on pages 285–286.

Build Fluency

Use page 200 and the steps on Procedure Card 2 to reinforce vocabulary and build fluency. Read each vocabulary word aloud and have students repeat it. Then have students work in pairs to reread the words. Follow a similar procedure with the phrases and sentences. Continue to help students build fluency by having them reread "You Are There" in the Student Edition.

Text Comprehension

BEFORE READING

Preview the Lesson Guide students in previewing the lesson using Procedure Card 3. Point out the following features of the lesson on Student Edition pages 516–523.

- **Pages 516–517** Read the "What to Know" question, and have students recall conditions in much of the South when the Civil War ended. Preview the time line, the photograph of Lincoln's funeral procession, and the portrait of the new President, Andrew Johnson.
- **Pages 518–519** Preview the painting and the chart comparing Johnson's and Congress's plans for Reconstruction. Have students identify points on which Johnson and Congress agreed and disagreed. Then have students examine the Primary Sources feature and discuss the document-based question.
- **Pages 520–521** Preview the photographs, and discuss what they show about the lives of African Americans in the South during Reconstruction.

- **Pages 522–523** Preview the painting of African Americans leaving the South. On page 523, preview the photograph of the school, the portrait of Booker T. Washington, and the Review questions.

During Reading

Build Comprehension of Expository Text Present the graphic organizer on page 201. Have students preview the organizer by filling in the lesson title and comparing the four main heads in the organizer with the matching subheads in the Student Edition pages 516–523. Tell students that the section subheads provide additional help with identifying important information. Use Procedure Card 4, the Reading Check questions in *Harcourt Social Studies*, and the directed reading suggestions below.

- **Page 516** After students have read "You Are There," point out that the death of President Lincoln not only made people very sad but also brought about a change in government.
- **Pages 517–519** Have students read "Plans for Rebuilding" and fill in the first box in the organizer. Point out the subheads in the organizer that match the section subheads in the text. Follow the same procedure for the next section of the lesson, "Reconstruction Politics."
- **Pages 520–521** After students have read "Hard Times," have them write information in the next box in the organizer. Point out that the section subheads can help students locate information in the text.
- **Pages 522–523** Have students read "Reconstruction Ends" and complete the organizer.

After Reading

Summarize Have students use their completed graphic organizers to summarize the lesson. Then have them compare their summaries to the lesson summary on page 523.

Review and Respond Work through the Review questions with students. If students need additional help with generalizing, use Focus Skill Transparency 6.

Write a Summary In a discussion, have students identify and list on the board the main points of each plan. Encourage students to look back at the text to recall or confirm information. Remind students to include only the most important ideas in their summary paragraphs.

Leveled Readers Use the Leveled Readers and Procedure Card 5 to build fluency and comprehension.

Name ______________________________ Date ______________

DIRECTIONS **Read aloud the words in Part A. Practice reading aloud the phrases and the sentences in Part B.**

Part A

Vocabulary Words		Additional Words
Reconstruction	acquit	rejoin
sharecropping	freedmen	corrupt
black codes	segretation	society
secret ballot		trade school

Part B

1. President Andrew Johnson's plan for Reconstruction / allowed the Confederate states / to rejoin the Union / after they abolished slavery.
2. After the Southern state legislatures / went back to work, / they passed laws called black codes / to limit the rights of former enslaved people.
3. The House of Representatives / impeached President Johnson / because of disagreements over Reconstruction, / but he was acquitted.
4. Many freedmen / worked at sharecropping, / but most workers' shares / were very small.
5. Many Southerners / believed that their state governments / were corrupt / because of Reconstruction.
6. Not all states / had secret ballots, / so secret societies formed / to keep African Americans from voting / or to make sure / they only voted in certain ways.
7. Over time, / state governments passed laws / that established segregation.
8. In 1881, / Booker T. Washington / helped found the Tuskegee Institute, / a trade school / for African Americans in Alabama.

YOU ARE THERE **Turn to Student Edition page 516. Practice reading aloud "You Are There" three times. Try to improve your reading each time. Record your best time on the line below.**

Number of words 46 My Best Time ________ Words per Minute ________

Name ______________________ Date ____________

Lesson Title ______________________

Plans for Rebuilding

Lincoln's Plan

What he believed

____

Johnson's Plan

What the Thirteenth Amedment did

____

____

Reconstruction Politics

Congress's Plan

What they wanted

____

Impeachment Result

____

New Elections Result

____

Hard Times

The Freedmen's Bureau

What it did ______________________

____

____

Sharecropping

What workers did ______________________

____

What they got ______________________

____

Economic Troubles

Why ______________________

____

____

Reconstruction Ends

When it ended ______________________

Effect on African Americans

____

____

What African American leaders did

____

Lesson 2 The Last Frontier

Vocabulary Strategies

Preteach Additional Vocabulary After teaching the Vocabulary words on Student Edition page 524, explain to students that there are several other important words they will see in this lesson. Use Procedure Card 1, along with the suggestions below, to introduce the words.

sheriff	Tell students that a sheriff today is a county official who enforces laws. In frontier times in the West, it was often the job of the sheriff to keep order in a community.
decline	Give *decrease* and *weakening* as synonyms for *decline* in the phrase *economic decline.* Have students give antonyms, such as *increase*, *growth*, and *strengthening.*
cowhand	Discuss the various meanings students know for *hand*, including "worker," as in the compound words *farmhand* and *dockhand.* Then have students give the meaning of *cowhand.*
plot	Students are probably most familiar with the meaning of *plot* in literature. Explain that another meaning for plot is "a piece of land."
range	Ask whether students know the song "Home on the Range." Talk about the meaning of *range* as a large area of open land where cattle and other livestock can roam and graze.

WORD CARDS To help teach the lesson vocabulary, use the Word Cards on pages 285–286.

Build Fluency

Use page 204 and the steps on Procedure Card 2 to reinforce vocabulary and build fluency. Read each vocabulary word aloud and have students repeat it. Then have students work in pairs to reread the words. Follow a similar procedure with the phrases and sentences. Continue to help students build fluency by having them reread "You Are There" in the Student Edition.

Text Comprehension

Before Reading

Preview the Lesson Guide students in previewing the lesson using Procedure Card 3. Point out the following features of the lesson on Student Edition pages 524–529.

- **Pages 524–525** Read the "What to Know" question, and have students predict possible answers. Preview the time line and the photographs of a mining town and mining families.
- **Pages 526–527** Preview the painting of a cattle drive on page 526 and the photograph of a sod house on page 527. Discuss the reason that many homesteaders on the Great Plains built sod houses rather than houses of wood.
- **Pages 528–529** Preview the painting of the Battle of the Little Bighorn on page 528, and the photograph of Chief Joseph on page 529. Then preview the Review questions.

During Reading

Build Comprehension of Expository Text Present the graphic organizer on page 205. Have students preview the organizer by filling in the lesson title and comparing the three main heads in the organizer with the matching subheads in the Student Edition pages 524–529. Tell students that the section subheads provide additional help with identifying important information. Use Procedure Card 4, the Reading Check questions in *Harcourt Social Studies,* and the directed reading suggestions below.

- **Page 524** After students have read "You Are There," have them recall what they have learned about the California gold rush. Ask them to predict what may happen if people learn about the discovery of a gold nugget in South Dakota.
- **Page 525** Have students read "Western Mining" and fill in the first box in the organizer. Point out the subhead, and explain that the dates and places students will write in the organizer are found after this section subhead in the text. Point out that the cause and effect relationships refer specifically to effects on the economy.
- **Pages 526–527** After students have read "Life on the Frontier," have them write information in the next box in the organizer. Point out that the section subheads can help students locate information in the text.
- **Pages 528–529** Have students read "Western Conflict" and complete the organizer.

After Reading

Summarize Have students use their completed graphic organizers to summarize the lesson. Then have them compare their summaries to the lesson summary on page 529.

Review and Respond Work through the Review questions with students. If students need additional help with generalizing, use Focus Skill Transparency 6.

Prepare a Question List Have students brainstorm and categorize the kinds of information a person planning to become a homesteader in the 1860s might need. For example, information might be grouped under headings such as food, shelter, dangers, and so on. Students can refer to these categories as they write their lists of questions.

Leveled Readers Use the Leveled Readers and Procedure Card 5 to build fluency and comprehension.

Name ______________________________ Date ______________

DIRECTIONS **Read aloud the words in Part A. Practice reading aloud the phrases and the sentences in Part B.**

Part A

Vocabulary Words		Additional Words	
prospector	boom	sheriff	plot
homesteader	bust	decline	range
reservation		cowhand	

Part B

1. When gold or silver / was discovered in a place, / prospectors / moved into the area / and set up mining camps.
2. At first, / the mining towns / had no sheriffs, / so law and order / did not exist.
3. Business owners / set up stores / to meet the needs of miners, / causing a boom.
4. When the gold and silver deposits / ran out, / a bust, / or time of fast economic decline, / often followed.
5. Cattle ranchers / on the vast grasslands in Texas / needed skilled cowhands / to deliver their herds safely to the railroads.
6. After the Homestead Act of 1862 / opened the Great Plains to settlement, / homesteaders / rushed to claim these plots of land.
7. Disagreements between ranchers and farmers / over land use / sometimes led to fights / called range wars.
8. By 1880, / almost all Native Americans in the United States / lived on reservations.

YOU ARE THERE **Turn to Student Edition page 524. Practice reading aloud "You Are There" three times. Try to improve your reading each time. Record your best time on the line below.**

Number of words 52 My Best Time ________ Words per Minute ________

Name ______________________ Date ____________

Lesson Title ______________________

Western Mining

More Discoveries

When ____________ Where ____________

When ____________ Where ____________

CAUSE → **EFFECT ON ECONOMY**

Gold or silver discovered ____________

Gold or silver deposits ran out ____________

Life on the Frontier

Cattle Trails

Where to ____________

How cattle got there

____

Where meat was taken

____

Challenges on the Great Plains

When ________ Law ____________

Challenges ____________

____

Western Conflict

Native American Resistance

Why ____________

Final outcome ____________

UNIT 6

Chapter 13

Lesson 3 New Industries

Vocabulary Strategies

Preteach Additional Vocabulary After teaching the Vocabulary words on Student Edition page 530, explain to students that there are several other important words they will see in this lesson. Use Procedure Card 1, along with the suggestions below, to introduce the words.

blast	Discuss how tunnels are constructed. Explain that machines may be used to dig through soil and that workers also may use explosives, such as dynamite, to blast through rock.
ledge	Tell students that a rock ledge is a narrow flat surface on a rock wall that resembles a shelf. Have a volunteer draw a sketch on the board to show what a ledge looks like.
investor	Explain that an investor is someone who invests, or puts money into a company in the hope of making a profit. Point out the suffix *-or*. Other words with this suffix include *inventor*, *actor*, and *sailor*.
laboratory	Ask students to describe what goes on in a laboratory. Students should understand that scientific experiments, tests, and observations take place in laboratories.
patent	Provide examples of objects, such as a stapler or pencil sharpener, labeled with a patent number or patent pending. Discuss why and how inventors and manufacturers patent their products.

WORD CARDS To help teach the lesson vocabulary, use the Word Cards on pages 287–288.

Build Fluency

Use page 208 and the steps on Procedure Card 2 to reinforce vocabulary and build fluency. Read each vocabulary word aloud and have students repeat it. Then have students work in pairs to reread the words. Follow a similar procedure with the phrases and sentences. Continue to help students build fluency by having them reread "You Are There" in the Student Edition.

Text Comprehension

Before Reading

Preview the Lesson Guide students in previewing the lesson using Procedure Card 3. Point out the following features of the lesson on Student Edition pages 530–535.

- **Pages 530–531** Read the "What to Know" question, and have students recall what they learned in Chapter 11 about how new industries and inventions changed people's lives around the time of the Industrial Revolution. Preview the time line and the photograph. Have students read the Fast Fact and trace the route of the Transcontinental Railroad on the map.
- **Pages 532–533** Preview the illustrated time line of industries and inventions. Discuss how some of the events shown on this time line changed people's lives.

- **Pages 534–535** Have students read Children in History and discuss the Make It Relevant question. Preview the photograph of labor union members and the Review questions on page 535.

During Reading

Build Comprehension of Expository Text Present the graphic organizer on page 209. Have students preview the organizer by filling in the lesson title and comparing the three main heads in the organizer with the matching subheads in the Student Edition pages 530–535. Tell students that the section subheads provide additional help with identifying important information. Use Procedure Card 4, the Reading Check questions in *Harcourt Social Studies,* and the directed reading suggestions below.

- **Page 530** After students have read "You Are There," discuss why the joining of the two sets of railroad tracks was such an exciting event.
- **Page 531** Have students read "The Transcontinental Railroad" and fill in the first box in the organizer by writing an effect for each cause.
- **Pages 532–533** Before students read "Industries and Inventions," have them set a purpose for reading by looking at the organizer. Point out that they will need to write an effect for the cause that is stated before the first section subhead. Have students match the three subheads in the chart with the section subheads in the text. Explain that students will add names to the chart under each subhead and write a very brief summary of what each person did.
- **Pages 534–535** Have students read "Workers Struggle " and complete the organizer.

After Reading

Summarize Have students use their completed graphic organizers to summarize the lesson. Then have them compare their summaries to the lesson summary on page 535.

Review and Respond Work through the Review questions with students. If students need additional help with generalizing, use Focus Skill Transparency 6.

Create a Chart Discuss how the charts that students create may be similar to and different from the chart they completed in the graphic organizer. Emphasize that starting a new business or industry is not the same as inventing a new technology. Point out that the time line on pages 532–533 may also be helpful to students in deciding what to include in their charts of inventors and inventions.

Leveled Readers Use the Leveled Readers and Procedure Card 5 to build fluency and comprehension.

Name ______________________ Date ____________

DIRECTIONS **Read aloud the words in Part A. Practice reading aloud the phrases and the sentences in Part B.**

Part A

Vocabulary Words		Additional Words	
collective bargaining	labor union	blast	laboratory
transcontinental railroad	skyscraper	ledge	patent
	petroleum	investor	
	strike		

Part B

1. In 1862, / Congress gave two railroad companies / —the Union Pacific / and the Central Pacific / —the right to build a transcontinental railroad.
2. Workers blasted tunnels / and cut ledges / into the Sierra Nevada / and the Rocky Mountains.
3. After Andrew Carnegie / saw a new method / for making steel, / he found investors / to help him build a steel mill.
4. In the 1880s, / William Jenney / used steel frames / to build skyscrapers.
5. When kerosene, / a fuel made from petroleum, / became widely used for lighting lamps, / the demand for petroleum / increased sharply.
6. The team / that worked in Thomas Alva Edison's laboratory / patented about one invention / every five days.
7. In the late 1800s, / workers began to join labor unions / to fight for better working conditions / and pay.
8. Sometimes / unions organized strikes.
9. Samuel Gompers encouraged / the use of collective bargaining.

YOU ARE THERE **Turn to Student Edition page 530. Practice reading aloud "You Are There" three times. Try to improve your reading each time. Record your best time on the line below.**

Number of words 59 My Best Time ______ Words per Minute ______

Name ________________________ Date ____________

Lesson Title ________________________

The Transcontinental Railroad

Building the Railroad

CAUSE Two railroads met. → **EFFECT** ____________________

CAUSE More railroads built. → **EFFECT** ____________________

Industries and Inventions

CAUSE New inventions → **EFFECT** ____________________

The Steel Industry

WHO	WHAT HE DID

The Oil Industry

Inventions Change Lives

Workers Struggle

Labor Unions Fight for ____________________

How ____________________ and ____________________

LESSON 4

Cities and Immigration

Vocabulary Strategies

Preteach Additional Vocabulary After teaching the Vocabulary words on Student Edition page 538, explain to students that there are several other important words they will see in this lesson. Use Procedure Card 1, along with the suggestions below, to introduce the words.

poverty	Tell students that this word is from the Latin *pauper*, meaning "poor."
qualified	Discuss who is qualified to drive a car and how to become qualified as a teacher. Be sure students understand that being qualified means having the necessary training and experience.
exclusion	Have students use this context clue to first define *excluded* and then the related word *exclusion*: "In 1882, Congress passed the Chinese Exclusion Act. This law excluded, or kept out, all Chinese immigrants."
migration	Students may be familiar with this term from science. Explain that when people migrate, they move from one area to another. Point out the similarity to *immigration*. Explain that *im-* means "in," so immigration is moving into a new country.
ideal	Tell students that this word, often used as an adjective, can also be a noun, meaning "principle, belief, or value."

WORD CARDS To help teach the lesson vocabulary, use the Word Cards on pages 287–288.

Build Fluency

Use page 212 and the steps on Procedure Card 2 to reinforce vocabulary and build fluency. Read each vocabulary word aloud and have students repeat it. Then have students work in pairs to reread the words. Follow a similar procedure with the phrases and sentences. Continue to help students build fluency by having them reread "You Are There" in the Student Edition.

Text Comprehension

BEFORE READING

Preview the Lesson Guide students in previewing the lesson using Procedure Card 3. Point out the following features of the lesson on Student Edition pages 538–543.

- **Pages 538–539** Read the "What to Know" question, and have students predict some challenges they may read about. Preview the time line and the photographs. Ask students what the photograph of Mulberry Street in New York City shows about challenges that some immigrants faced.
- **Pages 540–541** Preview the photograph of Asian immigrants and the boycott sign on page 540, and discuss challenges these immigrants faced. Preview the photograph on page 541. Explain that great numbers of African Americans moved to northern cities to take jobs in factories.

- **Pages 542–543** Preview the photograph and the graph on page 542. Have students identify the bar on the graph that shows the number of immigrants from Asia between 1991 and 2000. Preview the Review questions. On page 543, call attention to the biography of Jane Addams, who helped immigrant families.

During Reading

Build Comprehension of Expository Text Present the graphic organizer on page 213. Have students preview the organizer by filling in the lesson title and comparing the three main heads in the organizer with the matching subheads in the Student Edition pages 538–542. Tell students that the section subheads provide additional help with identifying important information. Use Procedure Card 4, the Reading Check questions in *Harcourt Social Studies*, and the directed reading suggestions below.

- **Page 538** After students have read "You Are There," discuss why the day an immigrant family arrived in America might be a great day in their lives.
- **Page 539** Have students read "Many Immigrants Arrive" and fill in the first box in the organizer. Point out the subhead "New Immigrants" that matches the section subhead in the text.
- **Page 540** After students have read "Reactions to Immigration," have them write information in the next section of the organizer. Point out the subheads that can help students locate information.
- **Pages 541–542** Have students read "Migration and Immigration " and complete the organizer.

After Reading

Summarize Have students use their completed graphic organizers to summarize the lesson. Then have them compare their summaries to the lesson summary on page 542.

Review and Respond Work through the Review questions with students. If students need additional help with generalizing, use Focus Skill Transparency 6.

Write a Diary Entry Have students recall the reasons that immigrants came to America and what they hoped to find here. Encourage students to look back at the text to help them remember this information. Discuss the feelings that a child might have coming to a new life in a new land, and remind students to write their diary entries from the child's point of view.

Leveled Readers Use the Leveled Readers and Procedure Card 5 to build fluency and comprehension.

Name ______________________________ Date ______________

DIRECTIONS **Read aloud the words in Part A. Practice reading aloud the phrases and the sentences in Part B.**

Part A

Vocabulary Words	Additional Words
tenement	poverty
reformer	qualified
settlement house	exclusion
	migration
	ideal

Part B

1. People / often came to the United States / to escape violence / and poverty.
2. Many lived in tenements / and struggled to find jobs / and learn English.
3. Some Americans / felt that because some immigrants / had little education, / they were not qualified/ to take part in a democracy.
4. In 1882, / Congress passed / the Chinese Exclusion Act, / which prevented any Chinese immigrants / from coming to the United States / for ten years.
5. Jane Addams and Lillian Wald / were reformers / who started settlement houses / to help immigrants.
6. Between 1910 and 1930, / so many African Americans / moved to northern cities / that this movement became known as / the Great Migration.
7. Although Americans / are different from one another, / they are united / by basic American ideals / —freedom, / opportunity, / and a belief in individual rights.

Turn to Student Edition page 538. Practice reading aloud "You Are There" three times. Try to improve your reading each time. Record your best time on the line below.

Number of words ___68___ My Best Time ________ Words per Minute ________

Name ______________________ Date ______________

Lesson Title: ______________________

Many Immigrants Arrive

When ______________ How many ______________

What they hoped for ______________________

New Immigrants

Where European immigrants arrived ______________

Challenges ______________________

____

Where Asian immigrants arrived ______________

Reactions to Immigration

Unfair Treatment Year ______________ Law ______________

Help for Immigrants Problems ______________________

Who helped ______________________

What they did ______________________

____

Migration and Immigration

African Americans Migrate When ______________________

To where ______________ Name of movement ______________

What many found ______________________

Immigration Today Where most are from ______________________

What unites Americans ______________________

Teacher Notes

Procedure Card  Vocabulary: Side A

Use the following steps to introduce the Additional Words in each lesson.

1. Write the word on the board or on chart paper.
2. Say the word aloud.
3. Track the word and have students repeat it.
4. Give the meaning of the word or context that makes the meaning clear. For example, you might
   - demonstrate or dramatize the meaning
   - point out meanings of roots, root words, prefixes, and suffixes
   - point out endings such as *-ed* and *-ing*
   - give examples
   - give synonyms or antonyms
   - relate to familiar concepts
   - draw a sketch or display a picture

Suggested Vocabulary Activities Use or adapt the following activities to give students further practice using Vocabulary Words and Additional Words.

FRAYER MODEL

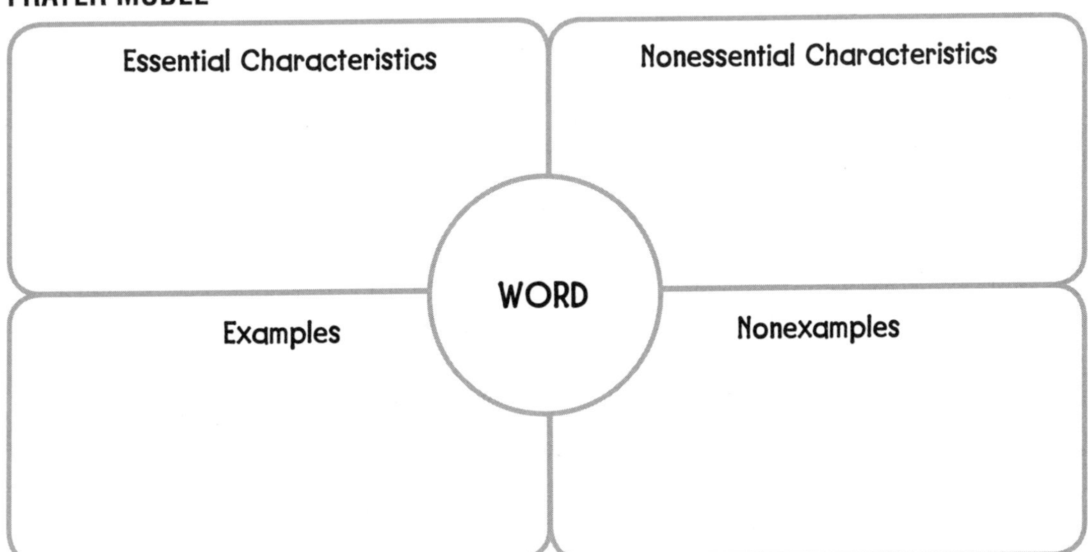

(continued)

Procedure Card 1 Vocabulary: Side B

Semantic Mapping

Category

Category

Major Concept

Category

Verbal and Visual Word Association

Vocabulary Term	Visual Representation
Definition	Personal Association or Characteristic

Word Sorts

Category 1	Category 2	Category 3

Procedure Card 2 Build Fluency: Side A

Use the following steps to help students build fluency.

Vocabulary Words

1. Read each vocabulary word aloud and have students repeat it.
2. Then have students work in pairs to read the vocabulary words aloud to each other.
3. Follow the same procedure with the additional words.
4. After partners have practiced reading aloud the words in each list by themselves, have them listen to each other as they practice the entire list.

Sentences

1. Read each sentence aloud and have students repeat it. As you read, model natural phrasing (intonation and rhythm), pacing, and tone.
2. Then read the sentences aloud as a coherent text. Point out that the sentences read together give a preview of the content of the lesson.
3. Have students practice reading the phrases and sentences with a partner. When the partners are satisfied with their progress, have them practice reading the sentences as a text several times.

(continued)

Procedure Card  Build Fluency: Side B

Help students continue to build fluency by having them do oral rereadings of "You Are There" in the Student Edition. Provide them with a stopwatch to time themselves on each reading.

Choose from the following options for the repeated readings.

- Students read the passage aloud to their partners three times. The reader rates his or her own reading on a scale of 1–4. The partner offers positive comments on the reader's improvement.
- Students read the passage aloud to themselves three times and rate their own reading on a scale of 1–4. Encourage students to note ways in which they have improved from one reading to the next.
- Students read the passage aloud into a tape recorder three times. After they listen to each reading, they rate the reading on a scale of 1–4. Then they listen to previous readings and compare to note improvements.

Procedure Card 3 Text Comprehension: Preview

Use the following steps to preview the lesson with students.

1. Read aloud the title of the lesson.
2. Have students look over each page. Call attention to text features such as the following:
   - the "What to Know" question
   - time lines
   - subheads
   - illustrations and captions
   - maps, charts, graphs, and other visual aids
   - features such as Primary Sources and Children in History
   - words that are highlighted in the text
   - Review questions
3. Discuss each text feature as needed to help students understand how it relates to the topic of the lesson.
4. Work with students to set a purpose for reading the first section of the lesson by turning the first subhead into a question. Remind them to use this strategy as they read each section of the lesson.

Procedure Card 4 Text Comprehension: Expository Text

Choose from the following options to have students read the text and complete the graphic organizer.

Reading the Text

- Have students read the lesson silently to themselves.
- Have students read together in pairs. Where possible, pair a struggling reader with a more proficient reader. Partners may take turns reading sections of the lesson aloud to each other.
- Have students read in pairs. Partners read together silently, pausing often to discuss and summarize what they have read so far.
- Have students take turns reading sections of the lesson aloud to the group.

Completing the Graphic Organizer

- If students are reading in pairs, they may work with their partners to complete the graphic organizer.
- If students are not reading in pairs, you may want to assign partners for the purpose of completing the graphic organizer.

Leveled Readers

Before Reading

1. Build background by talking about the topic of the book.
2. Discuss the cover illustration. Have children track the print as you read the title and the name of the author.
3. Preview the book by discussing the first few illustrations. Ask children what they think the book is about.
4. Help children set a purpose for reading.

During Reading

1. Have children read one or two pages at a time. If necessary, read the pages aloud as children follow along.
2. Ask questions about each page or set of pages to check children's comprehension.
3. Define any unfamiliar words, using illustrations, gestures, or context sentences.
4. Occasionally ask children to summarize or retell what they have read so far.

After Reading

1. Discuss what children liked about the book. Then guide them to summarize or retell the selection.
2. Have children respond to the book through discussion, drama, art, writing, or another appropriate activity.

Student Card  KWL Strategy

You can use a KWL chart to guide your reading. Follow the steps.

Step 1. Before you read the lesson, make a KWL chart like this one.

K What we know	W What we want to find out	L What we learned

Step 2. Read the title of the lesson. Discuss with your partner or group what you already know about the topic of this lesson. For instance, you may have information from previous social studies chapters or from other sources.

Step 3. Record the information you already know in the K column of the chart. Keep in mind that sometimes information that we think we know may turn out to be incorrect. As you read the lesson, look back at the K column to check whether each fact you listed is correct.

Step 4. Preview the lesson by reading the subheads and looking at time lines, maps, illustrations, and other special features. Discuss what you want to find out when you read the lesson. One way to do this is by asking questions about the subheads. Record your questions in the W column of the chart.

Step 5. Read the lesson. As you find information to answer your questions, record the answers in the L column of the chart.

Step 6. Use your completed KWL chart to review and summarize the lesson.

Student Card 2 SQ3R Strategy

You can use the SQ3R strategy to guide your reading. The letters SQRRR stand for the steps in the process—Survey, Question, Read, Recite, and Review.

Step 1. Survey

- Read the title of the lesson. Ask yourself what you know about the topic and what you want to find out about it.
- Read the lesson subheads and skim the first sentences of sections or paragraphs.
- Look over illustrations, maps, graphic aids, and special features.
- Read the first paragraph of the lesson.
- Read the lesson summary.

Step 2. Question

- Set your main purpose for reading by turning the title of the lesson into a question.
- Write down questions you thought of during your survey.
- Set a purpose for reading each section of the lesson by turning each subhead into a question.
- Ask yourself questions about illustrations, graphic aids, and special features.
- Write down unfamiliar words and find out what they mean.

Step 3. Read

- Read to find answers to your questions.
- Use the answers to your questions to be sure you understand each section of the lesson.
- If there are ideas or words that you don't understand, ask yourself more questions.

(continued)

Student Card 2 SQ3R Strategy

Step 4. RECITE

- Look away from the book and your questions to recall what you have read.
- Recite the answers to your questions aloud or write them down.
- Reread the lesson to find answers to questions that you have not already answered.

Step 5. REVIEW

- Answer the main purpose question that you formed from the lesson title.
- Look over the answers to the questions formed from the subheads and any other questions you had.
- Summarize the lesson by creating a graphic organizer, discussing the lesson with your partner or group, or writing a summary.

Student Card 3 QAR Strategy

What is QAR? The letters QAR stand for Question-Answer Relationship. You can use the QAR strategy to help you answer questions as you read and the Review questions at the end of each lesson.

Step 1. Read the information in the chart to learn about the four types of questions.

Question-Answer Relationships (QAR)

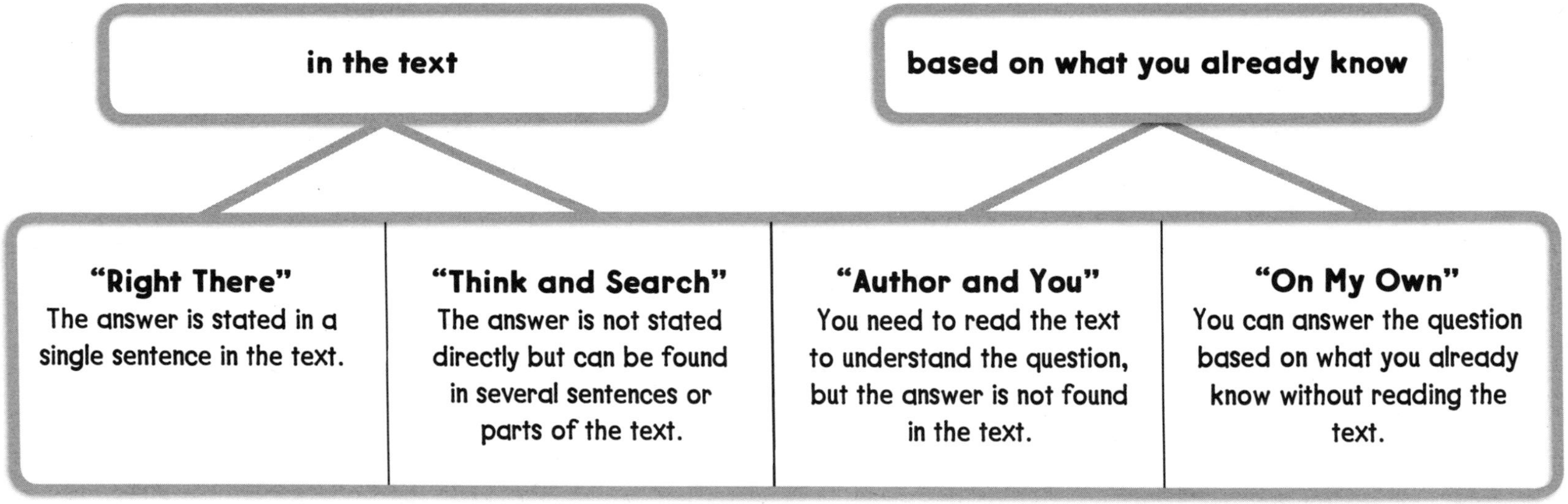

in the text		based on what you already know	
"Right There" The answer is stated in a single sentence in the text.	**"Think and Search"** The answer is not stated directly but can be found in several sentences or parts of the text.	**"Author and You"** You need to read the text to understand the question, but the answer is not found in the text.	**"On My Own"** You can answer the question based on what you already know without reading the text.

Step 2. Before you answer a question, identify which type of question it is. Decide what you will need to do in order to answer the question.

Step 3. Use the text, what you already know, or both to answer the question.

Build Fluency Words per Minute Formula

Use the following formula to calculate words per minute:

1. Count the words in the passage.
2. Record the student's reading time in seconds.
3. Divide the number of words by the number of seconds.
4. Multiply (number of words per second) by 60 to convert to words per minute.

Here is an example:

1. 90 words (in the passage)
2. 75 seconds (student's reading time)
3. 90 ÷ 75 = 1.2 (words per second)
4. 1.2 x 60 = 72 words per minute

Answer Key

Chapter 1

Lesson 1 States and Regions, p. 5

A Nation of 50 States 48; Alaska; Hawaii; West, Southwest, Midwest, Southeast, Northeast; kinds of land, how people earn their living, history, culture

A Country in North America both explored by the French and the British, were once under British rule; settlers came from Spain to Mexico and southwestern United States

Lesson 2 The Land, p. 9

Landform Regions because of the shape of its landforms; the United States

The Coastal Plain flat, low land; wider; south

The Appalachians the Piedmont; valleys and hills; from southern Canada to central Alabama; peaks worn down, highest about 7,000 feet

The Interior Plains Central Plains; tall-grass prairie; flat, few rivers, almost no trees

The Rocky Mountains and Beyond western; sharp, jagged peaks; the Great Basin

More Mountains and Valleys Sierra Nevada, Cascade Range, Coast Ranges; San Francisco

Lesson 3 Bodies of Water, p. 13

Inlets and Lakes Gulf of Mexico, Gulf of Alaska; harbors where ships can safely dock; the Great Lakes; five; the Midwest and the Atlantic Ocean

Rivers the Mississippi River and its tributaries

Rivers in the East where rivers flow into oceans; inland along the Fall Line; to make electricity

Rivers in the West the Atlantic Ocean; into the Pacific Ocean

Lesson 4 Climate and Vegetation, p. 17

Climate distance from the equator; distance from oceans and other large bodies of water; elevation; changes in seasons; different amounts of sunlight and heat at different times of the year

Vegetation soil; temperature; precipitation; forest; trees; grassland; grasses; desert; short grasses, low bushes, cactuses; tundra; mosses, herbs, low shrubs

Lesson 5 People and the Environment, p. 21

Patterns of Land Use physical features, such as climate, water, and landforms; desert, tundra, or mountainous regions; People use tools and inventions to live in those areas.

Using the Land farming; mining; cities with human features; renewable resources; nonrenewable resources; limited

Changing the Environment wells, dams, irrigation systems, modifying waterways; cut down trees, dig oil wells, build mines, plow land; by using natural resources carefully

Chapter 2

Lesson 1 Early People, p. 25

The Land Bridge Story Early people crossed a bridge of land from Asia to North America.

Other Theories recent discoveries; their people have always lived in the Americas

Early Ways of Life from hunting animals to farming and settling in one place; because climate became warmer and drier, and giant animals died out

The Olmec and the Maya strong trade system, systems of writing and counting, calendar; influenced by Olmec traditions, writing and counting system, social classes, built stone cities

Other Civilizations Mound Builders; large earth mounds; Ancient Puebloans; had many levels, often built against canyon walls or in caves

Lesson 2 The Eastern Woodlands, p. 29

Life in the Eastern Woodlands canoes, shelters, tools, weapons, food

The Iroquois near the Great Lakes; Iroquoian; on top of steep hills; longhouses; corn, beans, and squash; Iroquois League, Council to settle disputes

The Algonquians Coastal Plain or near Great Lakes; Algonquian; most groups had 1 to 20; longhouses or wigwams; crops, fish; leaders governed more than one village, some groups had two chiefs

Lesson 3 The Plains, p. 33

Life on the Plains (meat) raw, cooked, pemmican; (skins) clothing, moccasins, shelter, shields, drums; (hair) cord; (bones) tools, arrowheads, pipes; (stomach) bags to carry water; (hooves) glue; (horns) cups, spoons, tools

Farmers and Hunters beans, corn, sunflowers; deer, elk, buffalo

A Nomadic Society tepee; travois

Plains Cultures Cheyenne sent leaders to council of chiefs, every person equal; many groups shared traditions and beliefs, ceremonies to celebrate and give thanks

Lesson 4 The Southwest and the West, p. 37

The Southwest mesas, canyons, cliffs, mountains; corn, beans, squash; cotton; blankets and clothing

Pueblo Culture the desert environment; trade; medicine people; religion

Groups to the West Shoshone; hunted in Great Basin and mountains; Nez Perce; fished for salmon; Chumash; lived near Pacific Ocean; trade networks; to get goods from faraway places

Lesson 5 The Northwest and the Arctic, p. 41

A Region of Plenty forests and rivers; Kwakiutl, Makah, Chinook; coastal waters, salmon, whales

Resource and Trade giant trees; longhouses, all members of a clan; center of trade network, the Chinook; a celebration to show wealth

Lands of the North the Aleut; the Inuit; foxes, caribou, polar bears, seals, walruses, whales; beams of whalebone and walls of sod, igloos, tents of animal skin, sod houses; south of the Arctic; Cree; hunting, trees; long winters

Chapter 3

Lesson 1 Exploration and Technology, p. 45

A Rush of New Ideas 1400s; the Renaissance; to buy and resell Asian goods; did not have correct maps or technology

The World Awaits Prince Henry of Portugal; opened a school of navigation; better ships, maps, and navigational tools, made ocean exploration possible

The Business of Exploring Christopher Columbus; sail west to Asia; money for a ship, crew, and supplies; king and queen of Spain agreed to help him

Two Worlds Meet an island in the Caribbean Sea; Asia; treated like heroes

Lesson 2 A Changing World, p. 49

England Explores John Cabot (Giovanni Caboto); 1497; Asia; the coast of present-day Newfoundland and Labrador

A New Map of the World Amerigo Vespucci; coast of South America; had found lands not yet known to Europeans; South America and North America

Reaching the Pacific Vasco Núñez de Balboa; 1513; crossed the Isthmus of Panama and reached the Pacific Ocean

A New View of the World Ferdinand Magellan; Pacific Ocean; the first Europeans to travel around the world; Spain and Portugal

Lesson 3 Spanish Explorations, p. 53

The Spanish Explore Florida Ponce de León; Bimini, Fountain of Youth; landed in what is now Florida, claimed it for Spain

Early Conquistadors to find gold in the land of the Aztecs; conquered the Aztecs and built Mexico City; to find golden cities; explored lands in what is now the south-western United States, claimed lands for Spain

Expeditions Continue took control of the Inca Empire in Peru; explored the southeastern United States, claimed land for Spain

Missionaries to America the Reformation and Counter-Reformation; to gain new followers, to share in the wealth of the lands claimed by European countries, to convert Native Americans to the Catholic Church

Lesson 4 Other Nations Explore, p. 57

The Northwest Passage a shortcut to Asia; to gain wealth and power

Verrazano and Cartier met Native Americans, searched the coastlines of North America and South America; a passage; claimed land around St. Lawrence River for France, went as far as what is now Montreal; the Northwest Passage

Hudson's Voyages Henry Hudson; four; sailed through the Arctic Ocean, claimed Hudson River valley for the Dutch; claimed land around Hudson Bay for England; the Northwest Passage

Chapter 4

Lesson 1 The Spanish Colonies, p. 61

New Spain Spain formed colonies.

Slavery in the Americas They forced Native Americans into slavery. Many Native Americans died from hunger, work, and diseases.

Settling the Borderlands Spanish soldiers built presidios. Missionaries built missions. Settlers built haciendas.

Lesson 2 The Virginia Colony, p. 65

England Attempts a Colony 1584; Roanoke Island; ran low on food and returned to England; 1587; still a mystery, known as the Lost Colony; early 1600s; group of English merchants; to try again to start a colony in Virginia

Jamestown Captain John Smith; colonists had no interest in farming, but Smith made them plant crops; trouble between the Powhatan and colonists

Growth and Government John Rolfe; tobacco; indentured servants, Africans; 1619; Virginia's legislature; fighting between colonists and Powhatan, Virginia made a royal colony

Lesson 3 The Plymouth Colony, p. 69

The Pilgrims' Journey Pilgrims; North America; 1620, the *Mayflower*

The Mayflower Compact that fair laws would be made for the good of the colony; self-government and majority rule

Building a Colony Tisquantum; showed them where to fish and how to plant squash, corn, and pumpkins; helped them trade with neighboring tribes

Plymouth Grows from farming, fishing, and fur trading; after 1630; new colonists not friendly to Native Americans, settled on more of their lands

Lesson 4 The French and the Dutch, p. 73

New France wealth from the fur trade; start colonies in North America; Quebec; Champlain; 1608; slowly

New Netherland along Hudson River, parts of what are now New York and New Jersey; to profit from the fur trade; Manhattan Island; New Amsterdam; trade; many colonists and Native Americans killed, Algonquian almost wiped out

Exploring New France Marquette; Joliet; Mississippi River; La Salle; Mississippi River valley; France; Louisiana; settlement failed

Louisiana proprietary colony; 1712; New Orleans; failed to attract many people

Chapter 5

Lesson 1 Settling New England, p. 77

The Puritans Arrive John Winthrop; Massachusetts Bay Colony; along the Atlantic coast; to make it easier to get supplies from English trading ships

New Ideas, New Settlements Roger Williams; Providence; the consent of the people and cooperation with Native Americans; Anne Hutchinson; Providence; the colony of Rhode Island

New England Grows to find better farmland; because of their beliefs; Connecticut; looking for economic opportunities; New Hampshire

Growth Brings Conflict colonists and Native Americans; land; Pequot War; 1630s; King Philip's War; 1675; colonists moved onto lands that Native Americans had to give up

Lesson 2 Life in New England, p. 81

A Religious Life based on their religious beliefs; everyone had to attend, lasted most of the day

Everyday Life common; barter; voted on laws and elected leaders; cooking done in fireplace in main room, children helped adults with all kinds of work

Childhood in New England one room and one teacher, very strict; main subject, used a hornbook

Lesson 3 New England's Economy, p. 85

New England Farming surplus farm goods; free-market economy

Logging and Shipbuilding lumber; naval stores; shipbuilding

Colonial Trade trading; fishing and whaling

Triangular Trade Routes England; English colonies; Africa

Chapter 6

Lesson 1 Settling the Middle Colonies, p. 89

The Breadbasket Colonies good land for farming; good climate; large harbors; deep waterways; wheat, corn, rye

New Netherland Grows Peter Stuyvesant; 1647; expanded New Netherland; from Belgium, Denmark, France, Italy, Spain, Brazil, enslaved African, and free Africans

The English Take Over to control the Atlantic coast of North America; English took control without firing a shot

New York and New Jersey New York City; Quakers

Pennsylvania and Delaware William Penn; with justice

Lesson 2 Life in the Middle Colonies, p. 93

A Mix of People to escape war; religious freedom; better economic opportunities; more freedom than they had ever known

The Great Awakening a new religious movement; helped bring people together; greater religious toleration; equal participation; diversity of religious beliefs; more church members; free exercise of religion

Religion and Social Life religion; dances, plays, concerts, social clubs, horse races, sleigh rides, ice-skating, barn raising

Philadelphia Grows William Penn; ten houses; more than 28,000 people; Benjamin Franklin; printer, writer, scientist, inventor, leader in the colony's government

Lesson 3 Busy Farms and Seaports, p. 97

Rich Farmlands fertile soil; by farming; livestock and crops

Port Cities the colonies' prosperity; New York City; Philadelphia; England or English colonies

Colonial Jobs skilled trades; raw materials; by becoming apprentices

Chapter 7

Lesson 1 Settling the South, p. 101

Maryland the Calverts; to make money; a refuge for Catholics

Life in Maryland and Virginia mild; fertile; tobacco; governments; Toleration Act

The Carolina Colonies North Carolina; South Carolina; tobacco and corn; rice; enslaved people

Georgia James Oglethorpe; English debtors; plantations; labor of enslaved Africans

Heading West by the mid-1700s; backcountry in the Piedmont; the Great Wagon Road

Conflicts with Native Americans many killed, captured, died from diseases, forced to move west

Lesson 2 Life in the South, p. 105

Slavery and Society their owners; told stories and sang songs about Africa

A Farming Economy plantations; cash crops produced by enslaved workers; small villages; own enslaved people

Free Africans buy their freedom and start farms; in Spanish Florida; runaways who dressed like the Seminole and learned their language; a settlement for free Africans

Lesson 3 The Southern Economy, p. 109

Cash Crops tobacco; Maryland, Virginia, northern North Carolina; rice; southern North Carolina, South Carolina, Georgia; indigo; on drier land throughout South Carolina

The Economy Grows through a broker; on rivers or near ports; made it easier to ship crops; a major center for shipbuilding; forests; naval stores

Chapter 8

Lesson 1 Fighting for Control, p. 113

Conflicting Claims the Ohio Valley; both Britain and France; sent soldiers and built forts; to fight back

The French and Indian War Begins France and Britain with Native American tribes in the Ohio Valley; 1754; Albany, New York; colonial leaders; how to deal with the French forces; 1754; Fort Necessity

The War Expands 1763; most of Canada, all French lands east of the Mississippi River, and Spanish Florida

More Troubles colonists did not like British telling them to stay out of frontier lands; colonists angry about new taxes

Lesson 2 Colonists Speak Out, p. 117

The Stamp Act 1765; tax on paper documents in the colonies; no taxation without representation

Colonists Work Together to force Britain to take back the Stamp Act; the Sons and Daughters of Liberty; Parliament voted to repeal the Stamp Act; Committees of Correspondence; to spread information more quickly; to protest British policies

The Townshend Acts 1767; taxes on imports to the colonies; boycotted British goods; repealed all except tax on tea, sent more soldiers to the colonies

The Boston Massacre March 5, 1770; Some colonists were killed in a fight with British soldiers.

Lesson 3 Disagreements Grow, p. 121

The Boston Tea Party December 16, 1773; to protest the Tea Act; Sons of Liberty; boarded British ships in Boston Harbor and threw tea overboard

The Coercive Acts March 1774; new laws passed by Parliament; to punish Massachusetts colonists; against Britain

The First Continental Congress September 1774; Philadelphia; colonial leaders; sent a petition to the king; voted to stop most trade with Britain; asked the colonies to form militias

Lexington and Concord April 1775; fighting between Minutemen and British soldiers, beginning of the American Revolution

Lesson 4 The Road to War, p. 125

The Second Continental Congress May 10, 1775; Pennsylvania State House in Philadelphia; formed the Continental Army; chose George Washington as commander in chief; asked each colony to give money; printed its own paper money

The Battle of Bunker Hill June 17, 1775; Breed's Hill; Israel Putnam and William Prescott; The British won the battle but suffered heavy losses.

Trying for Peace July 15, 1775; Congress sent Olive Branch Petition to King George, but he promised to crush the rebellion.

Lesson 5 Declaring Independence, p. 129

Moving Toward Independence Common Sense; Thomas Paine; independence; a resolution of independence

The Declaration of Independence rights; grievances; free and independent

Congress Approves the Declaration July 4, 1776; members of the Second Continental Congress; freedom; equal rights

Forming a New Government John Dickinson; Articles of Confederation; the Confederation Congress; left most power with the states, limited power of national government

Chapter 9

Lesson 1 Americans and the Revolution, p. 133

Personal Hardships People faced hardships from taking sides and from British soldiers robbing and destroying towns.

Economic Hardships Problems included a shortage of imported goods, inflation, and profiteering.

Women and the War Women took on new roles in battle and at home.

African Americans, Free and Enslaved Many African Americans fought for the Continental Army, while others fought for the British to win their freedom.

People in the West Native Americans were divided, while many settlers wanted to help drive the British out.

Lesson 2 Fighting for Independence, p. 137

Comparing Armies no uniforms; many had no guns; most had no military training; needed a lot of supplies; experienced soldiers; 50,000 soldiers in the colonies; used mercenaries; long wait for supplies

Early Battles in the North Long Island; British won; Trenton; American victory

An Important Victory Saratoga; a turning point in the war

Winter at Valley Forge soldiers a ragged group, food running low; Lafayette; von Steuben

Contributions from Other Nations The French agreed to help the Americans. Bernardo de Gálvez gave guns, food, money, and helped fight. The Netherlands gave a loan to Congress. Russian leaders tried to keep the British from blocking trade.

Lesson 3 Winning Independence, p. 141

Revolutionary Heroes Nathan Hale; served as an American spy; John Paul Jones; battled larger British ships; Mary Ludwig Hays McCauley; carried water to soldiers and loaded cannons; Tadeusz Kosciuszko; helped design fort at West Point

The War Moves Savannah, Georgia; British victory; Charles Town, South Carolina; British victory; Cowpens, South Carolina; major American victory; Guilford Courthouse, North Carolina; British won but weakened

The War Ends October 19, 1781; General Cornwallis surrendered at Yorktown, Virginia, after being surrounded for weeks. September 3, 1783; named the United States of America as a new nation, set borders; George Washington retired.

Lesson 4 Effects of the War, p. 145

New Ideas began to write their own constitutions; that each person had the right to life and liberty; that slavery should be ended

Western Settlements more land; former soldiers and other settlers; Native Americans; south of the Ohio River

The Northwest Territory north of the Ohio River; 1785; ordinance about dividing land; 1787; Northwest Ordinance passed

Battles for Land Native Americans and new settlers; Native Americans gave up or sold most of their lands.

Chapter 10

Lesson 1 The Constitutional Convention, p. 149

Reasons for Change that the national government could not keep order or protect them; May 1787; to fix the Articles

The Work Begins needed a new Constitution; strengthen the existing federal system; American republic

A Major Debate how each state would be represented in the new Congress; state's population; equally represented

Working Together the population of each state; each state equally represented

Compromises on Slavery southern states and northern states; agreed to count three-fifths of the total number of slaves; 1808

Lesson 2 Three Branches of Government, p. 153

The Preamble We the People of the United States; to create a fairer form of government; individual liberty, other personal freedoms, justice, peace

The Legislative Branch to keep any one branch from controlling the government; House of Representatives; Senate

The Executive Branch President; veto bills passed by Congress; commander in chief of the military; "take care that the laws be faithfully executed"

The Judicial Branch federal court system; the Supreme Court; strike down any law that goes against the Constitution; amendments

Lesson 3 The Bill of Rights, p. 157

The Struggle to Ratify to limit the power of the federal government; to protect people's individual rights; to propose a bill of rights after the Constitution was ratified

The Vote of Approval Delaware; a strong federal government; that the national government would have too much power; June 21, 1788

The Bill of Rights ten; to protect the rights of the people; 1791; the states or the people

The New Government George Washington; 1789; Washington, D.C.; 1800; John Adams

Lesson 4 A Constitutional Government, p. 161

Sharing Powers among the legislative, executive, and judicial branches; to keep the federal government from becoming too powerful

Checks and Balances keeps any one branch from becoming too powerful or misusing its authority; ways to check the powers of the others

State Powers any powers not clearly given to the federal government or denied to the states

State and Local Governments federal, state, and local; collect taxes to pay for government services

Rights and Responsibilities from the people; voting

Being a Citizen to act with civic virtue, to help control the government

Chapter 11

Lesson 1 Exploring the West, p. 165

Immigrants and Pioneers to escape hard times, earn money, own land; the Wilderness Road

Americans Continue West Kentucky; Tennessee; Ohio

The Louisiana Purchase Thomas Jefferson; no ports on Gulf of Mexico; April 30, 1803; more than doubled the size of the United States

Lewis and Clark St. Louis, Missouri; May 1804; the Pacific Ocean; November 1805; added to the knowledge about the lands that became the West

Pike in the Southwest that people in Spanish territories needed manufactured goods; American traders traveled there to sell goods.

Lesson 2 Expanding Borders, p. 169

Troubles Grow on lands that belonged to Native Americans; fight the Americans; impressment of American sailors

The War of 1812 Battle of Lake Erie, Battle of the Thames; 1814, Washington, D.C. and Baltimore, Francis Scott Key wrote "The Star-Spangled Banner"; 1823; the Monroe Doctrine

Extending Democracy all white American men; Andrew Jackson; Jacksonian Democracy

The Indian Removal Act to take Cherokee lands; 1838; Cherokee and others had to walk about 800 miles to Indian Territory

Lesson 3 From Ocean to Ocean, p. 173

Texas Independence Mexican government raising taxes; 1836; the Mexicans

The Lone Star Republic April 21, 1836; Texans attacked, captured Santa Anna; Texas granted independence

Trails West Missouri; the Oregon Country; covered wagons, wagon trains; Brigham Young; Illinois; Great Salt Lake valley

Expanding Borders treaty that set Oregon Country border; dispute over border; Treaty of Guadalupe Hidalgo with Mexico; Mexican Cession; Gadsden Purchase

The California Gold Rush other parts of United States and the world; population growth, became a state

Lesson 4 New Ideas and Inventions, p. 177

Transportation National Road; the Appalachians; Erie Canal; Great Lakes and Atlantic; made it a center of trade

Steamboats and Railroads the main form of travel on large rivers; made it easier for people to travel and ship goods

The Industrial Revolution 1800s; a change to using machines for manufacturing large quantities of goods; Samuel Slater; built the first American textile mill; the beginning of large-scale manufacturing in the United States

More Inventions Eli Whitney; cotton gin; changed plantation farming; interchangeable parts for guns; mass production; Cyrus McCormick; mechanical reaper; John Deere; strong steel plow

Chapter 12

Lesson 1 The North and the South, p. 181

Different Regions small farms, slavery abolished, diverse economy, new industries; plantations, system of slavery

Division Over Slavery 1819; Missouri wanted to join the Union as a slave state; Henry Clay; number of free states and slave states remained equal

Different Ideas tariff helped North but hurt South; whether states or national government should have final say

More Divisions new lands not covered by Missouri Compromise; Fugitive Slave Act; law was very unpopular; fighting between groups for and against slavery; Kansas joined Union as a free state

Lesson 2 Resisting Slavery, p. 185

The Dred Scott Decision to try to win his freedom; that enslaved people were property; made disagreements over slavery worse

Challenging Slavery Samuel Cornish and John Russwurm; started a newspaper called *Freedom's Journal;* William Lloyd Garrison; founded the American Antislavery Society; Frederick Douglass; writings and speeches against slavery; Sojourner Truth; traveled the country speaking out against slavery; Elizabeth Cady Stanton and Lucretia Mott; called for equality for all Americans; Harriet Beecher Stowe; wrote a book about slavery; a system of secret escape routes to free lands; Harriet Tubman; slave catchers

Lesson 3 The Nation Divides, p. 189

Abraham Lincoln Illinois legislature; United States Congress; fight the spread of slavery; the Republican Party; made Lincoln well known

Events Further Divide the Nation divided the nation even more; slavery; they would secede if Lincoln was elected; Lincoln

The Nation Separates seceded from the Union; the Confederate States of America; torn between the two sides

Fort Sumter April 12, 1861; Confederate troops fired at the fort; divided the country, divided states, sometimes divided families

Lesson 4 The War Begins, p. 193

War Plans Anaconda Plan, blockade to weaken South, then invade; defend its lands, make the war last a long time

Early Battles first major battle, a confusing battle, Confederates won; many killed, neither side won a clear victory

The Emancipation Proclamation issued by President Lincoln, said that all enslaved people in areas still fighting against the Union were free

Americans At War took over factory, business, and farm jobs, also worked as nurses and even served as spies; about 180,000 served in Union army, led raids, served as spies and scouts, fought in major battles

Lesson 5 Toward a Union Victory, p. 197

Two Major Battles Ulysses S. Grant; major victory for the Union; victory for Confederacy

Union Victories July 1863; three days; Union victory, turning point in the war; November 19, 1863; President Lincoln; one of the most famous speeches in American history; September 1864; General William Tecumseh Sherman; Sherman's army cut a path of destruction through Georgia

The War Ends April 9, 1865; Lee surrendered to Grant, ending the war; many soldiers died, South in ruins, Lincoln assassinated five days after war ended

Chapter 13

Lesson 1 Reconstruction, p. 201

Plans for Rebuilding the South should not be punished; ended slavery everywhere in the nation

Reconstruction Politics to punish the South; Johnson was acquitted; African Americans elected

Hard Times gave food and supplies, built schools; farmed land owned by someone else; a cabin, mules, tools, seed; bridges, buildings, and railroads had been destroyed

Reconstruction Ends 1877; lost many of the rights they had gained; continued to work to help

Lesson 2 The Last Frontier, p. 205

Western Mining 1859; Comstock Lode in Nevada; 1860 to 1896; Idaho, Montana, Alaska; boom, fast growth; bust, fast decline

Life on the Frontier railroad stations; herded over trails by cowhands; to cities in the East; 1862; the Homestead Act; few streams or trees, bad weather, insects, range wars

Western Conflict did not want to be forced onto reservations; by 1880, almost all lived on reservations

Lesson 3 New Industries, p. 209

The Transcontinental Railroad trains could travel across country; helped the economy grow

Industries and Inventions helped economy grow rapidly; Andrew Carnegie; built steel mills; William Jenney; used steel frames to build skyscrapers; John D. Rockefeller; started Standard Oil Company, controlled industry; Thomas Alva Edison; set up first central electrical power station; Lewis Lattimer; directed the building of the power station; Alexander Graham Bell; started first telephone company

Workers Struggle better working conditions and pay; strikes; collective bargaining

Lesson 4 Cities and Immigration, p. 213

Many Immigrants Arrive between 1860 and 1910; about 23 million; freedom, safety, a better life; Ellis Island; were poor, lived in tenements, struggled to find jobs and learn English; Angel Island

Reactions to Immigration 1882; Chinese Exclusion Act; no clean water, garbage in streets; reformers Jane Addams and Lillian Wald; started settlement houses to provide food, health care, and classes for immigrants

Migration and Immigration between 1910 and 1930; northern cities; the Great Migration; jobs in factories; Asia and Latin America; basic American ideals

contiguous Unit 1, Chapter 1, Lesson 1	**climate** Unit 1, Chapter 1, Lesson 2
region Unit 1, Chapter 1, Lesson 1	**mountain range** Unit 1, Chapter 1, Lesson 2
relative location Unit 1, Chapter 1, Lesson 1	**erosion** Unit 1, Chapter 1, Lesson 2
continent Unit 1, Chapter 1, Lesson 1	**prairie** Unit 1, Chapter 1, Lesson 2
population Unit 1, Chapter 1, Lesson 1	**environment** Unit 1, Chapter 1, Lesson 2
landform region Unit 1, Chapter 1, Lesson 2	**inlet** Unit 1, Chapter 1, Lesson 3

The kind of weather a place has over a long time.	Next to each other.
A group of connected mountains.	An area in which many features are similar.
The gradual wearing away of the Earth's surface.	The position of one place compared to other places.
An area of flat or rolling land covered mostly by grasses.	One of Earth's seven largest land masses.
The surroundings in which people, plants, and animals live.	The number of people who live in an area.
Any area of water extending into the land from a larger body of water.	A region that has similar landforms throughout.

gulf Unit 1, Chapter 1, Lesson 3	**elevation** Unit 1, Chapter 1, Lesson 4
sound Unit 1, Chapter 1, Lesson 3	**natural vegetation** Unit 1, Chapter 1, Lesson 4
tributary Unit 1, Chapter 1, Lesson 3	**arid** Unit 1, Chapter 1, Lesson 4
river system Unit 1, Chapter 1, Lesson 3	**tundra** Unit 1, Chapter 1, Lesson 4
drainage basin Unit 1, Chapter 1, Lesson 3	**land use** Unit 1, Chapter 1, Lesson 5
fall line Unit 1, Chapter 1, Lesson 3	**natural resource** Unit 1, Chapter 1, Lesson 5

The height of land in relation to sea level.	A large inlet.
The plant life that grows naturally in a place.	A long inlet that separates offshore islands from the mainland.
Dry.	A stream or river that flows into a larger stream or river.
A cold, dry region where trees cannot grow.	A river and its tributaries.
How the land is used.	The land drained by a river system.
Something found in nature, such as soil, plants, water, or minerals that people can use to meet their needs.	A place where the land drops sharply, causing rivers to form waterfalls or rapids.

renewable resource Unit 1, Chapter 1, Lesson 5	
nonrenewable resource Unit 1, Chapter 1, Lesson 5	
modify Unit 1, Chapter 1, Lesson 5	
irrigation Unit 1, Chapter 1, Lesson 5	
efficiency Unit 1, Chapter 1, Lesson 5	

	Resources that can be made again by people or nature.
	Resources that cannot be made again by people or nature.
	To change.
	The use of canals, ditches, or pipes to move water.
	Using less energy to do the same tasks.

ancestor Unit 1, Chapter 2, Lesson 1	**class** Unit 1, Chapter 2, Lesson 1
theory Unit 1, Chapter 2, Lesson 1	**division of labor** Unit 1, Chapter 2, Lesson 2
migration Unit 1, Chapter 2, Lesson 1	**palisade** Unit 1, Chapter 2, Lesson 2
artifact Unit 1, Chapter 2, Lesson 1	**longhouse** Unit 1, Chapter 2, Lesson 2
civilization Unit 1, Chapter 2, Lesson 1	**wampum** Unit 1, Chapter 2, Lesson 2
tradition Unit 1, Chapter 2, Lesson 1	**confederation** Unit 1, Chapter 2, Lesson 2

A group of people in a society who have something in common.	An early family member.
Work that is divided so that it is possible to produce more goods.	An idea based on study and research.
A wall made of tall wooden poles to protect a village from enemies.	The movement of people.
A long wooden building in which several families could live.	An object made by a person.
Beads cut from seashells to make designs that showed important decisions, events, or stories, or traded and exchanged for goods.	A group of people with ways of life, religion, and learning.
A loose group of governments working together.	A way of life or an idea handed down from the past.

wigwam Unit 1, Chapter 2, Lesson 2	**council** Unit 1, Chapter 2, Lesson 3
lodge Unit 1, Chapter 2, Lesson 3	**ceremony** Unit 1, Chapter 2, Lesson 3
sod Unit 1, Chapter 2, Lesson 3	**adapt** Unit 1, Chapter 2, Lesson 4
scarce Unit 1, Chapter 2, Lesson 3	**staple** Unit 1, Chapter 2, Lesson 4
tepee Unit 1, Chapter 2, Lesson 3	**surplus** Unit 1, Chapter 2, Lesson 4
travois Unit 1, Chapter 2, Lesson 3	**adobe** Unit 1, Chapter 2, Lesson 4

A group of leaders who meet to make decisions.	A round, bark-covered shelter.
A celebration to honor a cultural or religious event.	A large round earthen house used by Central Plains Native Americans.
To adjust way of living to land and resources.	A layer of soil held together by the roots of grasses.
Something that is always needed and used.	In short supply.
An extra amount.	A cone-shaped tent made from wooden poles and buffalo skins.
A brick or building material made of sun-dried earth and straw.	A device made of two poles fastened to a dog's harness, used to carry goods.

hogan Unit 1, Chapter 2, Lesson 4	**potlatch** Unit 1, Chapter 2, Lesson 5
trade network Unit 1, Chapter 2, Lesson 4	**kayak** Unit 1, Chapter 2, Lesson 5
harpoon Unit 1, Chapter 2, Lesson 5	**igloo** Unit 1, Chapter 2, Lesson 5
clan Unit 1, Chapter 2, Lesson 5	
economy Unit 1, Chapter 2, Lesson 5	
barter Unit 1, Chapter 2, Lesson 5	

A Native American celebration meant to show wealth and divide property among the people.	A cone-shaped Navajo shelter built by covering a log frame with mud or adobe.
A one-person canoe made of waterproof skins stretched over wood or bone.	A system that allows people to get goods from faraway places.
A house made of snow or ice.	A long spear with a sharp shell point.
	An extended group of family members.
	The way people of a state, region, or country use resources to meet their needs.
	To exchange goods.

technology Unit 2, Chapter 3, Lesson 1	**benefit** Unit 2, Chapter 3, Lesson 1
navigation Unit 2, Chapter 3, Lesson 1	**Reconquista** Unit 2, Chapter 3, Lesson 1
expedition Unit 2, Chapter 3, Lesson 1	**isthmus** Unit 2, Chapter 3, Lesson 2
empire Unit 2, Chapter 3, Lesson 1	**treaty** Unit 2, Chapter 3, Lesson 2
entrepreneur Unit 2, Chapter 3, Lesson 1	**grant** Unit 2, Chapter 3, Lesson 3
cost Unit 2, Chapter 3, Lesson 1	**conquistador** Unit 2, Chapter 3, Lesson 3

A reward that is gained.	The use of scientific knowledge and tools to make or do something.
The movement to make Spain all Catholic; also called the Reconquest.	The science of planning and following a route.
A narrow strip of land that connects two larger land areas.	A trip taken with the goal of exploring.
An agreement between countries about peace, trade, or other matters.	A collection of lands ruled by the nation that won control of them.
A sum of money or other payment given for a particular purpose.	A person who sets up and runs a business.
Any of the Spanish conquerors in the Americas during the early 1500s.	The effort made to achieve or gain something.

reform Unit 2, Chapter 3, Lesson 3	
Reformation Unit 2, Chapter 3, Lesson 3	
Counter-Reformation Unit 2, Chapter 3, Lesson 3	
missionary Unit 2, Chapter 3, Lesson 3	
Northwest Passage Unit 2, Chapter 3, Lesson 4	
mutiny Unit 2, Chapter 3, Lesson 4	

	To change for the better.
	A Christian movement that began in sixteenth-century Europe as an attempt to reform the Catholic Church; resulted in the founding of Protestantism.
	A time when the Catholic Church banned books and used its courts to punish people who protested Catholic ways.
	A religious teacher sent out by a church to spread its religion.
	A waterway in North America thought to connect the Atlantic Ocean and the Pacific Ocean.
	Rebellion against the leader of one's group.

colony Unit 2, Chapter 4, Lesson 1	**hacienda** Unit 2, Chapter 4, Lesson 1
plantation Unit 2, Chapter 4, Lesson 1	**raw material** Unit 2, Chapter 4, Lesson 2
slavery Unit 2, Chapter 4, Lesson 1	**stock** Unit 2, Chapter 4, Lesson 2
borderlands Unit 2, Chapter 4, Lesson 1	**cash crop** Unit 2, Chapter 4, Lesson 2
presidio Unit 2, Chapter 4, Lesson 1	**profit** Unit 2, Chapter 4, Lesson 2
mission Unit 2, Chapter 4, Lesson 1	**indentured servant** Unit 2, Chapter 4, Lesson 2

A large estate or home where cattle and sheep are raised.	A land ruled by another country.
A resource that can be used to make a product.	A large farm.
Part ownership in a business.	The practice of holding people against their will and making them work without pay.
A crop that people grow to sell.	Areas of land on or near the borders between countries, colonies, or regions.
The money left over after all costs have been paid.	A Spanish fort.
A person who agreed to work for another person without pay for a certain length of time in exchange for passage to North America.	A small religious settlement.

legislature Unit 2, Chapter 4, Lesson 2	**majority rule** Unit 2, Chapter 4, Lesson 3
represent Unit 2, Chapter 4, Lesson 2	**demand** Unit 2, Chapter 4, Lesson 4
royal colony Unit 2, Chapter 4, Lesson 2	**supply** Unit 2, Chapter 4, Lesson 4
pilgrim Unit 2, Chapter 4, Lesson 3	**ally** Unit 2, Chapter 4, Lesson 4
compact Unit 2, Chapter 4, Lesson 3	**proprietary colony** Unit 2, Chapter 4, Lesson 4
self-government Unit 2, Chapter 4, Lesson 3	

The political idea that the majority of an organized group should have the power to make decisions for the whole group.	The lawmaking branch of a government.
A need or a desire for a good or service by people willing to pay for it.	To speak for.
An amount of a good that is offered for sale.	A colony ruled directly by a monarchy.
A partner.	A person who makes a journey for religious reasons.
A colony owned and ruled by one person who was chosen by a king or queen.	An agreement.
	A system of government in which people make their own laws.

charter Unit 3, Chapter 5, Lesson 1	**common** Unit 3, Chapter 5, Lesson 2
dissent Unit 3, Chapter 5, Lesson 1	**town meeting** Unit 3, Chapter 5, Lesson 2
expel Unit 3, Chapter 5, Lesson 1	**free-market** Unit 3, Chapter 5, Lesson 3
consent Unit 3, Chapter 5, Lesson 1	**industry** Unit 3, Chapter 5, Lesson 3
sedition Unit 3, Chapter 5, Lesson 1	**naval stores** Unit 3, Chapter 5, Lesson 3
frontier Unit 3, Chapter 5, Lesson 1	**export** Unit 3, Chapter 5, Lesson 3

A grassy area shared by the town's people, and used for grazing sheep, cattle, and other livestock.	An official paper in which certain rights are given by a government to a person, group, or business.
An assembly of people in a New England town that made laws and elected leaders.	Disagreement.
An economic system where people are free to choose the goods and services they buy and make.	To force to leave.
All the businesses that make one kind of product or offer one kind of service.	Agreement.
Products used to build ships.	Speaking in ways that cause other people to work against a government.
A product that leaves a country.	The lands beyond the areas already settled.

import Unit 3, Chapter 5, Lesson 3	
triangular trade route Unit 3, Chapter 5, Lesson 3	
Middle Passage Unit 3, Chapter 5, Lesson 3	

	A product brought into a country.
	Shipping routes that connected England, the English colonies, and Africa.
	The journey millions of enslaved Africans were forced to travel across the Atlantic Ocean from Africa to the West Indies.

refuge Unit 3, Chapter 6, Lesson 1	**Great Awakening** Unit 3, Chapter 6, Lesson 2
proprietor Unit 3, Chapter 6, Lesson 1	**religious toleration** Unit 3, Chapter 6, Lesson 2
trial by jury Unit 3, Chapter 6, Lesson 1	**militia** Unit 3, Chapter 6, Lesson 2
justice Unit 3, Chapter 6, Lesson 1	**prosperity** Unit 3, Chapter 6, Lesson 3
diversity Unit 3, Chapter 6, Lesson 2	**artisan** Unit 3, Chapter 6, Lesson 3
immigrant Unit 3, Chapter 6, Lesson 2	**apprentice** Unit 3, Chapter 6, Lesson 3

A religious movement that began in the Middle Colonies that changed the way many people practiced their religion.	**A safe place.**
Acceptance of religious differences.	**An owner.**
A volunteer army.	**The right of a person to be tried by a jury, or a group, of citizens to decide if the person is guilty or innocent of committing a crime.**
Economic success.	**Fairness.**
A craftworker.	**A group of people from many parts of the world.**
A person who lived and worked with an artisan's family for several years, learning a skill in order to earn a living.	**A person who comes into a country to make a new life.**

constitution Unit 3, Chapter 7, Lesson 1	**interdependence** Unit 3, Chapter 7, Lesson 3
debtor Unit 3, Chapter 7, Lesson 1	**broker** Unit 3, Chapter 7, Lesson 3
backcountry Unit 3, Chapter 7, Lesson 1	
planter Unit 3, Chapter 7, Lesson 2	
overseer Unit 3, Chapter 7, Lesson 2	
indigo Unit 3, Chapter 7, Lesson 3	

Groups of people who rely on each other.	**A written plan of government.**
A person who is paid to buy and sell for someone else.	**A person who was put in prison for owing money.**
	The land beyond, or " in back of," the area settled by Europeans.
	A plantation owner.
	A hired person who watched enslaved people as they worked.
	A plant from which a blue dye can be produced.

alliance Unit 4, Chapter 8, Lesson 1	**treason** Unit 4, Chapter 8, Lesson 2
delegate Unit 4, Chapter 8, Lesson 1	**congress** Unit 4, Chapter 8, Lesson 2
Parliament Unit 4, Chapter 8, Lesson 1	**boycott** Unit 4, Chapter 8, Lesson 2
proclamation Unit 4, Chapter 8, Lesson 1	**repeal** Unit 4, Chapter 8, Lesson 2
budget Unit 4, Chapter 8, Lesson 1	**imperial policy** Unit 4, Chapter 8, Lesson 2
representation Unit 4, Chapter 8, Lesson 2	**protest** Unit 4, Chapter 8, Lesson 2

The act of working against one's own government.	A formal agreement among groups or individuals.
A formal meeting of government representatives.	A representative.
To refuse to buy or use goods or services.	The lawmaking branch of the British government.
To cancel, or undo, a law.	A public announcement.
Laws and orders issued by the British government.	A plan for spending money.
To work against or object to a certain policy.	To have someone speak or act for you.

monopoly Unit 4, Chapter 8, Lesson 3	**commander in chief** Unit 4, Chapter 8, Lesson 4
blockade Unit 4, Chapter 8, Lesson 3	**earthwork** Unit 4, Chapter 8, Lesson 4
quarter Unit 4, Chapter 8, Lesson 3	**olive branch** Unit 4, Chapter 8, Lesson 4
petition Unit 4, Chapter 8, Lesson 3	**independence** Unit 4, Chapter 8, Lesson 5
Minutemen Unit 4, Chapter 8, Lesson 3	**resolution** Unit 4, Chapter 8, Lesson 5
revolution Unit 4, Chapter 8, Lesson 3	**declaration** Unit 4, Chapter 8, Lesson 5

A person who is in control of all the armed forces of a nation.	The complete control of a product or good by one person or group.
A wall made of earth and stone.	To use warships to prevent other ships from entering or leaving a harbor.
An ancient symbol of peace.	To provide or pay for housing.
The freedom to govern on one's own.	A signed request made to an official person or organization.
A formal group statement.	A member of the Massachusetts colony militia who could quickly be ready to fight the British.
An official statement.	A sudden, complete change, such as the overthrow of an established government.

preamble Unit 4, Chapter 8, Lesson 5	
grievance Unit 4, Chapter 8, Lesson 5	

	An introduction; first part.
	A complaint.

Patriot Unit 4, Chapter 9, Lesson 1	**enlist** Unit 4, Chapter 9, Lesson 2
Loyalist Unit 4, Chapter 9, Lesson 1	**mercenary** Unit 4, Chapter 9, Lesson 2
neutral Unit 4, Chapter 9, Lesson 1	**campaign** Unit 4, Chapter 9, Lesson 2
inflation Unit 4, Chapter 9, Lesson 1	**turning point** Unit 4, Chapter 9, Lesson 2
profiteering Unit 4, Chapter 9, Lesson 1	**negotiate** Unit 4, Chapter 9, Lesson 2
veteran Unit 4, Chapter 9, Lesson 1	**civilian** Unit 4, Chapter 9, Lesson 3

To sign up or to join.	A colonist who was against British rule and supported the rebel cause in the American colonies.
A soldier who serves for pay in the military of a foreign nation.	A person who remained loyal to the British king.
A series of military actions carried out for a certain goal.	Not choosing a side in a disagreement.
An event that causes an important change.	An economic condition which results in an increase in the price of goods.
To try to reach an agreement among different people.	Charging an extra-high price for a good or service.
A person who is not in the military.	A person who has served in the military.

traitor Unit 4, Chapter 9, Lesson 3	
abolitionist Unit 4, Chapter 9, Lesson 4	
abolish Unit 4, Chapter 9, Lesson 4	
territory Unit 4, Chapter 9, Lesson 4	
ordinance Unit 4, Chapter 9, Lesson 4	

	Someone who acts against his or her own government.
	A person who wanted to end slavery.
	To end.
	Land that belongs to a nation but is not a state and is not represented in the national government.
	A law or set of laws.

arsenal Unit 5, Chapter 10, Lesson 1	**legislative branch** Unit 5, Chapter 10, Lesson 2
federal system Unit 5, Chapter 10, Lesson 1	**executive branch** Unit 5, Chapter 10, Lesson 2
republic Unit 5, Chapter 10, Lesson 1	**electoral college** Unit 5, Chapter 10, Lesson 2
compromise Unit 5, Chapter 10, Lesson 1	**veto** Unit 5, Chapter 10, Lesson 2
bill Unit 5, Chapter 10, Lesson 1	**impeach** Unit 5, Chapter 10, Lesson 2
separation of powers Unit 5, Chapter 10, Lesson 2	**judicial branch** Unit 5, Chapter 10, Lesson 2

The branch of government that makes the laws.	A weapons storehouse.
The branch of government that has the power to enforce the laws.	A system of government in which the power to govern is shared by the national and the state governments.
A group chosen by citizens to vote for the President.	A form of government in which people elect representatives to run the government.
To reject.	To give up some of what you want in order to reach an agreement.
To accuse a government official of a crime.	An idea for a new law.
The court system, which is the branch of government that decides whether laws are working fairly.	The division of powers among the three branches of the national government.

justice Unit 5, Chapter 10, Lesson 2	**due process of law** Unit 5, Chapter 10, Lesson 3
rule of law Unit 5, Chapter 10, Lesson 2	**reserved powers** Unit 5, Chapter 10, Lesson 3
amendment Unit 5, Chapter 10, Lesson 2	**Cabinet** Unit 5, Chapter 10, Lesson 3
ratify Unit 5, Chapter 10, Lesson 3	**political party** Unit 5, Chapter 10, Lesson 3
Federalists Unit 5, Chapter 10, Lesson 3	**checks and balances** Unit 5, Chapter 10, Lesson 4
Anti-Federalists Unit 5, Chapter 10, Lesson 3	**union** Unit 5, Chapter 10, Lesson 4

The principle that guarantees that people have the right to a fair trial by jury.	A judge.
Authority that belongs to the states or to the people.	The principle that every member of a society, even a ruler, must follow the law.
A group of the President's most important advisers.	A change.
A group that tries to elect officials who will support its policies.	To approve.
A system that keeps each branch of government from becoming too powerful or misusing its authority.	Citizens who were in favor of ratifying the Constitution.
An alliance that works to reach common goals.	Citizens who were against ratification of the Constitution.

popular sovereignty Unit 5, Chapter 10, Lesson 4	
democracy Unit 5, Chapter 10, Lesson 4	
public agenda Unit 5, Chapter 10, Lesson 4	
suffrage Unit 5, Chapter 10, Lesson 4	
civic virtue Unit 5, Chapter 10, Lesson 4	
naturalization Unit 5, Chapter 10, Lesson 4	

	The idea that government gets its power from the people.
	A form of government in which the people rule and are free to make choices about their lives and their government.
	What the people need and want from the government.
	The right to vote.
	Qualities that add to a healthy democracy.
	The process of becoming a legal citizen of the United States.

gap Unit 5, Chapter 11, Lesson 1	**assimilate** Unit 5, Chapter 11, Lesson 2
pioneer Unit 5, Chapter 11, Lesson 1	**dictator** Unit 5, Chapter 11, Lesson 3
consequence Unit 5, Chapter 11, Lesson 1	**annex** Unit 5, Chapter 11, Lesson 3
impressment Unit 5, Chapter 11, Lesson 2	**ford** Unit 5, Chapter 11, Lesson 3
national anthem Unit 5, Chapter 11, Lesson 2	**manifest destiny** Unit 5, Chapter 11, Lesson 3
nationalism Unit 5, Chapter 11, Lesson 2	**cession** Unit 5, Chapter 11, Lesson 3

Adopted.	**A low place between mountains.**
A leader who has complete control of the government.	**An early settler of an area.**
To add to.	**Something that happens because of an action.**
To cross.	**The taking of workers against their will.**
Certain future.	**The official song of a country.**
Something that is given up, such as land.	**Pride in one's country.**

gold rush Unit 5, Chapter 11, Lesson 3	**cotton gin** Unit 5, Chapter 11, Lesson 4
forty-niners Unit 5, Chapter 11, Lesson 3	**interchangeable parts** Unit 5, Chapter 11, Lesson 4
canal Unit 5, Chapter 11, Lesson 4	
lock Unit 5, Chapter 11, Lesson 4	
locomotive Unit 5, Chapter 11, Lesson 4	
Industrial Revolution Unit 5, Chapter 11, Lesson 4	

A machine that could quickly remove the seeds from cotton.	A sudden rush of people to an area where gold has been found.
Parts that can be made exactly alike by machines.	A gold seeker who arrived in California in 1849.
	A human-made waterway that connects bodies of water.
	A part of a canal in which the water level can be raised or lowered to bring ships to the level of the next part of the canal.
	A railroad engine.
	The period of time during the 1800s when machines took the place of hand tools to manufacture goods.

sectionalism Unit 6, Chapter 12, Lesson 1	**fugitive** Unit 6, Chapter 12, Lesson 1
industry Unit 6, Chapter 12, Lesson 1	**Underground Railroad** Unit 6, Chapter 12, Lesson 2
free state Unit 6, Chapter 12, Lesson 1	**secede** Unit 6, Chapter 12, Lesson 3
slave state Unit 6, Chapter 12, Lesson 1	**Confederacy** Unit 6, Chapter 12, Lesson 3
tariff Unit 6, Chapter 12, Lesson 1	**border states** Unit 6, Chapter 12, Lesson 3
states' rights Unit 6, Chapter 12, Lesson 1	**artillery** Unit 6, Chapter 12, Lesson 3

Someone who escapes from the law.	Regional loyalty.
A system of secret escape routes that led enslaved people to free land.	All the businesses that make one kind of product or offer one kind of service.
To leave.	A state that did not allow slavery before the Civil War.
The states that left the Union to form their own national government called the Confederate States of America.	A state that allowed slavery before the Civil War.
States located between the North and the South that permitted slavery but had not seceded.	A tax on imports.
Large mounted guns such as a cannon.	The idea that the states, not the national government, should have the final say on all laws.

civil war Unit 6, Chapter 12, Lesson 4	
strategy Unit 6, Chapter 12, Lesson 4	
emancipate Unit 6, Chapter 12, Lesson 4	
prejudice Unit 6, Chapter 12, Lesson 4	
address Unit 6, Chapter 12, Lesson 5	
assassinated Unit 6, Chapter 12, Lesson 5	

	A war between people in the same country.
	A long-range plan made to reach a goal.
	To free.
	An unfair feeling of dislike for members of a certain group because of their background, race, or religion.
	A short speech.
	Murdered in a sudden or secret attack.

Reconstruction Unit 6, Chapter 13, Lesson 1	**segregation** Unit 6, Chapter 13, Lesson 1
black codes Unit 6, Chapter 13, Lesson 1	**prospector** Unit 6, Chapter 13, Lesson 2
acquit Unit 6, Chapter 13, Lesson 1	**boom** Unit 6, Chapter 13, Lesson 2
freedmen Unit 6, Chapter 13, Lesson 1	**bust** Unit 6, Chapter 13, Lesson 2
sharecropping Unit 6, Chapter 13, Lesson 1	**homesteader** Unit 6, Chapter 13, Lesson 2
secret ballot Unit 6, Chapter 13, Lesson 1	**reservation** Unit 6, Chapter 13, Lesson 2

The practice of keeping people in separate groups based on their race or culture.	Rebuilding.
A person who searches for gold, silver, or other mineral resources.	Laws limiting the rights of former enslaved people in the South.
A time of fast economic or population growth.	Not guilty.
A time of fast economic decline.	Men, women, and children who had been enslaved.
A person who settled on the land granted by the government.	A system of working the land in which the worker was paid by letting them keep a share of the crops they harvested.
Land set aside by the government for use by Native Americans.	A voting method that does not allow anyone to know how a person has voted.

transcontinental railroad Unit 6, Chapter 13, Lesson 3	**tenement** Unit 6, Chapter 13, Lesson 4
skyscraper Unit 6, Chapter 13, Lesson 3	**reformer** Unit 6, Chapter 13, Lesson 4
petroleum Unit 6, Chapter 13, Lesson 3	**settlement house** Unit 6, Chapter 13, Lesson 4
labor union Unit 6, Chapter 13, Lesson 3	
strike Unit 6, Chapter 13, Lesson 3	
collective bargaining Unit 6, Chapter 13, Lesson 3	

A poorly built apartment building.	The railroad that crossed North America.
A person who tries to improve society.	A very tall steel-framed building.
A place that provided food, healthcare, and classes for immigrants.	Oil.
	A workers group that fights for better working conditions and pay.
	The stopping of work to make employers meet worker's demands.
	A process that allows employers and workers to discuss and agree on working conditions.